READING AND SEEING
ETHNIC DIFFERENCES IN THE
ENLIGHTENMENT

READING AND SEEING
ETHNIC DIFFERENCES IN
THE ENLIGHTENMENT

FROM CHINA TO AFRICA

Birgit Tautz

READING AND SEEING ETHNIC DIFFERENCES IN THE ENLIGHTENMENT
© Birgit Tautz, 2007.

First published in 2007 by
PALGRAVE MACMILLAN™
175 Fifth Avenue, New York, N.Y. 10010 and
Houndmills, Basingstoke, Hampshire, England RG21 6XS
Companies and representatives throughout the world.

PALGRAVE MACMILLAN is the global academic imprint of the Palgrave Macmillan division of St. Martin's Press, LLC and of Palgrave Macmillan Ltd. Macmillan® is a registered trademark in the United States, United Kingdom and other countries. Palgrave is a registered trademark in the European Union and other countries.

ISBN-13: 978–1–4039–7641–3
ISBN-10: 1–4039–7641–4

Library of Congress Cataloging-in-Publication Data

Tautz, Birgit.
    Reading and seeing ethnic differences in the Enlightenment : from China to Africa / Birgit Tautz.
        p. cm.
    Includes bibliographical references and index.
    ISBN 1–4039–7641–4 (alk. paper)
        1. German literature—18th century—History and criticism. 2. Ethnicity in literature. 3. China in literature. 4. Africa in literature. I. Title.

PT289.T38 2006
830.9'920693—dc22   2006051388

A catalogue record for this book is available from the British Library.

Design by Newgen Imaging Systems (P) Ltd., Chennai, India.

First edition: April 2007

10 9 8 7 6 5 4 3 2 1

Printed in the United States of America.

For my parents

CONTENTS

Acknowledgments

Many institutions and individuals have supported me in writing this book. I am thankful for the resources provided by Franckesche Stiftungen (Halle), Herzog-August-Bibliothek (Wolfenbüttel), and Bowdoin College, as well as for the support I received from colleagues and friends. Special thanks are due to Joanna Bosse, Aviva Briefel, Helen Cafferty, Steven Cerf, Otto Emersleben, Pamela Fletcher, Rolf Goebel, Jonathan Hess, Alexander Honold, Peter Höyng, Charlotte Melin, John Noyes, Daniel Purdy, Jochen Schulte-Sasse, Linda Schulte-Sasse, Arlene Teraoka, Dharni Vasudevan, Liliane Weissberg, and Jack Zipes. They showed great interest in the project at various stages, shared their insights about its scope, read all or part of the manuscript and offered invaluable encouragement along the way. I am thankful to Samantha Altschuler, Dan Coogan, and Robin Jensen who worked as my research assistants. Thanks to Farideh Koohi-Kemali and Julia Cohen at Palgrave, and to Mary Fahnestock-Thomas and the staff at Newgen for preparing the manuscript and index for production. I have used reliable English translations of German texts when available; in all other instances, the translations, with assistance from Mary Fahnestock-Thomas, are my own, and exceptions have been noted.

An article introducing the project—and which was subsequently revised as part of chapter 1—first appeared in German as "Texturen und Farben: China und Afrika im Blick des deutschen Idealismus" (Honold/Scherpe, 63–82); I thank the *Zeitschrift für Germanistik* and Peter Lang Publishers for permission to use it here. An earlier version of a part of chapter 4 first appeared as "Fashionable Details: Narration in an Eighteenth-century Travel Account" in *The Germanic Review* 72.3 (1997): 201–13. It is reprinted here with the permission of the Helen Dwight Reid Educational Foundation and Heldref Publications. Copyright ©1997.

I could have never written this book, nor pursued my life, work, and passion without the support of my parents to whom I dedicate this book.

INTRODUCTION

This book is characteristic of our times in that it has recourse to the past to understand the present. When I began researching it, studies of the "Other" were in vogue, studies of people and fictional characters at the margins of Western society and literature. The principles, languages, and power structures of Western scholarship had saturated the non-Western world and it was now the turn of non-Western perspectives that started to flourish and began to influence Western scholarship. Edward Said's *Orientalism*, for instance, had already become a classic; a point of reference and an anchor for scholarly discourse, the book began to invite critical rereadings, revisions, and challenges.[1] It was a time when "the critique of the West ha[d] become not only possible, but mandatory" (Chow, xi). Books exposing the colonial and imperial entanglements of German literature and culture had just been published: John Noyes's *Colonial Space*, Susanne Zantop's *Colonial Fantasies*, and Russell Berman's *Enlightenment or Empire* are but a few examples. The field of German, or *Germanistik*, was in the process of reorganizing itself and making other, hitherto unheard voices heard; it has evolved—predominantly in the United States—as German Studies.

Nevertheless, within this moment of scholarly innovation, I intuited an inevitable impasse. What would the ultimate closure of this new scholarly narrative be? Would we see a proliferation of ever more critiques of Self-Other by practitioners and scholars alike? Would these critiques perpetuate, rather than deconstruct, the Self-Other constellation and its epistemological roots? Could everybody who fell outside the "Western norm"—among them women, nonwhites, non-Germans, and nonheterosexuals—be truly subsumed under one Other? For the Other's heterogeneity, multitude, and diversity of interest seemed all too often eclipsed in the critique of those forces that had originally conceived of it as "Other" from the Western Self. Conversely, the Other was on the verge of being perceived as responding in a monolithic voice. What processes and forces had ultimately led up to this seemingly stable, dominant configuration of Self-Other from which there appeared to be no escape? The answers to these questions remained elusive then, despite a growing number of scholarly books examining precisely the historical and discursive constructions of European Selves that produced correlating geographical, political, and racial Others. These books could not help but note the remnants of alterity that persisted in theories as much as in the literary (and often nonliterary) cultures that scholars sought to document (e.g., Lowe; Stoler; Pratt; Wheeler, *Complexion of Race*).

Simultaneously, as I started to conceive this book's scope, its sources and materials, I realized not only that twentieth-century German fiction might open a fascinating gateway to the historical problem of pre-Hegelian conceptualizations of cultural difference, but also sensed that the scholarly apparatus for approaching cultural alterity demanded historical specification (cf. Arens, 11–12). Contemporary fiction and postcolonial scholarship represent two sides of the same coin; they are late twentieth-century effects of what would become this book's ultimate subject: the materialities of and knowledge about ethnic difference in the "long eighteenth century" (1680–1830), the configurations of perceiving and representing non-German cultures that preceded the formulation Self-Other in Hegel's philosophical and historical thought. Clearly there were late twentieth-century texts that preserved older images, configurations, and linguistic formulations of cultural alterity and that suggested conflicting nuances of ethnic and racial otherness. Fantasies of the Enlightenment model of a Chinese "Orient" stood next to an Orientalist utopia first proposed by early German Romanticism that thought of Asia as a space where one could escape from a restrictive regime of space and time. Both imageries formed a sharp contrast to a variety of textual allusions to blackness encompassing depictions of wild behavior and outright danger, of physical, often sexual, seduction, and "appalling" noncivilization, and that could be geographically relocated to Africa.

As I began to scrutinize traces of eighteenth-century culture in contemporary German-language literature and culture through their textual presence, I began to consider their impact on the narrow realm of scholarly theories and on the broad, rather abstract level of power relations that have structured Western modernity. What distinguishes, for example, eighteenth-century representations of China from those of Africa? What happened, I wondered, when discursive—that is, material and communicative—practice and philosophical self-reflection intersected, or, more appropriately, what happened when diverse, mostly anonymous and often popular knowledge and events were met by assured, innovative, and institutionally powerful authors who created modern textual Selves full of an all-encompassing, seemingly homogeneous individuality? What happened at a historical juncture that subsequent scholarship has begun to interpret as the eclipse of the former diversity by the latter narrative of Self? These are the questions I answer in this book.

Representations of China and Africa are at the core of this study, but its focus is neither on the refining of a scholarly apparatus nor on the imaginary manifestations of Chinese and African ethnicities in today's German culture. These two approaches serve merely as pathways to the historical constellation to be explored: the discursive inception of the modern concept of ethnicity and its textual manifestations in eighteenth-century German literature, philosophy, and popular scholarly and scientific writing. By mapping out such a foundational moment in the genealogy of the modern concept of ethnicity, this book offers innovative readings that have, to the best of my knowledge, not been attempted before. My study no longer presumes an antagonistic Self-Other configuration as the underlying principle in the formation of ethnic difference. Rather, it concentrates on obscure processes of perception and representation which have only subsequently been interpreted through the attribution of clear-cut, albeit confining, binary oppositions applied to groups that share certain traits such as ethnic or national belonging and that, in turn, distinguish one group from others (Clifford; Ashcroft/Griffiths, esp. 80–84). As the book uncovers what turn out to be shifting and often conflicting ways in which selected eighteenth-century German-language texts constructed ethnic locales, it delineates historical variations of subjectivity which have not always been modeled on the construct Self-Other. Thus it examines interrelations between conceptualizations of community and personhood.

My discussion centers on the contrasting manner in which China and Africa were represented in eighteenth-century texts of varying popularity, institutions, and genres. I propose to describe this contrast through modes of perception, namely as a predominance of reading in the representation of China, versus a prevalence of seeing in the representation of Africa. The result is not just a complex, uneven arrangement between archived textuality and unmediated visuality in eighteenth-century constructions of ethnic difference. More importantly, the differences among these perceptions and representations expose fragile conceptual boundaries of ethnicity, which, in the case of China, emerge almost as synonymous with the Confucian bureaucrats and their ruler and which are, in the case of Africa, preempted (or expanded) to encompass a largely undifferentiated, continental mass (Ashcroft/Griffiths, 84, 89–90). We will also realize that the idea of

Enlightenment universalism, so central to facets of eighteenth-century culture and our preconceived notions of the period, evolved not only in opposition to material instances of ethnicity, but was also permeated by them.

To further delineate this distinction among modes of perception and their discernable effects, I employ two descriptive terms: *texture* and *color*. On one hand, they correlate with the primacy accorded to reading and seeing, while marking the interdependence of universality and difference or locality. Whereas reading signals the integration of difference, which I call texture, seeing incites the awareness of difference that is color. Texture refers to efforts to integrate ethnic differences into an Enlightenment notion of universalism, whereas color stands for differences perceived as irreducible and thus challenging claims of universality. On the other hand, I track the conceptual evolution of texture and color through two images that, in the long eighteenth century, appear tied to the depiction of China and Africa and, to this day, have engendered a distinct symbolism of these locales in German culture: texture refers to imageries of an exemplary, stable Chinese civilization modeled on books, whereas color pertains to blackness of the skin.

The imagined permanence and stability of China—which became a model for eighteenth-century German philosophy and politics, structuring fantasies of both enlightened universalism and enlightened absolutism—evolved from texts, from a fabric that undeniably entwined philosophy with social and religious life. These texts comprise the entire corpus of Chinese philosophies. Enlightenment writers appreciated China as a society that had established itself through these texts and continued to model itself on texts. They praised the larger, seamless texture that texts create. Accordingly, China's social fabric disclosed itself through reading, beginning with the philological and exegetic studies conducted by Jesuit missionaries. The imagery disseminated by the Jesuits influenced numerous philosophical studies in which China was correlated with the Western text, the biblical Scripture, and with European societies. These reading processes related differences to the construct of an infinite representation, causing Enlightenment thinkers to believe that the Eastern and Western hemispheres had been designed in perfect symmetry and that ethnic differences were equally accurate expressions of a universal order.

By contrast color—specifically blackness—designated not just a metaphor for the dark night, which opposes the bright day, nor a symbol for those people who remained uninitiated to reasoning and recognition, but a metaphor that condensed, in the psychoanalytical sense, the genealogy of an aspect of ethnicity, namely skin color and race. This genealogy was, as my argument will show, inevitably linked to the primacy accorded to sensual experiences, and to seeing in particular, by Enlightenment writers, scientists, and philosophers in their encounters with ethnic alterity. In these instances the immanence of experience caused new images of ethnicity to emerge, naturally confronting older ideas. Thus, while leading to an instability of representation through which a fundamental otherness manifested itself, sensual experience incited strategies of compensation. Scientific, ethical, or aesthetic in nature, these strategies culminated in the conceptual delineation of race.

Throughout the long eighteenth century, color and texture stood for constructions of ethnic difference marked by the "textualization of [sensual, especially visual] experience" in the case of Africa and the "experience [and function] of texts" in the case of China,[2] creating an interplay that has structured the images of China and Africa passed on through German (and often European) cultural history. This perceptual relationship helps to amend our understanding of ethnicity and, more generally, of alterity and otherness. It allows us to illuminate the distinct eighteenth-century institutions and subjects in German lands among which emerged images that stand out for their heterogeneity. Attention to ways of perception sheds new light not only on the forging of a German national imagination, but also on the widely debated and often misconstrued position of Germans vis-à-vis eighteenth-century European empires (cf. Zantop; Berman, 1–30; Arens, 22–27). To this day, the specter of eighteenth-century perceptions looms large, no matter how refined the use of scholarly language and concepts has become. Therefore, as I posit the concept of Self-Other as the ambivalent, but nevertheless structuring principle of scholarly discourse, I hope to challenge it in its predominance by exposing its genealogy, its heterogeneity and its deceptive effects.[3]

* * *

These reflections lead us to the theoretical framework and structure of this study. My initial thoughts on the perception and representation of ethnic locales, alterity, and difference point toward what Michel Foucault calls the operation of discourse (esp. *Order, Archaeology*), and it is discourse theory that has perhaps most profoundly influenced my lines of thinking in this book. Discourse and its theory, Foucault insists, mark an epistemological as well as a rhetorical and analytical break from intellectual histories and their interpretive frameworks.

Discourse theory opposes the conceptual foundations of traditional intellectual histories such as the progress of ideas (e.g., knowledge, reason, consciousness) and their illusionary, correlating capacities (e.g., the development of reality or history). Unlike interpretations that draw on idealist philosophy and its tendency to simulate continuity and rhetorical correspondence, discourse analysis concentrates on discontinuities, on the moment rather than the process. Foucault is interested in the statements through which any particular discourse connects linguistic entities, and in the ways in which limits of material environments, that is, preverbal practice or action, define these statements. For, as Foucault does not fail to remind us, discourse never establishes a metaphorical or causal correspondence between statement and environment, but merely a trace, a symptom, or an effect. Discourse entails subject positions, though it never predicates a Self through the identity of speech, body, and action: there is neither a conscious subject that knows (and thus produces objects of knowledge) without being an object of knowledge itself, nor a subject that creates statements and texts without being affected or even erased by them. To analyze discourse is, as James Clifford laconically remarks, "always in a sense unfair to authors. It is not interested in what *they* have to say or feel as subjects but is concerned merely with statements as related to other statements in a field" (27).

While I am fully aware of the irony and the potential for detriment that Clifford's observation entails for the "authority Foucault" himself, I do not wish to be sidetracked by considering the implications for my approach here, at least not at this point. Rather, I would like to suggest appropriating the concept of discourse in a little considered, historical perspective, namely as a precursor to the narrative of idealist philosophy (Brennan, 567–69). This suggestion naturally evolves from my aim to examine the nexus of sensual experience and textual rendering at a juncture where discursive practice not only intersects with philosophical reflection, but where the latter paradigm dissolves the former. For, philosophical reflection, which—historically speaking, suppresses or hides discursive practices of the eighteenth century—is tied to the narrative installation of the Self, characterized by the remarkably coinciding symbolisms of assertive speech, physiological and psychological unity of body, and teleologically conceived historical action. The Self and its narrative inception provide the foil for the literary concept of creative authorship, which, as we shall see in this book, has been in conflict with other, insurgent subjectivities.

Though Foucault himself locates this epistemological juncture in the Figure of Man that inaugurates historical modernity (*Order of Things*),

I will ultimately emphasize the aesthetic dimension of modern individuality (and community) over the collateral concept, its foundation in biology or history. The narrative Self anchors fiction. While affirming its centrality, the Self has authored and authorized its own critique; this reflexive turn has dominated both literary and nonliterary studies in recent years. This dual nature of aesthetic authorship, I propose, provides us with one—perhaps the chief—reason for the continued study of fictional and nonfictional texts for their rhetorical or particular linguistic qualities. Texts and the rhetoric they employ remain central; therefore, despite my critical engaging of other disciplines, I am committed to an analysis that acknowledges the uniqueness of individual languages and linguistic registers as well as the predominance of the imaginary and fictional—in short, of literature which, as a modern paradigm, was inaugurated at the end of the eighteenth century. Herein, I believe, this book distinguishes itself from historiographic, anthropological, sociological, and philosophical projects within German Studies (e.g., Eigen/Larrimore; Zammito, *Birth*) while entering a dialogue with them as well as with studies whose emphases are, for example, American, English, and French literature of the eighteenth century (e.g., Carretta and Gould; Douthwaite; Nussbaum; David Porter; Wheeler).

The result, then, is not a survey of ethnicity in eighteenth-century German literary and philosophical texts, nor any pretense to completeness or comprehensiveness. Instead, the six chapters that follow offer models for approaching textual manifestations of ethnicity. Each of the example texts captures a transitional moment in the perception of China and Africa, which elevates them over other, briefly mentioned or altogether omitted texts that preserve similar images but do not demonstrate change. I bring these texts together to map a variety of discursive fields in the eighteenth century. All of them address questions of perception and representation in preidealist discourse while exposing limits to and ramifications of thinking in the idealist, Hegelian tradition. Despite the deliberate noncontinuity among them, the texts are united by the trajectory they create—toward the ongoing divergence in the imagery of these two geographical locales, despite the appearance of confluence that emerges if we look at non-European alterity *only* from the perspective of the twentieth century.

Very few of the texts chosen here are "new discoveries." Several of my examples have served mostly illustrative purposes in published studies of specific genres, philosophical paradigms, and motifs (e.g., Aurich; Berger; Harris-Schenz; Hsia; Martin; Mielke). Others have been neglected by scholars despite the insights they yield for a historically more differentiating account of ethnic difference. Still others (e.g., Hegel, Kant, Herder) have been discussed widely, but only fairly recently examined for their foundational role in the emergence of particular epistemological moments, for example in critical debates on race (e.g., Honegger; Eigen/Larrimore) and aesthetics (e.g., Bindman). Therefore, in keeping with the intention to dialogue, each of my chapters engages pertinent critical studies that provide context for my readings—and often a critical, contrasting perspective.

In the first chapter, I analyze Hegel's *Philosophy of History* (1837) as a means of elucidating my notions of reading and seeing. Notwithstanding Hegel's attempt to conceive ethnicity as unified (i.e., sublated in the unity of spirit and Self), my reading lays bare two different logics underlying his argument: whereas he linked China by its *texture* to European Enlightenment, he saw Africa as a threat based on *color*. These accounts of Africa and Asia/China evolved out of different perceptual fields. They also entailed different subject positions. While the *viewing* subject struggled with the unsettling effects of sensual experience when embracing the geographical body of the African continent, the *reading* subject drew logical conclusions about Asia's usefulness in relation to Europe. By insisting on these discursive disparities, the chapter reveals the genealogy of a historical, epistemological, and methodological threshold, the homogenous configuration of Self-Other which has defined—and for a long time limited—ideas of ethnic difference since Hegel.

Chapter 2 locates eighteenth-century universalism in Leibniz's establishment of Chinese philosophy as the basis for the Enlightenment's emancipation of reason. Universalism evolved as the product of a reading subject, namely the philosopher's intellectual activity of relating texts to each other. I explore Leibniz's "Chinese writings," especially the major treatises on Chinese numerical systems and philosophy: "Das Geheimnis der Schöpfung: Neujahrsbrief an Herzog Rudolph August" (The Mystery of Creation: A New Year's Letter to Duke Rudolph August; 1697) and *Discourse on the Natural Theology of the Chinese* (1716). Read in the context of his correspondence with Jesuit missionaries and his position as philosopher and librarian for the Duke of Brunswick-Wolfenbüttel, these treatises attest to Leibniz's ethical stance on universal creation (and, as a consequence, to his obsession with the universalizing potential of translation, readability, and representation). We shall see that they assigned to the Chinese texts a position that was marked by both superiority (for its secularizing potential) and inclusiveness (for its confirmation of the universality of the same). Leibniz conceived ethnic difference as but one manifestation of infinite differences expressing, in the end, nothing more than the infinity of possibilities for reading the "world" as one and the same.

Chapter 3 distinguishes three "Chinese" models of subjectivity. In each instance representations of ethnic difference serve as a linguistic medium through which constraints and finitude were inflicted upon individuals. The chapter begins with an exploration of the "sovereign philosopher" in Christian Wolff's *Rede über die Sittenlehre der Sineser* (Lecture on Chinese Ethics; 1721), showing that China provided Wolff with a rhetorical mirror through which he narrated and legit-imized this new philosophical concept and its significance for the Enlightenment's public sphere. The chapter subsequently focuses on pedagogical tracts anonymously published in *Das Journal von Tiefurt* (The Journal of Tiefurt), a project conceived by Anna Amalia and Goethe's circle at the Weimar court between 1781 and 1784, and on *Das Rad des Schiksals oder die Geschichte Tschon-gsees* (The Wheel of Fate or the story of Tschon-gsees; 1783), a novel by Siegmund von Seckendorff, a member and critic of this circle. One of the treatises, "Der Chinesische Sittenlehrer" (The Chinese Morals Teacher), pro-posed a mode of communal conduct indebted to Chinese authority. Participating in a larger trend in eighteenth-century German and European fiction—here illustrated by recourse to Wieland and Lenz— "The Chinese Morals Teacher" drew on the imagery of China as a culture of discipline and order that revolved around ideas of filial piety yet was bound to the medium of the book. Another treatise published in *The Journal of Tiefurt*—incidentally called "Das Rad des Schicksals" (The Wheel of Fate) like Seckendorff's novel—critiqued the culture at the court while projecting motifs and forms of subjectivity that would guide the poetics of early Romanticism decades later. Thus, reading China produced paradoxical effects: the acceptance of individual limitations became both a new universal norm and a prerequisite for Enlightenment ideas about statehood and citizenship. At the same time, these texts dealt with death, a motif that they situated in China and that paved the way for the Romantic image of Asia as a space without any limitations.

My discussion in chapter 4 extends to travel literature, a genre con-cerned with instability. Georg Forster's *Reise um die Welt* (1784) and his *Voyage around the World* (1777), travelogues from the *Magazin von merkwürdigen neuen Reisebeschreibungen* (Magazine of Curious New Travelogues; 1790–1839), and especially the anonymously pub-lished "Reise des Herrn von M** nach China in den Jahren 1773 und 74" (Mr. M**'s Journey to China in 1773 and '74; 1775), an epistolary account, produced unstable representations on many levels: in the realm of perception and experience, in the seemingly sovereign traveler-authors, and in the communities of readers left behind. Instabilities arose as the protagonists' erudite image of China was confronted with a real visit to—that is, actually seeing—China. Experience undermined the impact of the textual tradition. The travelogues also shifted the study's emphasis to the second ethnic locale, Africa, as protagonists sailed around the African continent on their journey to China or the Pacific. The chapter emphasizes, on one hand, that the distinctions between China and Africa may be better described in perceptual rather than geographical terms. On the other hand, though fractured along gender lines, China continues to serve as a thread of universal texture: it now expresses "universal Woman," her beauty and domesticity, while Africa, in contrast, represents effects ascribed to black skin. Sight, materiality, and color induced a fundamental instability whose dispersed effects could only be captured in fractured structures of narration or as femininity. Ultimately this chapter becomes the centerpiece of my exploration of texture and color: by probing, via narrative, the conditions for a universal language (or texture), it establishes how this kind of universalism falls apart.

Chapter 5 places skin color literally on stage. By juxtaposing the performative elements of Peter Camper's tract on anatomy, *Rede über den Ursprung und die Farbe der Schwarzen gehalten in Groeningen auf der anatomischen Schaubühne den 14. November 1764* (Lecture on the Origins and Color of Blacks, held in Gröningen in the anatomical theater on November 14, 1764, with Schiller's drama *Fiesco* (1783–84), I explore eighteenth-century perceptions of skin color as a material threat. These ideas were conveyed in numerous popular, scientific, and poetic texts that form the context for my discussion. This unlikely combination of fiction and nonfiction illuminates how medical and aesthetic writings were allied in disseminating cultural ideas. It illustrates furthermore how a network of expert knowledge (e.g., anatomy, mechanics, and climate theories) was penetrated by both popular knowledge (e.g., body perception) and innovative technologies and philosophies of display. By placing these ideas in the framework of viewing and community, the chapter suggests that an aesthetic foundation of race and racism was "invented" to cope with these threats and that these aesthetic concepts complemented—perhaps even exceeded—the impact of scientific ideas. I demonstrate that this foundation not only relied on symbolic modes of identification, but, because of its resemblance to the formation of ideas such as "the individual" or "the nation," has left its mark in today's discussions of identity and difference, individuality and community, harmony and violence.

Chapter 6 underscores what has been my contention throughout *Reading and Seeing Ethnic Differences*: that although the eighteenth century's foundational moment of "ethnicity" embraced the idea of ethnic difference as the expression of a universal language through reading, discourse analysis reveals the ruptures in this kind of universalism once it confronted a palpable entity such as the body of the individual in acts of seeing. By tracing this contention through texts that have been widely discussed, such as Kant's anthropological writings on race and ethnicity (which spanned four decades, from 1764 to 1802), Herder's *Reflections on the Philosophy of History of Mankind* (1784–85), and a few early Romantic texts, chapter 6 forms a frame with chapter 1. Both emphasize the relationship between today's context of researching ethnic differences and its selected, yet multiple points of origin in eighteenth-century culture. Thus, chapters 1 and 6 relate in an explicit manner what the four middle chapters imply: while the idealist turn at the end of the long eighteenth century cut short richer possibilities for reading and seeing the world, these possibilities persist in the texts as we read them.

1

Hegel at the Limits
of Discourse

[By] making ourselves deliberately or unknowingly blind to Hegel or by trying to avoid him, we risk surrendering to his gaze all the more.
—Plotnitsky (71)

Africa proper, as far back as History goes, has remained—for all purposes of connection with the rest of the World—shut up; it is the Gold-land compressed within itself—the land of childhood, which, lying beyond the day of self-conscious history, is enveloped in the dark mantle of Night.
—Hegel, *The Philosophy of History* (91)

On the one side we see duration, stability—Empires belonging to mere space, as it were—[. . .] unhistorical History—as for example, in China.
—Hegel, *The Philosophy of History* (105–6)

Georg Friedrich Wilhelm Hegel's *Philosophy of History* is full of contrasting imageries. On one hand, the *telos* of Hegelian historiography, "the Germanic World," stands out against locales, nations, and regions that were left behind and that inscribe an insurmountable, ontological difference from history's ultimate purpose. On the other hand, depictions of the "other ethnic world" emerge as a noncoherent compilation, pitting against each other images that simulate either physicality or temporality only to convey, ultimately, a psychophysiological or a psychotemporal distance from the idealized "German" Self (Spivak, 1–111, esp. 7–8; Hartsock; Radhakrishnan; Bhabha, "Interrogating Identity"). In Hegel's narrative, empires such as China, stable to the extreme of being ahistorical, contest the condensed mass of land, Africa, which signifies childhood and marks, as we shall note, something of a rhetorical nuisance to the author. The lectures, I suggest, must have presented a representational problem for Hegel. For us they document the complexity of perceiving and representing China and Africa in the eighteenth century, as well as the gradual total eclipse of such complexity.

Delivered between 1821 and 1831, when Hegel was a professor in Berlin, the lectures on the *Philosophy of History* have been transmitted in hitherto controversial, nonauthoritative editions (Bernasconi, 172–74),[1] yet they have shaped reflection upon the effects of cultural differentiation to this day; indeed, they represent a pivotal "event," or threshold, in conceptualizing ethnic difference in that they epitomize an important, if not the ultimate, step in the genealogy of the Hegelian dialectic of Self-Other. Here the Self appears as the unfolding history of Spirit in relation to and over against what Hegel sought to unify in a profound, monolithic Other that was in turn modeled on the cognitive, physical, and psychological unity of the Self. This image of selfhood embodies key elements of modernity: organization and sovereign identity, history and interpretation (Foucault, *Order*, 217–21, 303–43).

Thus Self-Other evolved as the principle of modern thought whose binary opposition structures our interpretations of existence. While still exhibiting its origins in philosophical debate and writing, Arkady Plotnitsky reminds us, the cognitive figure Self-Other has operated elsewhere—really everywhere—in literature as well as in history, in political thought as well as in biological science (81). Today Self-Other has come to encompass all social narrative, for it not only allows us to imagine coherence and unity—that is, identity—as we envision our very own personhood, it shapes the narratives of the communities and nations to which we belong—both promoting and resisting unity—but always at the expense of an otherness that could truly transform the epistemological status quo. And, to put it bluntly, ethnic difference is but one symptom of Self-Other.

Yet perhaps most importantly, Self-Other also gives rise to its own critique: unfolding as an attempt to turn the gaze away from Hegel's dialectic—all too easily reduced to a predominance of the Self—such critique tries to adopt, instead, the gaze of the Other, forgetting that the Other itself is of the Self's making. As the Self's inferior reflection, it recurs as a mere product and intrinsic part of the Self. This is Plotnitsky's point; it is, moreover, a point reiterated by numerous scholars, who use, for example, psychoanalytic theories to account for concrete historical situations and ideological effects or, simply, to infuse historical narratives with material reality. Whether we think of Slavoj Žižek's reflection on the nexus of postsocialist states, social fantasies, and repression—he very eloquently states that "the opposition

between the One and its Outside is reflected back into the very identity of the One" (xxvi, 50–53)—or consider Homi Bhabha's rereading
of Fanon's concept of racial misidentification ("Remembering
Fanon," 112–23), we encounter figurations of Self-Other. Even when
we take into account recent discussions of the philosophical underpinnings of "race in the academy" (Krell, 103–34), it is the conceptual
genesis of Self-Other in Hegel's oeuvre against which today's discussions of ethnic difference and multiculturalism largely evolve. To paraphrase Gayatri Spivak, it is Hegel who imposed a normative
paradigm on colonial and postcolonial studies. His texts depended on
"ethnic moments," representations that allowed for "structural complicity" between Eastern and Western texts but that ultimately precluded access to "the true nature of the ethnic." Furthermore,
Hegel's texts simulated not only an intellectual and cultural Germany
that did not exist at the time, but also an authoritative European
presence (Spivak 39, 37–59). In this sense, the lectures on the *Philosophy
of History* have defined our consideration of ethnicity as much as they
have mandated our critique of Eurocentrism, a self-contained conflict
that shapes one dimension of this chapter.

A second dimension, though, is rooted in the historical place and
contingency of *The Philosophy of History*. In 1837, the lectures simulated much more than a cultural debate that would unfold roughly
150 years later. Only in hindsight do they represent both pinnacle and
closure, the epitome of Idealism. But more than their influential
beginnings, the lectures marked an end in that they curbed alternative
possibilities for perceiving and representing what we today, in an
ironic agreement with Hegel, call "the ethnic." Though Hegel did
not actually use this term, his narrative relies on images that defied the
logic of a universal "phenomenal people," his preferred term for
evaluating progress in the history of Spirit. Hegel's narrative sought
to manage these alternative, defiant images by integrating and
suppressing them in order to sustain the evolution of the Self against
the Other. Here is where our understanding of ethnicity comes into
play: if ethnicity as a discursive product resists universalizing narratives
of world, history, and intellectual spirit, it must expose, and at times
proliferate or even generate, alternate modes of origin, community,
and expression. While such alternate modes will be of interest throughout this book, in this chapter we will read them side by side with the
"new" Hegelian narrative. Because this narrative emerges as the product of a sovereign, self-asserted author-subject, enacting all nuances of
what Foucault reconstructed as the figure of Man, a closer look at
Philosophy of History will open up a path to Hegel's past—understood

not as a linear, chronological precursor, but as an archive of knowledge that reveals the discursive disparities that structured eighteenth-century representations of China and Africa.

The lectures draw our attention to the epistemology of ethnicity in European culture around 1800, mediating accounts of actually existing cultures, locales, and communities in a philosophically and linguistically constructed history. In other words, in Hegel's text ethnicity emerged from the discursive entanglement of materiality and narrative as an attempt to interpret and bring order to the still-extant, often ragged multitude of representations of culture in the eighteenth century. Reminiscent of bygone seeing and reading situations, these representations of Africa and China collided with the author's intention and his rhetorically forceful and compelling struggle for inner coherence and progress in the narration of human existence. While seeking a homogeneous meaning of ethnicity, Hegel's argumentation laid bare conflicting configurations that ultimately obstructed an understanding of ethnic difference that posits a unified Other as complementary notion of the Self.

History: Sustaining the Author's Narrative

This outcome notwithstanding, Hegel's authorial intention deserves closer scrutiny. After all, he set himself up as an ideal, as the sovereign author defined by a unified, solitary subjectivity whose expression matched what he sought to represent. The author Hegel wanted to tell a story, which was compelling not because of contemporary understandings of anthropology, geography, or ethnology, but because it challenged the authorial Ideal through the unrelenting presence of two competing senses of history. Hegel had to grapple with the "deeds and events" of history on one hand (Bernasconi, 177), and with the desire for historical narrative and its preconceived rationale on the other. Their unity would reflect the success of the author; everything else appeared subordinate to this force and intention. In the lectures, Bernasconi argues, Hegel "does not simply append his views about non-European peoples to his philosophy; [rather] these views are elevated above the level of mere prejudice by the logical framework [historical narrative] which helps sustain them and to which they in turn lend support" (172). If this statement is true, a look at the entwined operation of history and historical narrative may indeed prepare us for our subsequent investigation of the "ethnic events" that Hegel's narrative conceals. Moreover, we shall see that these two senses of history correlate—perhaps not surprisingly—with the rift between earlier, eighteenth-century manifestations of ethnic difference and the modern narrative of Self-Other.

But how did the author-subject put these two senses of history into play, all with the intended effect of producing ethnicity as a sustaining rather than a disrupting element of narrative? Early in *The Philosophy of History* Hegel provided a broad argument on the principles of historiography and the conceptual foundations of world history, followed by a section entitled "Geographical Basis of World History." Here he offered a geographical survey that, though somewhat disconnected from intellectual history, emerged as a basic element of his argument to which we shall return later. In the remaining four parts, however, Hegel quickly turned to a temporal division of world history along an abstract, idealized East-West axis combined with ethnographic and aesthetic accounts in the sections on "The Oriental World" and "The Ancient Greek World," respectively, and with commentary on military actions in Ancient Greece and the Roman Empire. The subsequent sections on Christianity and the Byzantine Empire created a transition to the final section and the ultimate purpose of historiography, "The Germanic World."[2] As this temporal geography mirrored developmental stages of the spirit, the *telos* of historical narrative came to the fore: the perceived unity of Spirit, a stage where Self and Other blissfully coincide.

Hegel, the sovereign author, wrote towards this goal, weaving into the text conventional accounts of actual people and documented lands that indeed sustained—not merely illustrated—intellectual history. While at first glance the philosophical narrative may appear to be infused with remnants of materiality, Hegel proposed a meaning that reduced instances of ethnicity to expressions of a progressing consciousness or, more precisely, to stages of recognition within the unfolding history of Spirit. To paraphrase Bernasconi, people and states appeared removed from prejudice and integrated into the logical framework of a historical narrative. Here, spatial and temporal coordinates disappeared in abstraction, making it possible for Hegel to elicit a notion of "a phenomenal people" and to suggest, thereby, the sublation of ethnic difference in history:

> But for the spirit the highest attainment is self-knowledge, an advance not only to the *intuition*, but to the *thought*—the clear conception of itself. This it must and is also destined to accomplish; but the accomplishment is at the same time its dissolution, and the rise of

another spirit, another world-historical people, another epoch of Universal History. (71)

As ethnicity first presented itself as a phenomenal people, it became a rhetorical device through which the differential moments of consciousness could be represented, giving content to the abstract configuration Self and Other running through Hegel's work.

Yet the syntactical link between historical spirit and phenomenal people suggested further conceptual renderings. It is not coincidental that the rhetoric of ethnicity simulated spatial coordinates. Despite and against its temporal impulse, it recalled its geographical location in the empirical orders; conversely, the rhetoric indicates another way of clarifying the difference between what I have called ethnic moments and Hegel's concept of phenomenal people. Usually this difference is described in temporal terms. "Hegel," John Noyes observes, "did hope for a picture of wholeness in which the untidy lives of historically and geographically remote individuals [read: ethnic moments] might disappear under the force of the here and now [read: phenomenal people]" ("Negativity," 3). I disagree with Noyes, however, with regard to the status of perception and representation. Hegel's text appears to have been not only driven by a desire to escape the necessary temporality of existence through language, but also profoundly affected by an overriding sense of spatiality that is cast in visual terms. For as "the phenomenal people" signaled a fundamental temporal otherness, a gap between what the spirit perceived and what it envisioned itself to be in the future, visuality appeared on the scene.[3]

It is here that we realize the true (inter)dependency of Hegel's thought and language: though both are allegedly all about temporality, that is, through the simultaneous capturing and counteracting of time, they draw on physical space and its expression in visual terms, that is, the ethnic instance. Spirit and otherness were seen to manifest themselves, respectively, in physiologically driven images of bodily wholeness and coherence on one hand, and the absence thereof on the other. Rhetorically, the history of Spirit—the configuration of Self-Other—marks vision, firmly placing Hegel in his time, a time when the conviction that "the ability to visualize something internally [was] closely linked with the ability to describe it verbally" had taken a lasting position in culture (Rivlin and Gravelle, 88–89, quoted in Jay, 8). It was this conviction that sustained Hegel's idea of the author and the manner in which he approached—not to say distanced—history's "deeds and events." Literally seeing difference, recognizing it as such, and nevertheless attempting to sublate it in a seamless texture of Selfhood sustained the concept of the ideal author as much as it authorized historical narrative. Ironically, this prevalence of vision also solidified the subject's negativity, its detachment from its own Ideal. That vision had not always had this status and subjectivity and had presented itself differently is a claim I merely wish to introduce at this point; I shall support it through the remainder of this chapter and throughout this book.

ETHNICITY: SUBVERTING THE AUTHOR'S NARRATIVE

The sensible challenge to the Self's narrative identity brings us to a second aspect of Hegel's philosophical mediation. Appearances of "phenomenal people" merely cover the empirical orders and material traces within which ethnic difference is arranged, for underneath philosophy's narratological structure, ethnicity breaks into locales, into random events that cannot be grasped by any unifying interpretation. Whereas in parts 1 through 4 of *The Philosophy of History* Hegel followed the narrative plot he had set up for the Spirit, the groupings in one part of the introductory section, "Geographical Basis of History," reveal different principles. Geography took on a special role in Hegel's text, forming on one hand "raw material for historical spirit" (Krell, 115) and, on the other, defying history and thus threatening to undo the Hegelian narrative or dialectic of Self-Other.

While the discovery of the Americas represented the threshold event in distinguishing the New from the Old World in *The Philosophy of History*, it evidently did not amount to a new quality of Otherness. The New World appeared, as Krell argues, as a mere reconfiguration of the Old World, a reflection or mirror of the Old World's defining parts: Africa, Asia, and Europe (124). Therefore, Hegel subjected only the Old World to geographical description and classification, and it is in these passages that Hegel's narrative authority is challenged in an encounter with bygone manifestations of subjectivity that asserted their own proliferations of ethnicity, modes of perception, and constructions of cultural difference. These manifestations point to a heterogeneity in constructing ethnic difference throughout the eighteenth century, turning *The Philosophy of History* into an archive that reflects a deeper, older order. The traces of these various representations of ethnicity—in pervading the narrative—undermined the author's intention of reducing ethnic difference to a phenomenological or metaphorical status. At the same time the author responded to his own historical context. He appeared compelled to supplant his strictly historical perspective with alternate disciplinary viewpoints—which in turn, of course, betrayed contemporaneous tendencies toward the emergent, modern social sciences.

From an anthropological point of view, Hegel regarded Africa as a land of children, hence still precluded from the history of the world. In contrast, China exhibited an ontological stability that Hegel expressed in the image of a space eliminating time. Economically, he acknowledged Africa's wealth of unexplored natural resources while praising China as a nation of merchants, where property and trade flourish (91, 100). Physiologically and socially, he perceived Africa as an unordered, primitive mass, constituting the opposite of meticulously ordered Chinese society. As we shall see, the result was a variety of contexts that, while indeed expressing ethnic difference, had diffuse points of origin and unsettling effects. Betraying their material and discursive origins, these expressions of ethnicity point to other histories that escaped the order of teleological narratives and the authority of an individual author-subject. Instead, they preserved eighteenth-century moments of perceiving Africa and China that stressed the sensual over the intellectual, and seeing, smelling, and hearing over reading, philosophizing, and politicizing—in short, that link Africa to the body and China to the mind.

Accordingly, Hegel spoke ill of the cruelty and mercilessness of African people, attributing their brutality to their untamed instincts, carnal fixations, and fanaticism: "The destruction which is the consequence of their excitement is caused by the fact that it is no positive idea, no thought which produces these commotions—a physical rather than a spiritual enthusiasm" (98). The African existed, in Hegel's view, in a sensuous, wild singularity (93), lingering in an animalistic state and bare of any bonds that would assure morals or civic laws. He ultimately concluded: "From these various traits it is manifest that want of self-control distinguishes the character of the Negroes. This condition is capable of no development of culture, and as we *see* them at this day, such have they always been" (98; my emphasis).

China, on the other hand, had a state system that resembled an organism or a perfect, sophisticated machine (113). But the very perfection of this machine precluded any development of consciousness and therefore any historical progress:

> The laws of the state are partly civil ordinances, partly moral requirements; so that the internal law—the knowledge on the part of the individual of the nature of his volition, as his own inmost self—even this is the subject of external statutory enactment. The sphere of subjectivity does not then, attain to maturity here, since moral laws are treated as

legislative enactments, and law on its part has an ethical aspect. All that we call subjectivity is concentrated in the supreme head of the State, who, in all his legislation has an eye to the health, wealth, and benefit of the whole. (112–13)

In China morals had taken an abstract form because state and politics functioned in accordance with civic and moral codes derived from century-old books. "These books are the groundwork of the history, the manners and the laws of China" (117), maintained Hegel, suggesting that every social phenomenon had been predetermined by these books and that the material limits of the books explained the static character of Chinese society. Books defined people's position in the world, even the position of the patriarchal sovereign, who in turn was the sole interpreter of the books. His task consisted in communicating the rules of the book to the people. Their knowledge of themselves remained, in turn, confined to what the books told them, and their desires were never outside the scope of the recorded laws. Ultimately, by penetrating every aspect of life, codifications and books conferred a static character upon that society.

Hence, by relating Africa to sensuous appetites, instinctive behavior, and evolution, and China to literal authority, a meticulous social machinery, and nonprogress, Hegel assessed the historical importance of these geographical regions. In a way, the representations of Africa and China functioned in a highly ambiguous manner: while Hegel's Africa, for all its physical concreteness and descriptive qualities, threatened to rip historiography apart, China sustained it in more than one way, first and foremost by tying Hegel's narrative to tradition. More significantly, however, the characteristics attributed to Africa ("dark mantle") and to China ("durability, stability") conveyed a meaning that reached well beyond any positioning of these geographical regions in Hegel's narrative of history. They indicated the primary qualities or metaphors that distinguished Africa from China in eighteenth-century discourses and that still prevailed in Hegel's *Philosophy of History*: sensuality and physicality still dominated representations of Africa, while rationality and philosophical inquiry remained confined to China. These characteristics were reflected in the correlating imageries of skin color and books representing textual authority.

GENEALOGIES

Indeed, Hegel's depiction of Africa and China displays some striking similarities to eighteenth-century accounts of these geographical regions; more importantly, though, rather than preserving these accounts in an intertextual way as citations, Hegel's text reworked genealogical processes. Exposing epistemological shifts through the intrinsic link between perception and representation, between knowledge production and philosophical language, the lectures mirrored the genealogy of texture and color through their narrative inscriptions of temporal and visual distances. At the same time, they embraced and perpetuated a new status of reading and seeing.

A wide range of textual accounts come to mind when reading Hegel's Africa, including several that will play a role in subsequent chapters of this book: Kolb's eighteenth-century description of the Cape region, popular scientific texts on race, Forster's travelogues. Their traces are ubiquitous. The same can be said of Jesuit reports on China and idealized fictional accounts of Confucianism, which flourished in Goethe's Weimar and influenced Hegel's thesis of China's exclusion from historical progress. Though they are not cited as sources, descriptive passages in Hegel's lectures bear subtle traces of these older texts: while they did not take up motifs or images, they preserved stylistic features, modes of presentation, and genres that serve to demonstrate perceptual relations in the text.

For example, vivid adjectives detail the account of Africa, intensifying their graphic potential by signaling ultimate death in a virulent nature. Through emanating energy that forces Europeans' decay, this space also seals off its interior. Swamps, lush vegetation, and wild dangerous animals penetrate a space that confronts Europeans through its manifest otherness. It therefore remains inaccessible to European conquest, to naturalist observation, and to economic exploitation:

> Next to this towards the interior, follows to almost the same extent, a girdle of marsh land with the most luxuriant vegetation, the especial home of ravenous beasts, snakes of all kinds—a border tract whose atmosphere is poisonous to Europeans. This border constitutes the base of a cincture of high mountains, which are only at distant intervals traversed by streams, and where they are so, in such a way as to form no means of union with the interior; for the interruption occurs but seldom below the upper part of the mountain ranges, and only in individual narrow channels, where are frequently found innavigable waterfalls and torrents crossing each other in wild confusion. (92)

By linking the omnipresence of venomous creatures in a territory shut off from the outside world, the description joins conflicting versions of late eighteenth century-knowledge in a symbolic hybridity. On one hand, this symbolism reflects popular beliefs about the threatening impact of the body, which, as Barbara Duden has shown, until the eighteenth century, was thought to interact with its environment through the constant exchange of substances and energies (11–12). These images of permeable bodies run through Hegel's text, beginning with stories about the boisterous and unrestrained nature of African people, which the author interpreted as indicative of a primitive stage of nonalienated consciousness. Accordingly, everything African posed a threat. For Africa would either spread into the bodies exposed to it and thereby violate their physical integrity, or threaten to confuse the observer's recognition through the nonclarity and disorder of the subject it presented. On the other hand, this passage of Hegel's *Philosophy* depicted African vegetation and geography accurately as a result of scientific curiosity and the observational skills associated with eighteenth-century natural history. Intended to make nature's universal reason transparent, accurate descriptions shared the ultimate intent of Enlightenment philosophy, namely to achieve clear recognition. The claim to clarity is evident in all Enlightenment discourses with regard to speech, recognition, and, evidently, the representation of knowledge (Wellbery, *Laokoon*; von Mücke, *Virtue*).

Hegel's text coped with complex hybridity by arriving at a mode of reading based on a new understanding of body and visuality and involving a process of invoking aesthetic convention and judging its functionality. This strategy becomes clear if we take a closer look at the descriptions of Africa. Although they condense two paradigms of science, the science of Man and natural history, they form a balanced narrative as they define the textual dynamic of the account. Interrupting the text's narrative movement, the descriptions eventually culminate in the aesthetic construct of the tableau. A common rhetorical device in eighteenth century-narrative (see Caplan), tableaux frequently occurred in travelogues—a few of which I shall discuss in chapter 4—where they mediated sense perception and textual strategies. Here, by establishing the firm boundaries of the narrative image, Hegel's text evokes a tableau-like landscape in the eye of the reader. At once repulsive (because of its decentering permeation) and inviting (because of its educational intention), it directs the reader's gaze. But rather than making him/her part of the image as many eighteenth-century accounts do, this tableau keeps the reader at a contemplative distance. Unlike older accounts that engaged readers through aesthetic recognition and ultimate transparency of textual images, Hegel's narrative required a reader to judge the functionality of an object's composition by relating its qualities to an ideal.[4] For this to work, reader and tableau had to remain separate. And, more importantly, some guiding intervention and interpretation by the author were required.

Asserting that Africa lacked any material coherence for perfection, Hegel evaluated the continent's natural conditions. He claimed that its geographical features were so imposing that Africa's interior remained inaccessible to Africans as well as Europeans; after all, Africa was, as the opening of this chapter suggests, a "land compressed within itself." From there, Hegel took the leap to suggest that, unlike Europe, Africa could not be recognized. He ultimately concluded that such a continent must be functionally deficient in comparison with Europe. In order to substantiate this conclusion, Hegel destroyed the spatial arrangement placing the reader vis-à-vis the object, for in the end, contrary to numerous eighteenth-century portrayals of the African continent, his did not strive for a representation that would encourage readers to evaluate its appropriateness, accuracy, and distinction. The relations of the textual representation to both the object (the "true" African landscape) and the reader (possessing an idea of Africa) were distorted.

Hegel's account of the continent referred the reader back to his self-image by evoking a description that alludes to organic, physical integrity. Several natural boundaries, whose images constantly recur in the passage, indeed strengthen the impression of the continent's inaccessibility to the reader. Like two distinct bodies—one that reads, one that is read—the pictorial continent and the reader face each other. Therefore, from this point on, it was neither the distinct quality of a representation nor the manner in which it preserved traces of perception that shaped the image of Africa. That role fell to an idea constructed in accordance with the figure of Man and communicated through an author functioning as both the creator and the medium of knowledge. Through this epistemological shift, indicating the sovereign subject's imaginary doubling of Man, a discursive event was transformed into a narrative.

But this transformation was not always successful. The textual interplay among the conflicting perceptions of bodies in the field of vision, among representations and interpretations of knowledge, reflects the presence of eighteenth century-genealogies of blackness in the cultural unconscious. At any point this profound otherness might erupt and reenter experience; the awareness thereof directed Hegel's efforts to write a normative history. Drawing on the graphic and emotive potential of representations of blackness, Hegel resorted to comparisons with a permeable body when speaking about Africa's interior and violations of the interior's order. The continent, though presented as a geographical body with demarcated boundaries, was shaped from within, through its confrontation with the living Africans: "In the sixteenth century occurred at many very distant points, outbreaks of terrible hordes which rushed down upon the more peaceful inhabitants of the declivities. Whether any internal movement had taken place, or if so, of what character, we do not know" (92).

Again, the author's voice aimed to transform the sensual effects of the imagery into knowledge, anchoring the image in history and thus explaining the relation between cause and effect. Knowledge became at the same time origin, meaning, and destiny, as Hegel asserted an empirical origin ("the sixteenth century") and posed questions that lead eventually to the formation of knowledge ("whether," "if"). Despite attempting, in this textual instance, to create historical narrative and inventing himself as a sovereign subject, the author failed: against sensual distractions he activated the Cartesian belief in the absolute power of individual recognition, but the act of knowing remained unfinished ("unknown").

In the end it did not matter that Hegel had textual accounts (e.g., missionary reports) he could rely on when writing about Africa (93). He could not help but find himself engulfed in a sensual reaction to the communicated information and provoke a similar response in his readers. Like Hegel's narrative, readers could not rid themselves of older body perceptions that threatened to disturb the recognition of Africa. Hegel's description evoked distinct images but simultaneously erased them by dispersing their form into the formlessness of immanence. His eagerness to know was not rewarded because the "African presence" surfaced in a manner that escaped the causal logic of the historical narrative. These "ponderous" details merely disrupted the narrative flow and dialectical movement of Spirit, hindering Hegel's philosophical argumentation. Ultimately he recommended: "At this point we leave Africa, not to mention it again" (99).

This sentence has become legendary in colonial and postcolonial studies. It has frequently been interpreted as the most overt sign of Hegel's latent racism and as an early and rather blunt expression of Eurocentrism (Kukendall, esp. 571–81; also Said; Spivak; El-Tayeb). Here I suggest reading it also—and perhaps first and foremost—as an inflection of a profound epistemological shift. This sentence is marked by a breakdown of authorial intention and the persistence of a bygone moment of perceiving Africa; in an instance of lapse it expressed the incipience of modernity in all its complexity. While Hegel failed to integrate representations of Africa in a manner that fully supported the logic of historical narrative laid out in the lectures, making it impossible for him to reduce Africa to a space accommodating phenomenal peoples, he nevertheless created a narrative whose modernity revolves also, in a seemingly paradoxical manner, around the representational status of Africa, for Hegel was, it turns out, as much interested in "the bodies of black folk" as he was fascinated by African geography. True to what Foucault has described as the modern paradigm of knowledge formation, geography is modeled on the body. Hegel displaced or transferred the physical features of the black body's genealogy onto the geography of the African continent; consequently, African geography appeared as a mere metaphor for an eighteenth-century black body, its image and its assumed effects on other bodies. By preserving, condensing, and radiating the old fear associated with blackness, "the body Africa" could not be subsumed under the new narrative of history and instead threatened to rip it apart. In other words, the body of the Self only read bodies like itself, not bodies of alterity.

In contrast, Hegel's account of Asia resembles a carefully structured report; it is concise, fast moving, and informative. A parallel, fairly efficient syntax lists criteria for the comparison of geographical areas:

> In regard to Asia the remark [. . .] respecting geographical differences is especially true; viz. that the rearing of cattle is the business of the Upland—agriculture and industrial pursuits that of the valley-plains— while commerce and navigation form the third and last item. Patriarchal independence is strictly bound up with the first condition of society; property and the relation of lord and serf with the second; civil freedom with the third. (100–01)

By compiling facts and comparing and arranging them in accordance with geographical conditions and social stratification, Hegel created an account of Asia that reflects the assumption of a universal condition for human existence. In correspondence to early Enlightenment thought, where universalism was perceived as a relation between the world's immanent reason and its articulation through signs, certain natural conditions entailed specific occupations that seemed well suited to those living in the environment. Coincidentally, these correlations could be found on the Asian continent.

On a deeper level Hegel's Asian tale unveils a categorical division along humanist ideals (such as patriarchal independence, master-slave relations, and freedom). It reflects events in the genealogy of German philosophy and culture that—as chapters 2 and 3 will illustrate— gradually detached the philosophical subject from the transparent relation to signs and reason in the course of the eighteenth century, when

Leibniz's universe of signs, expressing a unity of creator and creation, gave way to disciplined subjects produced through moral education and erudition and aspiring to embody Confucian principles. Only in retrospect are these ideals combined with specific, meticulously classified (pre)bourgeois existences in agriculture, manufacturing, trade, and travel. In short, these ideals were interpreted as expressing the possibility of a perfect correlation among nature, individuals, and societies because they implied functional relationships between natural, economic, and political spheres and stressed their formal functions and mutations within history rather than their present reality. Predicated upon development, these ideals sustained the absolute notion of subjectivity that propelled the narrative of *The Philosophy of History*: in seeking to achieve a correspondence between "phenomenal people" and history's *telos* of sublating ethnic difference, between history's deeds and events and historiography, they perpetuated Enlightenment notions of reading that wove signs into a texture of coherence.

In other words, although this passage reflects an understanding of universalism that is different from the universalism of the early Enlightenment, it still relied on the same medium to claim its truth: the book. Critics have shown that in the first half of the eighteenth century, ideas of enlightened universalism emanated from China's literal authority and book culture, which established links not only to European texts, predominantly religious and linguistic treatises, but also to the blossoming secular philosophies (Figueira, 8–26; David Porter, 15–77). Hegel resorted to the same authority. Not only did universal recognition depend on the reading of texts, texts also enclosed China and Europe in a universe: the Chinese had certain ancient canonical documents from which their history, constitution, and religion could be gathered (117). Within China the appreciation of books gave rise to the strata of philosophers (*literati*). They became a model for Enlightenment intellectuals since their writings taught Europeans how to imagine the emancipation of reason from religion: "Although every Chinaman is at liberty to study these philosophical works, a particular sect, calling itself *Tao-tse*, 'Honorers of Reason,' is isolated from civil life" (136). Books about China counted as an old but reliable source of information: "In the thirteenth century a Venetian [Marco Polo] explored it for the first time, but his reports were deemed fabulous. In later times, everything that he had said respecting its extent and greatness was entirely confirmed" (118). For these two reasons, Hegel asserted, the relationship between China and Europe was as predetermined as Chinese society. China and

Europe were linked through the reading of texts, just as China's well-being depended on reading.

Dorothy Figueira has reminded us of the fictionality of such a construct while demonstrating the significance and authority of an absent text for the subsequent Orientalist project and for the Asian participation and collaboration in this project. David Porter has pointed out the nexus of linguistic legitimacy, language theory, and interpretation of Chinese culture in eighteenth-century Europe, showing how Chinese books and philosophy became the medium through which the universal language of the early Enlightenment expressed itself. In Hegel's text, the role of the book seems slightly altered. It retains its authoritative status, but this authority is no longer grounded in linguistic transparency, but rather corresponds to Man's historicist and interpretive mode of existence. For Hegel, books became an origin, a static sign to which modern philosophy could repeatedly refer, even when part of the book's original importance seemed lost. Accordingly, his imagery of China designated a developmental stage of humankind. Like the book, Chinese civilization constituted a point of origin to which other people could relate; China was absorbed by the web of historical existence. Thus, compared to the perception and representation of Africa, the grammar of identifying sameness created opposite effects when it came to reading and integrating and translating Chinese philosophy. A desensualized discourse, the perception of China remained remarkably unaffected by the body, a direct result, perhaps, of both the obsession with the ideogram, a written character that was thought to express an idea perfectly, and the textually sustained construct of Enlightened China.

In any case, Hegel's ethnic accounts engaged the figure of Man in illustrating the logic of history. The imagery of Africa drew on Man's organic wholeness and his self-image of physical integrity, while Hegel employed Man's constant interpretation of himself to construct China's and Asia's position in history. Yet the perceptual situation distinguished the representation of Africa from the representation of China in such a way that the former remained excluded from history while the latter was part of it. Evolving out of different perceptual fields, the accounts of Africa and Asia/China entailed divergent subject positions. Unlike the subject of vision that struggled with the dispersing effects of permeance when capturing Africa, the subject of reading drew (logical) conclusions when representing China. Unlike the subject of vision that encompassed the geographical body of the African continent, the subject of reading transcended the physicality of Asia's organic structure in order to recognize Asia's phenomenology. The subject of vision observed, whereas the subject of reading related. Reading compared, divided, combined, and concluded, establishing coherent textures between Asia and Europe, whereas color designated Africa's irrefutable otherness.

As perceptions and representations of Africa and China evolved in accordance with and against the image of the body, they produced contradictory ways of reading ethnicity and ethnic difference. In the process, ethnicity in Hegel appears as either an inflection of Enlightenment reason (in the case of China) or as a fundamental otherness, the Other of reason (in the case of Africa). Nevertheless, most readings of Hegel's *Philosophy* have neglected the discursive complexity of ethnicity pervading the text; therefore, they have positioned Hegel's text at the limits of discourse.

In an epistemological sense the limits of discourse mark a discontinuity since they empty out the content of eighteenth-century constructions of ethnicity. Indeed, the material and perceptual foundations of the constructions of ethnicity are eclipsed by the narrative mode of the text. Operating upon an imaginary doubling of the figure of Man, these acts of narration establish, in Foucault's words, "the sovereignty of the subject, and the twin figures of anthropology and humanism" (*Archaeology*, 12). The sovereign subject—posing here as Spirit and as the author Hegel—relates a moment where Man's philosophical ideal of selfhood lives, whereas his material condition is suppressed. This moment defines, in Foucault's words, the end of discourse and the beginning of history.

In *The Philosophy of History* the sovereign subject mediated the accounts of Africa and China through the lens of a self-induced narrative. Indicating a unity of speech, body, and action, the subject's position was often identical with the author's voice and intention. This subject depleted ethnic difference of its local foundation—and thus situated its own universal claim—by attempting to dissociate expressions of ethnicity from the perceptual and material situation of their initiation. Defining itself simultaneously as the point of origin, as agency of movement and as destination, the subject occupied the position of narrative closure, but also the positions indicating that this point of closure had not yet been reached. In this light, differences were naturally perceived as an expression of the temporary otherness of this self-same subject. Difference stood, then, for an Other that belonged to the Same. Yet, as my reading of blackness has shown, discourse imposed limits on this narratological foundation; as older modes of seeing broke through, they ultimately impeded modern modes of reading.

Finally, limits of discourse can be understood in yet another way. In a strict chronological sense, Hegel's lectures were the last of a series of "eighteenth-century" accounts of ethnic difference considered in this study. By analyzing this text in the first chapter, I hope to have emphasized not only the rise of the sovereign subject, but also the origin of a heavy legacy. The idea of sovereign subjectivity, modeled on the figure of Man, links our century to the eighteenth century as it collapses the differential particularity of an event into the continuity of history. In this function, it has maintained a persistent presence in our current discussions of ethnicity. The configuration of Self and Other, inevitably linked to sovereign subjectivity and its model, continues to influence studies of eighteenth-century representations of ethnic difference. This insight prompts me to reconsider to what extent today's view of eighteenth-century cultures has been distorted by the narratives of emancipation and liberalization attached to this figure. (Alternatively, I could ask—with Gayatri Spivak—to what extent this figure and its narratives have shaped "the voice" of colonial and postcolonial subjects.) The following four chapters represent an attempt to shake up a cultural critique that by now has run the risk of preempting the "Other," depriving it of its multiple genealogies and rendering it a merely rhetorical figure. They are an attempt at resurrecting eighteenth-century moments of perception and representation that may suggest alternate histories.

2

THREADS OF A TEXTURE: LEIBNIZ'S
TRANSLATION OF CHINA

LEIBNIZ AND CHINA IN THE REPUBLIC
OF SCHOLARS

A first such moment where the perception and representation of ethnic locales might suggest alternatives for conceptualizing ethnic difference arrived in the writings of princely librarian, mathematician, and philosopher Gottfried Wilhelm Leibniz (1646–1716), especially in his treatises, editions, and correspondence on China. In the course of four decades of his writing, Leibniz frequently mentioned China, beginning in 1670, when he first showed interest in Jesuit Anasthasius Kirchner's writings on China, and culminating in a substantial piece on the subject, *Discourse on the Natural Theology of the Chinese* (1716), a treatise he drafted in French shortly before his death. Aside from this final text, Leibniz's Chinese writings comprise an extensive correspondence with Jesuit missionaries, an exchange with Andreas Müller on the legendary *Clavis sinica* (1679), an edition of Jesuit writings about China, *Novissima Sinica* (1697–99), and, curiously, a letter he wrote to his patron for the New Year in 1697 entitled "The Mystery of Creation: A New Year's Letter to the Duke Rudolph August of Brunswick-Lüneburg-Wolfenbüttel."[1]

These writings illuminate central tenets of Leibniz's encyclopedic enterprise: linguistically they chronicle the search for a universal language; ontologically they document an interest in natural principles of Creation; morally they examine the relationship between divine and human power, especially that of the monarch; and scientifically they reference the binary arithmetic, a system that allows for any positive, whole number to be represented through mathematical operations using only 1 and 0. Ultimately this system took on special significance for Leibniz because he considered it the perfect medium for representing and explicating the universe of the world in its dual unity of divine predetermination and infinite recognition. As he understood this latter dimension to be a key aspect of reading and representing the world, Leibniz provided us with a "translation" of China that marks a threshold in defining European subjectivity and, by extension, ethnicity. Thus, these writings capture—looking back from Hegel's *Philosophy of History*—a bygone way of reading and defining the ethnic.

Nevertheless, they amount to more than a moment in Hegel's past. Leibniz's cultural translations show, as David Porter has argued, that China occupied a unique place in Europe's geographical and cultural imagination in the late seventeenth and early eighteenth centuries, and that its celebrated status represented more than an aberration in a discourse of colonization, exploitation, and subjection to a new imperial narrative of conceptualizing the world (3). Porter not only offers a series of historical case studies that attest to eighteenth-century Europe's preoccupation with ancient Chinese texts, he also demonstrates, by implication, why we should reconsider this preoccupation in the same terms that eighteenth-century writers reserved for their project: as a striving for a universal language and a grammar of similarity and correspondence rather than an expression of imperial, linguistic invention.

Porter sees Europe's semantic overinvestment in the Chinese language, especially in its intercultural and interethnic legibility, as a unifying response to Europe in turmoil. After a century of wars (the Thirty Years' War, 1618–48; English Civil Wars, 1642–51) and tormented by the subsequent religious and political decline, Europe was ready for "order and stability." Everything—descriptive systems, collections, inventions, and so on—reflected an "ordering impulse" (16), and the attention given to the Chinese language was no exception. It was a witness to the cultural desire for a shared language that would remedy what contemporaries saw as a problematic linguistic deterioration: Learned Latin, the European lingua franca of the erudite elites, no longer had the power it had possessed for centuries, but gave way to French and Italian at princely courts, to the vernaculars of the emergent literary markets at the beginning of the eighteenth century, and, more broadly, to the oral forms of communication that began to dominate social interaction. Amidst this social and communicative instability, Porter contends, Europeans looked elsewhere for an organizing and ordering principle of knowledge and life, and they projected it onto the Chinese language. To the mind of the European scholar, Chinese characters could recapture what the Latin alphabet, syntax, and rhetoric had once represented, namely a unity of European scholarship that was based on the unquestioned validity of text and writing.

As the alleged economy and exactness of the Chinese writing system testified to durability and stability over time, the subsequent linguistic integration of China into European language theory expressed the firmly held belief that religious and political stability could spring from linguistic and intellectual coherence.

Porter is not alone in claiming that Leibniz shared this belief, asserting that Leibniz's quest for a universal language evolved from his desire for universal peace, a contractual agreement shored up by religious unity. In fact most scholars agree, linking Leibniz's interest in China to his desire to heal the rift within the Christian Church and "to reconcile Catholics and Protestants" (Cook/Rosemont, 3; see Schrecker/Schrecker, vii–xxii; Needham, 496–505). To be sure, because of his lengthy service at Duke August's court, Leibniz is thought of as a politician and advisor as often as he is singled out for his "discoveries" of differential and integral calculus. I suggest considering Leibniz less for his alleged intentions than as *primus inter pares*. He was as much a product of the scholarly exchanges in which he participated as he was a contributor to them. Like his contemporaries he quoted freely and attributed little to other authors, truncating some texts and expanding others. Thus he appeared as an almost anonymous figure to whom authorial significance has been affixed only in retrospect and who can illuminate the epistemological constellation that, according to Friedrich Kittler, characterized Leibniz's time: the Republic of Scholars ("Gelehrtenrepublik"; 8).

Far from signifying a political or geographical idea of community, but connoting an unmistakably intratextual network, the Republic of Scholars serves as an important cognitive figure in this chapter. Anchored by the idea of a unity-forming text, it simulated a reality of scholarship where any verbal expression was regarded as an exterior sign of God's work. Scholars neither crossed out expressions nor suppressed them; they neither invented information nor articulated responses to observation; rather they produced rhetorical paraphrases: expressions were rearranged in sentence and paragraph, extrapolated from texts and interspersed in others, paraphrased, and translated (Kittler, 3–24, esp. 12, 15; cf. also Elias, 166). Every scholar contributed to writing a larger fabric of world, which of course took as its model the exegesis of the biblical text. In this world, where a text (a chain of signifiers), and not an outside object (a signified), shaped scholarly activity, "knowledge [consisted]," according to Foucault, "in relating one form of language to another form of language; in restoring the great, unbroken plain of words and things; in making everything speak" (*Order*, 40). As a text-centered discourse, every discursive act or verbal expression—conversation and disputation, treatise and aphorism—became a commentary, an element in the endless proliferation (or paraphrase) of texts, never finished or complete.[2] Consequently, scholars were enfolded by and endlessly reproduced what could be described as a text reading and interpreting God's infinite knowledge. Their own reading process, while infinite, could only approximate this knowledge and never surpass it through creativity or invention. Accordingly, recognizing the world's perfection—"the ultimate reason, superior to the world," wrote Leibniz in 1697—resembled the copy of a book that had been reproduced multiple times, and to which generations of readers referred, without ever being able to examine the book's subject in an exhaustive manner ("Origination of the Universe," 84, 90–91).

Not surprisingly, then, the book became a preferred metaphor for imagining the production of knowledge in the Republic of Scholars. While books establish relations to other books and texts, they never surpass their respective material limits and always confine knowledge production to acts of reading. A book was thought to mirror perfectly the relationship between scholar and text in that it contains a small segment of the "infinite or seamless conversation" and reiteration of paraphrase and commentary. At the same time, the writing of books reproduces the limits of the social world and retranslates and contextualizes them in texts. Norbert Elias observes that everything that scholars fashioned as a book, a treatise—in short, as scholarship—represented nothing but a figural extension of their social lives: they were mere appendices of their patrons, commentators if you will, whose books were hindered expressions and conversations that never happened for lack of like-minded partners in conversation (cf. 161). In this respect the book contained the effacements taking place in the Republic of Scholars, with the erasures dissolving the scholar in the sense of the presumed, retroactively projected individuality and autonomy that come with sovereign authorship. In turn, as the medium of the book defined the limits of reading and recognition, it also became the foil against which new models of subjectivity evolved.

The larger cultural setting of the Republic of Scholars constituted the backdrop for Leibniz's Chinese writings. At the same time these writings reflected the material conditions and rhetorical conventions of a small segment of the culture, the Christian mission that like courtly patronage and the universities provided a center for early modern scholarship. Yet unlike the Republic's domestic version that barely extended beyond the European courts and universities, the mission lent an imperial dimension to its scholarly enterprise. While the Republic of Scholars drew on "the historical possibilities afforded by colonialism" (Rajan, 12), it concealed this complicity by remaining outside the colonial institutions—rhetorically, morally, and practically. Scholarship cloaked itself in innocence. Accordingly, Leibniz's Chinese writings represented rewritings of Chinese historiographies that were mostly written or translated by Jesuit missionaries in open disregard of any imperial enterprises that were not involved with the mission.

Almost always, Leibniz's texts drew on several instances of mediation en route to the rhetorical paraphrases they offered, and these sources have been extensively documented (Cook/Rosemont, 10–18; *Zwei Briefe*, 11–18). Aside from linguistic theories addressing the role of Chinese characters, Leibniz resorted to the writings of the Jesuit missionaries Matteo Ricci (1552–1610), Nicholas Longobardi (1565–1655), and Martino Martini (1614–61), and of the Franciscan Antoine de Sainte-Marie (1602–69), and he was strongly influenced by his personal contacts and correspondence with Claudio Filippo Grimaldi (1638–1712) and Joachim Bouvet (1656–1730), also Jesuit missionaries. Their accounts, as well as Leibniz's subsequent writings on China, presume three historical periods: the era of sage kings, the period of Confucius, and the period of Neo-Confucianism (Cook/Rosemont, 19).[3] Of these periods the first stands out because of the unique role it has played in the Western reception of Eastern philosophies. Since the missionaries and Leibniz held the period of sage kings in especially high regard, they fostered a belief in the authority of an absent text dating back to this era and a widespread confidence among European scholars that that text contained a founding myth, which assured Europe and Asia of their shared tradition (Figueira, 8–10).

But there were also important differences between Leibniz and the missionaries. Whereas Leibniz enjoyed the benefits of patronage, with no other obligations than occasionally celebrating his benefactor, missionaries' renderings of ancient Chinese texts were naturally influenced by the challenges they faced in daily missionary work, as well as by the agendas and ideologies that shifted with transitions in missionary leadership and the vanishing Jesuit dominance among Christian missionaries. For example, whereas Ricci advocated an accommodating position—considering the Chinese rites as secular expressions of cultural tradition and allowing the Chinese to study their ancient books—his successor to the mission, Longobardi, regarded the rituals as manifestations of atheism and sought to eradicate them, as did the Dominicans and Franciscans who later gained influence in China

(Cook/Rosemont 10–16). Yu Liu has recently drawn renewed atten-tion to the major phases of the Jesuit mission to China and the dis-tinctions among them. In an essay on Jesuit and non-Jesuit influences on Leibniz's Chinese writings, she discusses the intellectual relations between Leibniz and the Jesuits in an attempt to revive the debate on whether there was "a causal relationship between Leibniz's intellectual association with China and the development of his own ideas" (163). Discerning two phases in Leibniz's Chinese writings, Liu distin-guishes between China's supporting role in the first and its profound influence on his thought in the second. Accordingly, both phases evolved in response to Jesuits' representations of China and their changing impact in the context of the Christian mission. Yet the increasing influence of an anti-Jesuit element, namely the Franciscans, forced Leibniz to examine critically, rather than merely reiterating, his sources on China.[4] He had to develop an argument that refined the Republic of Scholar's ideas of China and challenged their limitations.

My suggestion, then, is that Leibniz's privileged status at the court enabled him to transform the missionary text, which he received with all the distortions and ideologies inflicted upon it and which changed with every shift in the administrative powers among the missionaries. But Leibniz was not the only one engaged in acts of paraphrase. In fact, missionary practice was steeped in it as rhetorical paraphrase ascended to a dominant method of conversion. Not only was the ethnic read through paraphrase, Christianity was spread through this particular form of translation. Leibniz commented on it in his corre-spondence with missionaries (cf. Widmaier, *Leibniz*) and in the pref-ace to *Novissima Sinica* (Cook/Rosemont, 45–60), going so far as to recommend a series of readings for potential converts. Even more illustrative is an anonymously published catalogue of instructions for missionaries entitled *Observationes* written around 1700 in German, a three-page manuscript that remained quite obscure in terms of its author(s), the sponsoring religious order, and the geographical area of missionary activity; nevertheless, the piece reveals how the textual principles of the Republic of Scholars unfolded in practice.

The different needs and backgrounds of the locals played a crucial role in proselytizing, as did tricks to get young people interested in technical gadgets, optical instruments, and Western devices that could be sold, rhetorically, as products of Western—that is, Christian—civilization. Yet among the various procedures intended to convert the "heathens," those concerned with books, with writing and copying, were deemed particularly successful because of their subtlety and the elegance with which they were disguised as education. These techniques conceived of successful conversion as a process that completely detached language, representation, and thought from discriminating sounds and images, and that restricted them, instead, to a system of literacy, writing, and reading (Ong, 90–93). In its emphasis on writing, this moment of conversion recaptured—not quite coincidentally— the elevation of Learned Latin, thus simulating, through the technologies it employed, its roots within the Republic of Scholars.

Although its title, *Observationes*, alluded to visual perception of the native culture, any traces thereof were completely suppressed in the treatise, which begins, not surprisingly, by recommending appropriate recording techniques for documenting the native language in a book. Though on the surface the title of the treatise appears to be an aberration, it enshrines, in fact, the shift from aural perception to literal representation that is defined by the visual space of the inscribed page. Appropriately then, the missionaries were instructed to listen carefully to the idioms used by the natives and to record them as a resource available for reading by their potential successors in the next phase of the mission. The technologies of mission not only translated what was *heard* into what could be *read*, they also imposed a new system of writing. The Chinese idioms, the treatise instructs, had to be transcribed in an alphabetized writing system so that the locals could be asked to copy them. Once they had acquired writing skills and recorded their own language in Latin characters, they would be given short Christian pamphlets or excerpts from the Scripture to copy. Writing and copying, the text suggests, would allow the locals to become literate and eventually assure their growing interest in the teachings of the Bible. As literacy became highly instrumental, it provided the material base and ideal medium for a European understanding of universal translatability.

This understanding of literacy acknowledges different characteristics of individual languages, but its implementation leads to erasing cultural alterity. Since literacy denotes a complex phenomenon relating sounds to letters, or spoken to written language, it levels cultural differences once it is equated with the alphabet as its primary writing system. In this respect, the presumed pictorial nature of Chinese characters and their intercultural legibility seemed to be eclipsed by a writing system whose use and accessibility spread with the technological advances of printing, the revolutionized mediality of the book market, and the emergence of broader school systems. Elitist in its sociological genesis and democratic in its potential, literacy became an important goal of (not only missionary) instruction. As it adopted the ideal of fostering a transparent language representing the order of world, it resurrected an ideal that Leibniz's contemporaries perceived as real in the Chinese language and political process. Thus "authentic" recommendations in *Observationes* for an effective mission corroborated long-standing scholarly opinions about the role Jesuits played in China.

By assimilating the information he received through Jesuit missionaries, Leibniz helped secure them an almost fairytale-like presence in philosophical thought: after all, these Jesuit reports enabled Europeans to reconstruct ancient China. Though not the first to report on China, the Jesuits gained a unique reputation. Their status within the Republic of Scholars, their scholarly method of missionary work, and their hitherto little-appreciated linguistic proselytizing assured their legacy. Their familiarity with European sciences created an alternative framework for evaluating the Chinese belief system, leading, perhaps, to praise of Chinese morals and state systems as a model for Europe. By perceiving China as a society where their own ideals might prosper, the Jesuits found effective ways to convince their fellow Europeans of the mission's significance (Dawson, 43; *Discourse*, 105). Leibniz greatly appreciated the Jesuits' rigorous training in the sciences and their mode of scholarly conduct (Hsia, 369–74), comparing—especially in his *Discourse*—the missionaries' readings of and their writings about China with his own interpretations.

READING LEIBNIZ, THE READER OF CHINA

Although Leibniz's Chinese texts resonate with the learned nature of missionary discourse, they are distinct in that they engendered what David Porter calls an "inassimilable alterity" (241), a textual image of China that arose and was fortified throughout eighteenth-century Europe, that referred not only to subject matter and to the reception they received, but also and especially to the notions of subjectivity they generated. They installed, as we shall see, a subject that *knows* because it reads between and across several "books." In that, Leibniz's texts distinguished themselves from missionary writings that chronicled and instructed about the supplanting of Chinese culture through one book, the Scripture.[5] In Leibniz's case, alterity indicated a manner of reading and translating that produced a different conceptualization of an ethnic locale, a moment incongruent with imperial subjection. His Chinese texts signaled an epistemic shift: they planted the seeds of Enlightenment universalism by anchoring the idea of universality in Chinese philosophies—effectively intellectual imperialism.[6]

By closely examining Leibniz's texts and the ways in which they understood and translated China, the remainder of this chapter demonstrates that the Enlightenment's universal claims were not merely constituted in opposition to ethnic alterity, but were permeated by it: the idea of Enlightenment universalism became legitimate, legible, and plausible through acts of reading China. These acts would eventually morph into a philosophical intention that did not equal a notion of autonomous subjectivity, but that did allow it to emerge. Put differently: reading and writing the ethnic became a foundation for proclaiming the sovereignty of reason, rather than positing reason as the product of a rational, sovereign, and entirely autonomous writer-subject. In this sense, alterity entailed possible alternatives to Cartesian subjectivity.

Leibniz began his *Discourse* by drawing attention to the Jesuit premises in representing China:

> I have taken the pleasure of looking through the books you sent me on Chinese thought. I am inclined to believe that the [Chinese] writers, especially the ancient ones, make much sense. There should be no difficulty in granting that to them despite the opinions of some of their own modern writers. It is comparable to the Christians, who are not always obliged to follow the meaning which the Scholastics and later commentators have given to Scripture, the Church Fathers or the ancient laws. *A fortiori*, concerning the Chinese, where the Monarch, who is the leader of all sages and the living embodiment of the law, appears to reveal rational expressions of ancient doctrines. Therefore the grounds upon which Father Nicholas Longobardi (successor to Father Ricci, founder of the mission to China) most often supports himself in order to combat the accommodationist explanations of his predecessor, namely that the Mandarins did not take such ancient writings seriously (something which made for considerable difficulty in Ricci's time) are no longer valid today by authority of this prince and many knowledgeable members of his court. (75)

Defined and essentially limited by missionary intentions, the received information resembled a translation into the language of Scripture, for it contained extensive linguistic commentary and spurred discussions, theses, and debates on how to reconcile Confucianism—dubbed interchangeably "Chinese philosophy," "Chinese theology," or "Chinese doctrine"—with Christian theology. That this reconciliation was possible was hardly doubted; neither the so-called Rites Controversy nor the later, somewhat more divisive question of whether there is a Chinese equivalent to God undermined the assimilatory technique of conversion (Cook/Rosemont, 8–10).

At first glance Leibniz's commentary seems to be an extension of this practice. His critical references to sources, his analysis and inter-pretation of words and concepts, and the titles of the first three parts of the text all point to a scholarship rooted in Christian theology: the first part is "Chinese Opinion Concerning God," then "Chinese Opinion Concerning the Productions of God or of the First Principle, Matter, and Spirits," and finally "Chinese Opinion Concerning the Human Soul, Its Immortality, Rewards and Punishments." But when writing about his renewed interest in the ancient Chinese texts, Leibniz invoked Jesuit commentary mainly to criticize their overre-liance on modern, Neo-Confucian interpretations and commentary rather than the ancient writings themselves. As Leibniz revealed an at times complicated relationship between those individuals who could read ancient Chinese texts and those who translated and interpreted them, he firmly placed the ancient book at the center of his *Discourse*. The materiality of the book and its preserving qualities transcended human interest and distortion. Nevertheless, the section ends by glorifying Scripture-inspired reading and commentary as an effective means for recognizing the "truth," and it emphatically reiterates Leibniz's focus on "doctrine" rather than the "ceremonies of worship" (76).

Thus the first section of the *Discourse* creates an overall sense of epistemological uncertainty. Conflicting readings were indeed inevitable in a text relating information about the ancient Chinese but colored by Jesuit missionary accounts. Witnessing to scholarly exchange rather than subjugation in the textual relations between Europe and China, Leibniz's *Discourse* contains notions of ethnicity that suggest secular reading and that code subjectivity and knowledge correspondingly. Leibniz set out to combine reading with considera-tions of mathematical, political, and philosophical systems of repre-sentation because the ancient books of the Chinese were paired with the well-informed Chinese court as their intellectual safeguard and interpreter.

To assume the perspective of an autocratic ruler, either real or rhetorical, was a commonplace of early modern texts. On a mundane level, textual inscriptions of monarchs allowed writers to pay homage to their patrons. In the symbolic system of society, the monarch stood, of course, simultaneously for the limits of worldview and tentative, nonblasphemic thought-experiments pushing these limits. "The social position of the king," writes Norbert Elias, "encourage[d] the image of independent, self-sufficient individuality" (319). The monarch oscillated between two worlds, symbolizing the divine world order in everyday life by being God's representative in his principality, and also simulating the essentially modern concept of the individual. Leibniz's Chinese monarch was more radical, however, for his importance arose not from his assumed place in a divine order or his presence in the historical imagination of his subjects, but solely from his relationship to the sacred and mundane writings of his culture. By being the sages' principal, the Chinese monarch held a position that exceeded the executive and legislative role of European sovereigns. As an intellectual authority, a blend of political sovereign and scholar, the monarch embodied a force that thwarted textual corruption, false readings, and general abuse of tradition on the part of Neo-Confucian authors. Through his great level of erudition, he restored the ultimate authority of the ancient text. Alternately, the unique combination of politics and scholarship assured a rightful, conscious relationship of a people to its past and to the books telling the story of a people and defining its place in the world.

Evidently the importance and appreciation of a particular monarch was not defined sociologically (i.e., by the political power relationships at the court) or hereditarily (i.e., by royal kinship), but through the sovereign's access to books, his position within the community of scholars, and the common understanding that he was the wisest in reading and interpreting the ancient texts (Liu, 167). In Leibniz's view the Chinese monarchy resembled an intellectual community. After the sovereign the community included, in hierarchical order, the *literati*, a group of philosophers whose "prestige [. . .] consisted in a knowledge of writing and of literature as such," and *mandarins*, a class of highly educated bureaucrats who acquired their official rank after passing a series of imperial exams. "Orderly government" emanated from this community, as well as "a public morality admirable in certain regards, conjoined to a philosophical doctrine, or rather a natural theology, venerable by its antiquity, established and authorized for about 3,000 years" (*Discourse*, 78). Here Leibniz accomplished more than merely refuting dogma: by insisting on a more accurate reading of the Chinese texts than Ricci (and Longobardi) provided, he also proclaimed the greater authority and wisdom of these ancient books; he suggested that, based on their age, they might turn out to be more valuable than the Bible and comparable only to Ancient Greek and Roman texts (78).[7]

That superb public morals, leaders with impeccable ethics, and traditionally sanctioned laws shaped Chinese society were beliefs that, according to David Porter, seventeenth-century Jesuits and their contemporaries merely read into the texts (16, 229). This assessment is correct from today's point of view, but warrants some expansion. Throughout the seventeenth century—and in full agreement with the epistemology of the time—Chinese sacral books, their reading as well as their rewriting were imagined to establish correspondences of *relation*. Different forms of representation, be they verbal or social expression, were thought to be in perfect correspondence with each other, "interwoven in the same fabric" (Foucault, *Order*, 88). The political order of China and the public ethics of the Chinese people were perceived as modeled on these books, in perfect accordance with the text. Only much later in the history of Western philosophy, namely in Herder's *Reflections on the Philosophy of History of Mankind* (1784–85) and in Hegel's *Philosophy of History* (1837) were these correspondences regarded as a limitation because they could not escape the static character of their model.[8]

For Leibniz, though, to insinuate that the monarch's political leadership and the moral fabric of society could arise from engagement with text and tradition transformed the ways in which the Republic of Scholars had treated the Christian dogma of a Scripture-based world. It laid the groundwork for models of individual subjectivity that were not based so much in introspection or cognitive sovereignty as in a reader's relation to texts. Thus, Leibniz began to construct a basic element in the Enlightenment narrative that gained special significance in the German context: the enlightened monarch who could be educated and, once knowledgeable, would foster public discourse toward an all-encompassing community and, eventually, toward national unity. Hence the Chinese emperor embodied an ideal that simulated the elusive reality of the Brunswick-Hannover dukedom, where, on one hand, many of the perfect material conditions for an enlightened principality existed—an extensive library, a duke interested in collecting, Leibniz's systematic approach to cataloguing books, and so on—yet where, on the other hand, Duke Rudolf August showed no interest in relating to and through books (cf. Green et al.). To emulate the Chinese ideal in a German reality was implicit in Leibniz's writings, however, and certainly guided their subsequent reception.

Situated between Jesuit texts and the ghostly ideal of an enlightened ruler, Leibniz embarked on his project of reading. As we have seen, his first technique was selection, aimed at returning to what he deemed to be historically original, and this was entirely consistent with dominant language theories of the time. On one hand was the belief that a text's inherent reason—the relation between *word* and *thing*—shone through in the translations and proved the text's authenticity. Inherent reason, historical origin, and a single appropriate and unobstructed use of the word became synonymous, the distinguishing marks of the text's authentic nature, contrary to the criterion that would define authenticity a hundred years later, namely the author's original intent. Though efforts at discrediting the textual truth certainly existed during Leibniz's times, no profane author-intention could corrupt a text's or language's natural transparency. (Leibniz's criticism of Jesuit and neo-Confucian manipulations of the originals attests to this conviction.) On the other hand was the idea that the essence of the text evolved from what Leibniz perceived to be the ideographic nature of the Chinese language. He frequently pointed to the identity of word and thing: "as is well-known Chinese characters aim not at words but things" (Widmaier, *Rolle*, 212). Skeptical about a fully pictorial or mimetic nature, he was convinced of their potential for absolute transparency. Claiming that Chinese characters have complex meanings because they are composed of smaller primitive signs arranged in a reasonable order and mirroring the essence of life (Widmaier, *Leibniz*, 60), Leibniz proposed that an isolated character might indeed serve as a model for an entire text. The "truth" of the text would prevail accordingly, since such a text would resist accidental misreadings as well as corrupt reading strategies. Leibniz ultimately concluded: "But to examine these things more closely, these explications are best sustained by the texts" (*Discourse*, 76). And although the unity of word and thing, which in Leibniz's mind symbolized the unbroken surface or unity of the world, was ensured hermetically through reading, what was read was no longer God's words, but the natural clarity and effectiveness ascribed to Chinese characters.

Peter Fenves's *Arresting Language* proves helpful in discerning Leibniz's textual practice further. Though Fenves does not specifically address the Chinese writings, he attempts to explore possible connections between what Leibniz considered to be a divine or in any case natural transparent language and the effects of reading this language; thus he directs us toward the conditions of knowledge production in Leibniz's work. To Fenves these conditions expressed themselves as "philosophical style" and its variations, without which there could be no extrapolation or advancement of knowledge. Accordingly, Leibniz's philosophical style was characterized by (1) meandering among a variety of genres and thus creating open spaces where knowledge could flourish without being choked by the rules of rhetoric, and (2) the inevitable liberation of subjectivity on the level of the word, the phrase, or the isolated expression, precisely by untying language from the word "God." In a series of attempted detachments, knowledge and philosophy arise through a variety of figural replacements: in the *Theodizee*, Fenves's main subject of analysis, fictional identities for the author (e.g., pseudonyms, taking on a character's name) stand beside numerals, or a small fable. Nevertheless, as Fenves demonstrates, philosophy cannot fully liberate itself from a way of reading that is modeled on the divine text, without creating pure fiction.

To what extent, then, do the Chinese texts untangle knowledge and subjectivity from the word "God"? Did Chinese symbols, authorities, and ways of knowing really penetrate European knowledge formation? Leibniz's insistence on using the translation closest to the ancient Chinese text, on going beyond the multiple renderings, transformations, and interpretations that existed, reflected the simple, foundational principle of his language theory: that any language originates from either a natural or a divine order (Fenves, *Arresting*, 16). Hence Leibniz's belief in the natural clarity of the Chinese character amounted to more than a natural theology. Chinese characters, Leibniz's correspondence suggested, might simulate the traces of a technical language, that is, invention, but unlike technical language, which is prone to corruption and obliqueness by elevating itself above nature and the divine, these characters portrayed clarity. Leibniz had hitherto attributed such clarity only to historical languages, believing that they "constitute a place where chance and reason, so far from excluding each other, are curiously combined. Every element of language is thoroughly grounded and is for this reason, if only for this reason, 'rational' " (42). Similarly, the Chinese characters' foundation appeared to be rational and contingent rather than prophetic or invented through a divine act. The same logic was thought to pervade the ancient Chinese texts and the relation between book and monarch, who reads according to the inherent reason of the book but also according to the probability and freedom appropriated through his intellect and wisdom:

> What we call the light of reason in man, they call commandment and law of Heaven. What we call the inner satisfaction of obeying justice and our fear of acting contrary to it, all this is called by the Chinese (and by us as well) inspiration sent by the Xanti (that is, by the true God). To offend Heaven is to act against reason, to ask pardon of Heaven is to reform oneself and to make a sincere return in word and deed in the submission one owes to this very law of reason. (*Discourse*, 105)

Nevertheless, Leibniz's *Discourse* was necessarily indebted to the mediating character of representation. Believing that there is no truth outside language and representation, he conferred authority upon the medium of the book, presuming that the Chinese scholars "knew" without the rationale of individual judgment, and were obligated to no authority other than the reading and deciphering of ancient books and interpretations (108).[9]

In the end Leibniz regarded the inherent reason of the Chinese character as a milestone, if not a presupposition of his larger project: the discovery of a universal language that is first and foremost natural, not invented, and that forms the basis of ethics. He believed it to be the logic of original or inherent reason that joined China and Europe in the world, and that it was still to be uncovered in Europe, through reading. The resulting relation, then, no longer stood for the one-dimensional and abstract, albeit all-encompassing unity of world expressed in God's Word, but also for an ongoing process of reading and translation that did not always refer back to the exalted divine. Relation comprised more than the image of an ideal China linking the book as the material basis of public morals to its deciphering through an erudite leader. Rather, acts of reading embedded China and Europe in the same fabric, the same texture of relation. The *Discourse* accordingly suggested that, by carefully weighing all conclusions and readings, the close-knit texture of the world, and reason as its universal cause, could be recognized and discerned in a reasonable, rational process drawing only on cognitive abilities and precluding *Anschauung* or *Empfindung*, the sense-based modes of recognition (79).

Conversely, Leibniz considered the subjectivity of the writer to be produced by this reading, evolving through the juxtaposition and combination of several textual authorities; hence another idea of modern subjectivity began to loom large, if in the background: that the text subverts the very idea to which it clings rhetorically, "the unbroken surface" of the sovereign's body (Foucault, *Order*, 39), which represented, in the view of premodern Europe, the unity of the world according to God's universe. Such textual subversion allegorizes another ideal: in alluding to the sage-like qualities of the Chinese monarch, the treatise paved the way for the European philosopher's self-stylization as reader, moral adjudicator, and political architect of society.

Though far from being asserted daily in the Republic of Scholars, this ideal resonated within the social, political, and cultural context of early eighteenth-century Europe, which gradually moved away from the "hereditary privilege" of aristocracy and church hierarchy and toward a society of *philosophes* (Dawson, 55). But because this ideal is confined to "intellectual training" (i.e., does not signal an epistemological intervention or the philosopher's autonomy), it affirms a unity-creating texture (Weber, 112). Enacting it was at the core of Leibniz's style; while paving the way toward enlightened secularization, it always characterized the texture woven by the Republic of Scholars. Never completely severing the ties to older, exegetic models of reading, this style allows us to read philosophical invention instantaneously, through allegories and translation.

TAMING THE EFFECTS OF TRANSLATING CHINA: THE SAGE-PHILOSOPHER IN A PREESTABLISHED HARMONY

As this bifurcated manner of reading arose, representations of China unfolded accordingly. Though Leibniz explicated the Chinese notions of macro- and microcosm as corresponding manifestations of heaven and earth, he moved closer to an idea of autonomous subjectivity by fusing the image of the Chinese king with that of ancient Chinese sage-philosophers (e.g., Confucius), even allowing the latter to depose the former. But whenever Leibniz's reading produced moments of ethnicity that threatened to rip the universal texture apart, those moments were tamed.

One such instance is Leibniz's account of the social impact of the king-sage-philosopher in passages advocating Confucian morality and politics, and calling upon the allegorical figure of the enlightened monarch to sustain their rhetorical legitimacy. Yet in constructing such allegories, Leibniz always avoided their appearing to reflect directly on the Brunswick-Wolfenbüttel court by retreating into the material foundation of the allegory, the unsurpassed authority of the old Chinese texts, and claiming that these texts created the monarch. What appears to be a shrewd deflection of Leibniz's compromised position vis-à-vis the court in fact indicates intellectual individuality cloaked in cosmopolitanism, as he fully adopted what was handed down to him as the literati's view of society: a perfect machine based on kinship, monarchy, and books. This view, which would dominate European accounts of Chinese society for decades to come (Dawson, 43; David Porter), was not just a European invention, but was also sustained by representational patterns across the Chinese literary tradition emphasizing relationships between processes of reading and natural ethics, between the individual ruler's microcosm and the macrocosm of world (Ames, 41). Thus the allegory of the reading scholar-monarch affected and defined the limits of the Republic of

Scholars in multiple ways, shifting the emphasis from the reader to what was read, hence replacing the Scripture with another, equally defining text, since Leibniz' *Discourse* refers to the historically codified materiality of ancient Chinese texts. At the same time, by conferring reasonable authority on Confucius and his successors, Leibniz simulated the future idealized role of the philosopher at German courts without having to accept the position, rhetorically, for himself.

But Leibniz's reading also advanced an understanding of ethnicity as something that could sustain universal thought and pave the way toward secularization, reverberating most strikingly in the practical or ethical application of reading Confucius. In an effort to explain Confucius's persistent silence on several epistemological topics, Leibniz agreed with most commentators, saying that Confucius had to remain silent on certain questions because of their complex nature (117). He argued that Confucius and his pupils must study clearly stated phenomena, including everything that could be perceived sensually, whereas everything beyond experience constituted forbidden territory (117–18). Furthermore, Leibniz asserted that Confucius considered the common people unable to liberate themselves from sensuous relationships to the objects surrounding them, and that he defined leadership as the ability to endow such relationships with respect and distance rather than sensual engagement and exploration of the sensual world.

Here Leibniz opened himself to discussing the conditions of social theories and political practice, but the ideas remained confined, even in their Chinese context. For Leibniz, they became legitimate only when he managed to "naturalize" them (105). He read them as an intricate part of the larger, societal fabric of the Chinese macrocosm, or heaven and universe, and its microcosmic pendant, that is, social relations among people. The *Li* governing their relation to each other, according to Leibniz, evolved in an unregulated, entirely natural way; in other words, he neglected to mention the intervention of sage-philosophers who had "devise[d the *Li* as] formal rules of conduct (Ames, 50).[10] For him, macrocosm and microcosm existed in perfect structural correspondence, though independent of each other (90), and the macrocosm reflected people's actions in that they were related to the supranatural powers, the Heavenly King, through the power of the *Li*.

Since the *Li* played a significant role in establishing "the natural theology of the Chinese," Leibniz devoted a significant portion of the *Discourse* to delineating correspondences and limits between the *Li* and the Divine (79, 83). He described the *Li* as an embodiment of the original cause of unity: itself not creating, it nevertheless proclaimed the almighty presence of a universal order. Citing ancient Chinese writings, Leibniz claimed that order is preestablished *in* and *through* the *Li* that, in turn, expresses itself through microcosmic singularities, that is, through individual people and natural and societal phenomena. They not only emanate from the *Li* but expose its otherwise hidden, macrocosmic force (91). A force or principle *beyond* human life, the *Li* structures life yet remains excluded from it. Life, knowledge, and authority are mere effects of this force, symptoms or fading "copies of a book," to borrow the rhetorical phrase Leibniz used in his essay on the origin of the universe.

Leibniz regarded these effects as the only means of assessing the power of the *Li*, discernable evidence of a rational order, allowing him in turn to deduce the inherently reasonable qualities of the *Li*: "Thus do I understand the Chinese, who say, according to Father de Sainte-Marie [. . .], that the *Li* is the law which governs, and the intelligence which guides things; that it is, however, not itself intelligent, but through natural force, its operations are so well regulated and sure, that one could say it is intelligent" (91). He opined that the *Li*, in and of itself perfect, had reached perfection through "its nature to choose, from several possibilities, the most appropriate" (93). Its intelligence produced, on one hand, the possibility of human choice since humans could read and recognize it; their actions constituted the macrocosm's polar supplement, a subjectivity that followed the law of force. On the other hand, because of its inherent predetermination, the *Li*'s intelligence confined this subjectivity. Constituting and erasing itself through endless variations of reading the original order, subjectivity thus replicated layers of commentary and the world's texture, but was incapable of reflecting upon the acts of cognition.

The flip side of these correspondences between microcosm and macrocosm was an autoinduced obedience among the Chinese people, suggested Leibniz, observing further that such behavior led to stable, stratified societies not susceptible to change. Rather, China's sacrificial structures stabilized social hierarchies, and, conversely, these stable societies created predictable reading situations for philosophers and the monarch, who furthered the insight into the macro- and microcosm by relating notions of "life," "knowledge," and "power" in human form (90–91). To many Europeans at the time, such conclusions seemed naturally like secularism, if not atheist propaganda, as is evident from the fate of Christian Wolff, a philosopher whom I will discuss in the next chapter. Leibniz himself, however, preempted an epistemological break with the Republic of Scholars by emphasizing that force, not matter or origin of creation, constituted the central element in his reading of the Chinese world.

A similar notion of force runs through Leibniz's writings on preestablished harmony, suggesting to some scholars that Leibniz's key philosophical concepts were indeed influenced by his engagement with Chinese thought (Needham, 496; cf. Liu on opposing arguments; see also Cook/Rosemont, 141–48). While I do not seek to establish or reject a causal relationship among his various writings, I do believe that Leibniz very deliberately constructed a relationship of representational correspondences throughout, making those adequate translations of each other. In this sense, Leibniz's reading of the *Li* links the Chinese writings to other texts and genres including the aphoristic *Monadology* and the *Theodizee*, both of which espouse the system of a preestablished harmony. Within this system "force" is characterized by spontaneity and receptivity as well as by its actual (and lawful) effects. Because of an inherent force, life follows "certain established rules of operation" (Schrecker/Schrecker, xix; cf. Deleuze, 11, 18–24). Force realizes life's potential for harmony between freedom and limitation, though this harmony is not always recognized and sometimes not even actualized. In this respect, "force" both absorbs and mirrors the primary qualities of the *Li*.[11]

The idea of a preestablished harmony reflects most clearly Leibniz's coming to terms with the problems of knowledge, the languages of representation, and the overall finite possibilities of subjectivity existing in the Republic of Scholars, and it structured Leibniz's encyclopedic enterprise, providing a grid for classification, that is, all his other philosophical ideas, images illustrating these ideas, and entire representational systems can be projected onto this grid.[12] Obeying its own inherent reason, every expression of creation is perfect and so perfect in fact that it never interferes with any other expression. If this system is universally valid, allowing, in Leibniz's sense, for an explication of the world, its consequences for representational systems are indeed far-reaching. In the realm of language, for example, every "commentary" must agree with every other, thus making languages universally translatable, and by relating one language to another, commentary produces an infinite number of systems of representation, all of which are equally legitimate expressions of the order of the world, or, as Leibniz has it, "different arrangements of the same truths" (*New Essays*, 625–26). Put differently: an infinite series of translation and paraphrase enables access to finite knowledge. This understanding, I propose, influenced the conceptualization of ethnic differences in Leibniz's texts: equally valid and unmistakably unique, ethnicities add up to a universal whole and represent—each by itself as well as all of them together—the coherence and truth of the universe.

1 AND 0: EXPRESSION OF A UNIVERSAL TEXTURE THROUGH READING

The last section of the *Discourse* ("Concerning the Characters which Fohi, Founder of the Chinese Empire, Used in His Writings, and Binary Arithmetic") epitomizes Leibniz's style of translation and paraphrase, illustrating that his writing devolved on reading and commentary while simultaneously pursuing a notion of ethnicity that actually sustained universalism. The *Discourse* concludes with an almost separate treatise on binary arithmetic in which Leibniz demonstrated the necessity for and—as he had believed for some time—the actual existence of a system of universal representation suited to entwine natural theology with reading the ethnic.[13]

"Concerning the Characters" brings into focus all the discreet, representational elements introduced before. The Chinese monarch, principal among a community of enlightened scholars, figures prominently, and the binary 1 and 0, to which the explication of the *Li* in the first part of the *Discourse* only alluded, comes to the fore. At last the *Discourse* addressed its own epistemological roots in a culture of commentary. As it set out to prove the intrinsic value of the most ancient sage-king's writing, the *Discourse* not only proclaimed a genuine philosophical tradition between this king, "Fohi, founder of the Empire," and Confucius superior to Neo-Confucian revisions, it also affirmed the hitherto merely alleged authority of the ancient Chinese books by discerning the manner in which they represented, unequivocally, the natural order of the universe. Appropriately, as this final section became the site where various textual authorities intersected and competed with each other, the *Discourse* proposed an innovative configuration of knowledge. By installing a newly arranged hierarchy among epistemological authorities, Leibniz's argumentation had come full hermetic circle. He, the European philosopher of the early Enlightenment, had finally brought to light the world's inherent universalism by reading China correctly:

> It is indeed apparent that if we Europeans were well enough informed concerning Chinese Literature, then, with the aid of logic, critical thinking, mathematics and our manner of expressing thought—more exacting than theirs—we could uncover in the Chinese writings of the remotest antiquity many things unknown to modern Chinese and even

to other commentators thought to be classical. Reverend Father Bouvet and I have discovered the meaning, apparently truest to the text, of the characters of Fohi, founder of Empire, which consist simply of combinations of unbroken and broken lines, and which pass for the most ancient writing in China in its simplest form. There are 64 figures contained in the book called Ye Kim, that is, the Book of Changes. Several centuries after Fohi, the Emperor Ven Vam and his son Cheu Cum, and Confucius more than five centuries later, have all sought therein philosophical mysteries. Others have even wanted to extract from them a sort of Geomancy and other follies. Actually, the 64 figures represent the Binary Arithmetic which apparently this great legislator [Fu Xi] possessed, and which I have discovered some thousands of years later. (132–33)

Clearly, in Leibniz's view, the characters of the Chinese language derived their semantic and semiotic transparency from more than their intercultural legibility as his contemporaries (and many scholars following them) believed. Earlier in the *Discourse* Leibniz himself had insinuated that the characters' clarity resulted from their perfect depiction of nature; now he maintained that their clarity stemmed from their relation to other systems of representation, that they were perfectly translatable into the language of formal logic as well as into the language of politics.

In pursuing this line of reasoning, Leibniz dissolved one of the central paradoxes of his time: on one hand, he adhered to the dogma that texts express the all-comprising, universal power of creation because God speaks through them; on the other, he demonstrated, by resorting to non-Western systems of representation, that the signs of the text (letters, words, and sentences) are arranged in a reasonable, additive order that reaches beyond the exalted word to the thing or object the words denote. They thus render possible the greatest transparency of expression, though the signs' accumulation adds to their complexity and density. In this respect texts must represent a natural order. Consequently, Leibniz amended his initial statement on Chinese books. In order to substantiate his thesis of their universal translatability into other systems of representation, he actually listed the strategies of reading that he deemed necessary for discerning the complex character of Chinese writing systems, namely "logic, critical thinking, mathematics, and our manner of expressing thought—more exacting than theirs" (132). Thus, Leibniz refined his understanding of the *clavis sinica*, which he had hoped to receive ready-made some decades earlier; now, deciphering the Chinese language became possible through a natural "key," a combination of logic and commentary through reading. Readily at the disposal of early modern scientists, these processes could be applied to what they perceived to be the self-revealing nature of the Chinese language (see Palumbo-Liu; David Porter).

The sixty-four characters of Fohi sustain this model of reading because they combine transparency, or linguistic preciseness, with the accuracy of calculus. Pictorially they incorporate binary arithmetic, thus enabling an understanding of a numerical system as a privileged realm for representation. The binary—or, as Leibniz frequently called it Chinese—arithmetic enables an infinite notation of numerical singularities and multiplicities through nothing but 1 and 0; "[I]n Binary Arithmetic," wrote Leibniz, "there are only two signs, 0 and 1, with which we can write all numbers" (133). This system of dyadic progression distinguishes itself from decimal progression, where 0, 1, 2, 3, 4, 5, 6, 7, 8, and 9 generate an infinite series of numbers through mathematical operations; the numbers comprise positives and negatives, decimals and fractions.[14] By contrast, dyadic progression remains restricted to an infinite series of positives, excluding decimals and fractions from the outset. In this system, all numbers can be easily counted and written using a recurring periodicity of 0 and 1 arranged in columns, beginning at the right-hand side of a page, and progressing in a dual manner, as table 2.1 shows.

Table 2.1 Dyadic Progression of Numbers in the Binary Numerical System

0 = 0
01 = 1
10 = 2
11 = 3
100 = 4
101 = 5
110 = 6
111 = 7
1000 = 8
1001 = 9
1010 = 10
1011 = 11
1100 = 12
1101 = 13
1110 = 14
1111 = 15
10000 = 16

Far more central than this "rediscovery of the binary arithmetic," which Leibniz claimed, is the representational power that numbers acquired. They continued to fulfill perfectly their conventional role of expressing an arrangement of relation, but they also exceeded it, coming to signify the conditions of existential being and its origin, as well as of possibilities and limitations. The latter was most important to Leibniz, because numbers came to provide the material substrate for representing the presence of things, for expressing what exists, not what is lacking. Accordingly, all numerical (as well as corresponding nonnumerical) representations start out with 1, a full entity indicating a given, empirically perceivable amount. In Leibniz's writings on Chinese philosophy, 1/One stands for the world's unity, "the Being, the Substance, the Entity" (80). It ultimately demarcates the *Li* and defines its unique relation to force and predetermination. And just as this primary unity or cause is a necessity of being without depending on matter, unity, or Oneness, is the foundational principle of all numbers without having a constituent outside itself. While 0 in contrast seems empty, it too functions in a highly ambiguous manner, being at once a sign within a numerical system and hovering outside this system as a "sign-about-signs," for 0 "signifies nothing," while enabling all kinds of signification (Rotman, 13). It is 0, not 1 that propels the dyadic progression forward. It constitutes a point to which all kinds of references can be made while by itself being unable to signify anything without other numbers.

By deciphering the binary or, in his words, "Chinese" arithmetic, Leibniz believed he had solved the puzzle of representing the universe. Within the decimal system, 0 marks the void; however, in binary arithmetic this void is filled with the unfolding of numbers that can be accumulated ad infinitum through combinations of 1 and 0. By producing relations among numbers, 0 takes on a crucial, signifying role and transcends its own predetermined emptiness as the series of numbers eradicates a void, even though they depend on the "character of emptiness" for both designation and notation. Similarly, an infinite series or quantity of numbers can be produced from a finite cause or inventory of signifiers.

Just as the binary 1 and 0 can express every number and every numerical operation, the corresponding representations create a precise identity between signifier and signified. They are never obscure or invented (or technical), but always clear and natural. Not surprisingly, one system of representation easily translates into another; moreover, Leibniz observed, one system even contains and condenses another: "When I communicated this system to the Reverend Father Bouvet, he recognized in it the characters of Fohi, for the numbers 0 and 1 correspond to them exactly if we put a broken line for 0 and an unbroken line for the unity, 1" (*Discourse*, 133).

Evidently the expression (and preservation) of binary arithmetic in the characters of Fohi acquired an important status in Leibniz's philosophy of universalism. The mutual reflection of numerical system and characters suggested that every event, phenomenon, or concept could be represented in a universally accessible language that, in the end, restores an unbroken surface between words and things. However, the ideal, transparent language no longer relates God's exalted word but nature's order. It therefore reconciled Leibniz's position within the Republic of Scholars with an early Enlightenment worldview in which every representation constituted a reference to the universe. Accordingly, any particular expression or language, be it a linguistic sign, a scientific axiom, or mathematics, symbolized universality; thus ethnicity—in this case Chinese ethnicity—engendered both the effects of universalism and its representational anchors.

This becomes clear from an example of Leibniz's prenational thought. A letter to Duke Rudolph August von Braunschweig-Lüneburg-Wolfenbüttel, "The Mystery of Creation," in fact reiterates the value Leibniz attributed to the binary arithmetic and Chinese characters. Like the *Discourse*, this much shorter and much older text established textual links between Europe and China. Leibniz had composed the letter in German in 1697 and addressed it to his patron. At first glance, the text seems rather ordinary: a New Year's greeting expressing Leibniz's deep gratitude and implying his profound hope that the duke would continue to support his studies (*Zwei Briefe*, 19–23). In the midst of the letter, Leibniz informs the duke that he had written to the Jesuits in China, imparting the same ideas he was about to share with the duke and hoping that the arithmetic-enthusiastic Chinese emperor would love them and, perhaps, show more interest in Christianity.

Leibniz, however, devoted most of the letter to a medallion or coin he had designed and dedicated to the duke. Like the letter, the coin does not call attention to itself, at least not on its obverse: a portrait of the duke, meant to signal Leibniz's devotion, featured prominently, expressing the duke's supreme power over him, his dedicated scholar-subject, as well as over everyone in the dukedom; it also represented the duke's place within God's universe. The coin's reverse appears a little more mysterious. It includes Arabic numerals and their binary equivalents, in addition to a Latin maxim, demonstrating the universal order in numbers in that they are identical in meaning to the words. Alternately, the numbers underscore the absolute role Oneness (1) or unity played in Leibniz's thought, while implying the reference point zero, a signification of relation and choice:

2.3.4.5. &C   0   [1]
OMNIBUS. EX. NIHILO. DUCENDIS. SUFFICIT.UNUM (21)

Together with the commentary provided in the letter, the imprint revealed the ultimate purpose of the medallion and its allegorical meaning: the search for a medium through which the mystery of Creation, "the creation of all things out of nothing, through the almighty God" (19). By designing the coin Leibniz wanted to reiterate the philosophical thoughts on Creation he had shared with the duke a few weeks earlier, rendering material and comprehensible what had then seemed like a mere belief or an abstract, nonrepresentable axiom. The imprint, thus, encapsulated Leibniz's translation theory.

According to Leibniz, God the Creator equals God the Determined Knowledge in this letter, thus constructing Scholastic truism. But this truism finds its perfect and natural expression in the Chinese arithmetic. In accordance with Baroque aristocratic fashion, the binary arithmetic—via the Roman and Arabic numerical systems—inscribed a maxim; accordingly, the medal's central motto, engraved on the coin's obverse, reads: IMAGO CREATIONIS (image or representation of Creation). By placing the duke in the divine line through an allegorical representation, the medal translated a universal order into the particularity of the German principality:

> Hence one of the main principles of Christianity, especially among the principles that are least understood by the learned men of this world and hardly teachable to the heathens, is the creation of things through the almighty power of God. And one can well imagine that nothing in this world represents this power more adequately, even exhibits it, than the origin of numbers as it is presented here: by expressing it through 1 and 0 or Nothing. It is hard to imagine finding a better epitome of this mystery in nature. (19)

By introducing a dominant opinion about the nature of numbers likening them to unordered accumulations and combinations of single digits, Leibniz revealed the preestablished order and harmony within numerical systems. He believed that the work of creation reveals itself through this harmony: like creation, the harmony of numbers cannot be improved upon; it is therefore stable and complete. However, because of its meaningfully organized design, this harmony can apply to an infinite series of numbers and indeed generate new numbers; in that sense, numerical systems produce infinite knowledge and progressing ways of reading (20).

Furthermore, just as the intrinsic link between stability and the infinity of the numerical system expressed Leibniz's belief in determination and freedom, the corresponding design on the medal's reverse asserted the symmetry of creation and represented it in an exemplary way. Linking the language of Learned Latin to a numerical language and natural religion to the monarch of a German dukedom restored the texture of the world (or, as I have frequently called it in this chapter, "the unbroken surface of the world"). The capacity of numbers to represent everything in a precise way assured the identity between signifier (1) and signified (the unity of the world), thus turning the ideal of universal translatability into an attainable objective and, ultimately, into a statement relating a truism. Admittedly, the Latin sentence, the numerical sequence, and the duke as the medal's recipient stood for different systems of representation, but they expressed the same organizing principle of the "world's texture." Despite rendering it into different languages and materials, these representations designated the unlimited power of creating and reasoning. At the same time, the representation through different material objects defined the position of humans in the world. Be they coins or books, Leibniz concluded, these objects produced a text that, grounded in either the Divine or in Nature, penetrated every aspect of worldly existence.

Through the etching on the coin, Leibniz's patron took on the characteristics of the enlightened monarch, modeled on his Chinese counterpart. Thus various systems of representation and the analogy and interplay between two of Leibniz's writings linked two monarchs who embodied their respective societies in the all-encompassing texture of world. In other words, Leibniz's style espoused the dominant configurations of knowledge production and subjectivity of his time, capturing their limitations while implying possibilities for transgressing these boundaries. Whereas the *Discourse* characterized the Chinese sovereign as an intellectual who actively interacted with the community of scholars and incorporated the centuries-old wisdom of books into daily politics, the medal's representation of the duke placed him in a divine line; accordingly, he resumed the role of God's representative on earth and embodied divine power. Leibniz emphasized this aspect by praising the duke and attributing to him ultimate authority over education, scholarly research, and the learned conversations in which he participated, and in which Leibniz functioned only as a commentator and translating reader, not as inventing philosopher. In the *Discourse* then, the more progressive allegory of the monarch indicated not so much a regression (Härtel, 105–8) as a disguise and the anticipation of the future role of the philosopher, while not permitting Leibniz to pursue this role for himself.

Ultimately, "The Mystery" and the *Discourse* marked a threshold, a transition to a new epistemological authority. The texts reiterated the claim to a universal language, to a world in which Europe and China complemented each other, by combining the Western writing systems of alphabet and Scripture with the Eastern writing system of the binary arithmetic. Leibniz's writing replicated a thus-conceived universal texture, but not without an essential paradox. As it entwined the rhetorical paraphrase of divine creation with renderings of nature's inherent reason, his commentary remained caught within the epistemological confinements of the Republic of Scholars while simultaneously advancing secularization and the emancipation of individual subjectivity and autonomy. Subjectivity was seen as limited, because it could only encompass what was given and imposed by God. However, the subject could approximate the infinite, divine knowledge through reading and recognition. Reading, in turn, could continue *ad infinitum*, so in this respect, Leibnizian subjectivity is free and unlimited. Furthermore, by posing a challenge to his patron in the New Year's letter, Leibniz asked that he appreciate learned conversation and reading and, in claiming that a society's history reveals itself through reading and that society progresses through intellectual activity, Leibniz embraced enlightened absolutism and introduced a program of *Fürstenerziehung*, a philosophical-educational ideal of societal evolution that would become popular in German principalities in the second half of the eighteenth century and that would shape the view of the eighteenth century for subsequent generations (see chapter 3).

Leibniz's "Chinese writings" represent an early sign—and a unique manifestation—of what Russell Berman has called the German *Sonderweg*, a particular instance of Enlightenment alterity that surfaced as Germans encountered other cultures (7–10). As a participant in the deterritorialized and inter-European but text-bound culture of the Republic of Scholars, Leibniz anchored his prenational hopes for the central German principality of Brunswick-Wolfenbüttel in an idealized Chinese text (and wrote it mostly in French or Learned Latin). Subjectivity arose not from an assertive Self, but through a perpetual reading of a transparent texture through which the world's inherent reason and inner coherence shine. Whereas Berman locates the causes for national differentiation and multiplicity within the European narrative of imperialism and the nexus of individual observation and writing—a thesis to which we shall return in chapter 4—Leibniz's writings on China point toward an element of the Enlightenment that has been disputed in recent decades. This is its claim to universalism, the roots of which lay in China's textual tradition, without which Jesuit and Protestant missionaries would probably not have shown any interest or success in the Chinese empire. Both written documents and the intellectual nature of the Chinese culture appealed to missionaries, the first of whom arrived in China in 1583. They probably expected to encounter an illiterate, "oral" culture such as missionaries and other travelers had found on the African continent, and that may explain why, for example, the systematic Herrnhut mission to the African Cape region did not begin until more than 150 years later, in 1731 (Mielke, 177, 222 n. 201, 336).

3

READING SOVEREIGN SUBJECTIVITY
VIA CHINA

To read and, ultimately, to translate China enabled Leibniz to proclaim the existence of universal reason; nevertheless, he never gave up on the metaphysical principle of predetermination. To him, China expressed its essence in a writing system and culture of historical literacy—and legibility—driven by reason and literally depicting the *things* behind the *words*. As reason articulated its worldly presence through the Chinese characters, reading the characters—that is, engaging in an act by which people related themselves to signs as well as signs to signs—advanced reason over time. Hence, Leibniz concluded, ancient Chinese books continued to direct the actions of Chinese emperors, who assured moral order because of their roots in a literary culture. Texts obligated the ruling class to lead a knowledgeable existence and to uphold public ethics. The result of Leibniz's translation was a representation of China that combined aspects of language, history, and moral order and that, if read properly by Europeans, could help restore inherent reason, order, and stability on the war-torn continent. Reading thus linked China and Europe in a universe of texts.

According to Leibniz, reason expressed itself not only in the clarity of the Chinese characters, but also in the microcosmic social stratification of Chinese society; hence he regarded the potential of the philosopher-scholar as a force that could both disrupt and promote the prearranged unity of the world without forcing him to leave behind his patron's court and the intellectual confines of the Republic of Scholars. And enlightened monarchy functioned accordingly: as a shield upholding the epistemological authority of one individual and guarding against the excess of widespread "philosophizing" activities at the same time. (Of course, there was always the risk of a corrupt or overzealous reader who might include other texts or infuse with dogma both the ethnic text and the idea of deciphering a predetermined reason. And if the reader strayed from texts, reading, and translation, the established network of knowledge production would break down completely. Yet, as with every crisis, with this breakdown would come innovation as well.)

Leibniz noticed the liberating effects that such an epistemic rupture might have on philosophy and knowledge even in his Chinese writings. With the publication of *Novissima Sinica*, more than a decade before he finished writing his *Discourse*, Leibniz introduced a genre of writing and a notion of the philosopher that inevitably, if unintentionally, brought with it the possibility of leaving the Republic of Scholars. In his preface to this edition of Jesuit writings, he cautioned against the adverse effects that reports about China, the intercultural exchange, and the Jesuits' teaching of sciences to Chinese monarchs might have upon Christianity in Europe (Cook/Rosemont, 51–52). While his tone and content showed him fully in the Republic of Scholars, he had compiled a new model of scholarly communication. Naming influential scholars and contributors in the preface, he acknowledged their patrons and dependency on court and church; however, by envisioning as readers a broader public composed of all those interested in China, he appealed also to a new type of scholar: the specialist. Leibniz sensed the increasing tendency toward specialization among scholars and the need to enlist the help of others if he wanted to succeed in his ultimate project, the translatability of the universe. Perhaps he was already keenly aware of what Luhmann would describe almost three hundred years later as the onset of a functionally differentiated society; in any case he seemingly began to realize that the authority of knowledge resides not necessarily in a text. This realization fueled Leibniz's interest in creating academies of science and encouraged him to promote them actively (see Schrecker/Schrecker, xix).

Most importantly, in his analysis of "the latest news from China," Leibniz noted the same areas of specialty among the Chinese. Comparing European and Chinese expertise in areas as diverse as crafts, trades, agriculture, cameralism, and the natural sciences, he distinguished practical from theoretical occupations and singled out Chinese practical philosophy (ethics) as a model. That became one of *Novissima Sinica*'s most long-lasting impacts, but the text is equally significant for the emergence of a new concept of the philosopher whose product, though still a text, no longer chronicled the divine word but the human task. By legitimizing both the epistemological situation and the public role of the philosopher, *Novissima Sinica* paved the way for understanding intellectual activity as something inspired by a community of people and their shared interests. The intellectual enterprise derived its *raison d'être* from social interaction among humans rather than from the parameters of a text and a textually sustained social hierarchy; it was reflected in the innovative genre of collaboration, editing, and publishing that *Novissima Sinica* initiated. The habit of communication among small communities of scholars eventually led to the modern public forum. Put differently, Leibniz's *Novissima Sinica* was both a seed for and the product of what we have come to consider a staple of Enlightenment discourse: the public sphere (Zammito, *Birth*, 17, 23–35; Habermas; Hess).

As I explore contours of the Enlightenment public sphere in this chapter, its reliance on China remains of central interest: Was China an image? A geographical space? Had it become—not unlike 0 in Leibniz's treatise on numbers—a unique signifier? Which transitions, if any, would the Chinese cipher undergo? At the same time, the notion of the public sphere also invoked sovereign subjectivity and projected a new relation among reading, constructions of China, and subjectivity.

In what follows I shall examine three models of sovereign subjectivity from German philosophical and literary texts of the eighteenth century. China emerges as a cipher in these texts, continuously conjuring up a universal order while still becoming linked to these different expressions of subjectivity. The Chinese cipher projects these subjectivities elusively: through cognitive identity, individuality and authority, communal reference, and personal limitation. While engendering the sovereignty of subjectivity, the Chinese cipher never names it explicitly. Moreover, as we navigate through the texts, we notice that the Chinese elements become more and more ornamental in the philosophical and didactic prose, novelistic fragments, and dramatic texts: while we can very easily recognize some attributes of the traditional imagery of China, others appear obscure or detached from the institutional, cultural, or historical situations from which they emerged. "China" was on its way to an empty signifier in texts that simultaneously enlarged the exemplary nature and stature of the distant culture. At the same time, subjectivities evolved around and against China. As they were produced in relation to community, these subjectivities shifted authority away from the text and toward individuals, engendering new textual dynamics that henceforth characterized attempts at theorizing ethnicity as well. However, the results evince an equal desire for universality and universal norms.

We shall see a tension arise from the collusion of two modes of perceiving and representing cultural alterity. Though there is the ongoing

effort to identify symptoms of universalism by reading and interpreting ethnic difference, ethnicity appears as a distorting, segregating,
and particularizing element that emanated, I submit, from the altered
focus on the individual and its self-articulation in texts. We can discern
processes that insert the philosopher's individuality—and, literally, his
physical identity—into the text. A prominent speaking voice, an "I,"
evolves into the first model of sovereign subjectivity: the philosopher.
Christian Wolff's *Lecture on Chinese Ethics* (1721) demonstrates the
sovereignty of the philosopher by taking recourse to a Chinese counterpart of enormous pedigree, Confucius. I will then investigate filial
piety as a model for enforcing limitations upon individuals, and as an
early effort to mediate individual and communal intent. Here and in
the chapter's last portion, on an expression of the individual's ultimate
liminality—death—I will expand the discussion to one of the most
prominent communities in eighteenth-century Germany that negotiated the relationship between the public sphere and individuality, jug-
gling social, class, and group expectations: the Weimar court society.
By addressing communal aspects of creating the *Journal of Tiefurt*
(1781–84), the publishing venue for "The Chinese Morals Teacher"
and "The Wheel of Fate," and examining competing ideas of individuality in these texts and in contemporary novels, short prose, and
dramas, the prenational intentions of Weimar aristocracy become
abundantly clear. From then on, the body and individual subjectivity
played an important role in eighteenth-century attempts at theorizing
ethnicity.

THE PHILOSOPHER

Like Leibniz, his younger contemporary Wolff (1679–1754), in his
Lecture on Chinese Ethics, directed his attention toward China. He was
less concerned with a linguistic unity of the world and, from the
beginning, stripped his writing of the foundational text of the
Republic of Scholars, the Bible. The consequences of this "translation"
were drastic: Wolff's adversaries at the University of Halle, where he
was a professor, made the *Lecture* a centerpiece of philosophical and
legal debate, even accusing him of blasphemy. The controversy led
to Wolff's dismissal from his academic position and exile from Prussia
in 1723.

Originally delivered in Latin on the occasion of passing on his leadership at Halle to a successor, Wolff's *Lecture* was translated and published in German in 1726, with annotations and extensive commentary
tying the treatise into his larger philosophical system.[1] It became an

indication of his efforts to combine mathematics with philosophy, public lecture and private inquiry, as well as German text and Latin treatise. Thus I believe that the *Lecture* provides a condensed version of Wolff's philosophical genesis, at the center of which a new subjectivity—rather than an atheist worldview—emerges. Like the Jesuits and Leibniz before him, Wolff spoke of the exemplary administration of the Chinese, the emperors and monarchs, who themselves had been philosophers and who had become models to their people by studying ancient texts. Yet unlike his predecessors, Wolff not only praised an almost mythical, nonlocalizable past, he also noted a subsequent decay in public ethics among the Chinese—due less to "misreadings" than to human fallacy—that pervaded all strata of society and that persisted until Confucius retrieved the honorable past. According to Wolff, Confucius restored the glory of the Chinese empire by becoming a great teacher to his people. Ultimately, the philosopher's task as a teacher emerges as a central tenet of the treatise.

Wolff's *Lecture* has been discussed predominantly as either advancing an understanding of ethics emancipating itself from religion (e.g., Berger), or, more recently, as an example of antivoluntarist religious ethics (e.g., Larrimore, "Orientalism"; cf. Sorkin). Both lines of interpretation engage the wider context of the early eighteenth-century discourse on China. The former sides with Wolff's contemporary critics: one interpreter, Willy Berger, equates with atheism the eighteenth-century idea of highly developed, "oriental" cultures (read: enlightened, secular cultures) that stood in sharp contrast to Africa's uncivilized state of existence. This reading brings into focus my interest here, namely, to demonstrate how such an imaginary juxtaposition came into existence. Similarly, the latter tendency, reading Wolff's "Chinese text" as a religious paradigm, underscores, I believe, the necessity for examining the rhetorical construction of sovereign subjectivity—that is, the philosopher. How did the subject depart from the text without abandoning belief and religion completely? Reading the *Lecture* as an indicator of Wolff's larger cognitive system—in which philosophy took a decidedly ethical turn provoked by the *epistemological* battles at Halle University—rather than as an accurate (or false) reading of Chinese philosophy, confirms that Wolff differed from his contemporaries. By inventing a mode of inquiry and an epistemology that rested on the individual unity of body and soul and not on a divine voice speaking through a text, he liberated the philosopher and gave him the freedom to serve either secular reason or religious belief. Accordingly, revelation had a place in philosophy only if it served the discovery of multiple truths (Zedler, 58:575).

Though the *Lecture* began by reiterating the Jesuit accounts of China, its argument quickly changed direction. Initially, Wolff claimed that the Chinese society reached its prime with the emergence of Confucian philosophy, because "Confuz," as he called Confucius, dedicated himself to the meticulous study of ancient books (*Rede*, 28). Pointing out a shared bibliophilic inclination, Wolff then related ancient Chinese to early modern European culture. He spoke highly of the Jesuits, especially of Franz Noel, whose (mostly Latin) translations made the Chinese teachings accessible to Europeans (208–10), and he combined praise of "Confuz" and of his "invaluable writings" with reflection about the nature of Sino-European relations. Crediting the Jesuit mission with rightly recognizing the virtuous interactions among the Chinese people, he acknowledged that the nature of these interpersonal relationships—elsewhere called public ethics—fueled the notion of an exemplary Chinese state in European eyes.

But then Wolff abandoned this Leibnizean model of reading. Resorting to books in a quest for personal legitimacy, Wolff turned to his individual philosophical opinion, theory, and even invention. He used the images books create to validate this new role of the philosopher. Constructing an analogy between Confucius and himself, Wolff envisioned his Chinese counterpart as a mirror of the role of the philosopher in Europe's text, a role that he established. This transformation of a Baroque motif that in the seventeenth century had stood for the allegorical reflection of the cosmos in the worldly particularity pointed to the hybrid epistemological nature of Wolff's times. No longer an exclusive means of reproducing cosmic order in human life by locating divine traces, the rhetoric of the mirror projected the relation between China and Europe as one among individuals while emphasizing the effects of reading. Thus, the geographical counterpart was consistently more than an Other to the Self, absorbing the traditions of reading and relation, and the philosopher's roots in this tradition. Just as Confucius was finding himself unable to step out of the sequence of textual order and obligation that constituted Chinese history and tradition, European philosophy was barely stepping out of "the shadow of theology" (Zammito, *Birth*, 19). But Confucius was also an outstanding individual; as he assumed democratic, public tasks; he set up a new model for the philosopher as well: the reader with a mission who took on the duty of teaching and pursued this duty outside the realm of political power (*Rede*, 52–53; Schmidt, 4, 9).

Evidently Wolff's turning to Confucius revealed a new understanding of philosophy altogether. Confucius found himself charged with a communal task: mediating among the common people, between their drifting toward the immanence of sense perception and the emperor's derivative, cognizing reading of books. In the process he espoused a model of clarity, "rigorous demonstration and absolute certitude," and he embodied philosophy, because he interpreted the texts of human wisdom correctly, eliminating impurities within a philosophical practice and doctrine intended to support people's humility. The laws Confucius imposed ultimately cultivated the ideal of an active life among humans and superb morals in correspondence with the devotion prevailing among his disciples (60–61).

It is here that Confucius' status and importance solidified the place Wolff envisioned for himself. Like a mirror, the Chinese figure reflected back upon the German philosopher and his advancing of both *cognitio philosophica* and *cognitio historica*: "Although the Chinese inventions did not contribute anything to my own, since they were largely unknown to me, my own inventions, the products of my sheer thought alone, helped me understand the inventions by the Chinese" (223–24). Whereas Leibniz had emphasized the philosopher's role as reader, Wolff carved out a slightly different, and certainly superior role for the philosopher by stating repeatedly that the ancient Chinese books contained plenty of discernable truth and reason. Although both men were highly suspicious of unfiltered sense perception and favored "transparent representation" (the manifestation of reason in and through language), they located transparency differently. While Leibniz praised the Chinese character and text for its inherent transparency, Wolff found transparency in the process of cognition. But only the philosopher could recognize the systematic truth that is hidden beneath a chaotic surface, and expose it in the process of artful reading. Through his cognitive powers and the products of his intellect, the philosopher could make judgments perceived as universal. Accordingly, authority shifted from texts to persons, to "the retriever" of the world beyond the text (59), and, albeit latently, from reading to invention. Or, to modify one of Foucault's central observations about the onset of modernity: "the body of the philosopher [had come between the texts] to affirm his own law" (*Discipline and Punish*, 91). Transparency became the essence of philosophy as system and academic discipline. Such a "grounding," states John Zammito in his account of Wolff, "was what distinguished philosophy, drawing it close to the lucidity of mathematics" (*Birth*, 19).

Wolff discerned the task of individual scholars—who were not monarchs—as putting forth appropriate, reasonable political systems. Moreover, he proposed a concept of Chinese philosophy that literally implied—in keeping with the contemporary German term for philosophy—"universal wisdom," which in turn echoed "cosmopolitanism"—clearly a human construction. Indeed, he set forth an understanding of Chinese "philosophical virtue" (Ching/Oxtoby, 49) which, though not amounting to atheism on Wolff's part, provided an ethical foundation for the Enlightenment public sphere. As Julia Ching observes: "[Wolff believed] in a new system of morality, based on man's natural capacity for perfection rather than God's positive command and grace. [. . .] Yet he was careful to distinguish between 'philosophical virtue,' which he granted the Chinese, and 'theological virtue,' accessible only to believers and Christians" (49). Reason, public ethics, and religion were seen as independent yet interrelated. Corresponding notions of virtue inhabited distinct hemispheres of the universe, but existed as different manifestations of universal reason.

The philosopher attained, then, a unique position in discerning and asserting these intricate details. His task consisted neither in the historical explication of a divine authority or revelation nor in providing a sense of history. Rather it involved the mediation (and interpretation) of causality, change, and human actions, that is, the furthering of public ethics, with an orientation toward happiness (*Glückseligkeit*). As Wolff developed this argument, he suggested a model of reading Chinese philosophy entailing recognition and classification of knowledge and, not coincidentally, including the entire repertoire of Enlightenment metaphors: truth and clarity, light and distinction. He proposed "to examine with some care the mysteries of Chinese philosophy, to draw out the hidden principles of their ethics and politics, from a depth that is perhaps not accessible to everyone. We shall bring to light what we have selected, and we shall make an evaluation of what we have brought to light" (Ching/Oxtoby, 157; *Rede*, 81–83).

Wolff explicated three motivations that might cause, or at least influence, human action: (1) the motivation by outcome (which roughly corresponds to utilitarian thought); (2) the belief in the divine origin of reason in human existence (which equals the eighteenth-century definition of a natural religion); and (3) the belief in the Gospels' claim that thoughts and actions depend on God's mercy:

> Those who regulate their actions according to events have no other guide than reason, and their virtues, purely human, are due only to the strength of nature. Those whose actions are determined by the consideration of divine perfections and of Providence, seen only by the light of reason, derive their virtues from natural religion. And finally, those who act in conformity with revealed truths for which there is no natural

evidence have, as principles of their virtues, the strength coming from grace. (Ching/Oxtoby, 161; *Rede*, 105–06)

The first type of action prevailed among the Chinese, if only because God was unknown to them. Their idea of virtue, Wolff implied, had to be inspired by the possibility of human perfection, a strictly human ideal since the old Chinese knew nothing about the Creator and were unfamiliar with the (Western) concept of divine revelation. Therefore, he concluded, the Chinese kept in mind the consequences when acting, thus behaving in an ultimately reasonable, virtuous manner. Conversely, they lacked any sense of imperfection that might give rise to vice or disgraceful or wrong actions, attending only to reason's perfection as the ultimate goal of human existence.

The Chinese, Wolff suggested, perceived the consequences of their actions as manifestations of virtue and vice: virtue as what provided pleasure, vice as what caused pain. Yet rather than locating these feelings in the body, Wolff maintained that they were ultimately transformed into cognitive, intellectual patterns. Once people recognized the pleasurable, they would attempt to be virtuous and stop thinking about committing sinful actions, thus becoming cured of vicious behavior: "Whoever learns virtues, by so doing unlearns vices, since virtues and vices as contraries cannot coexist" (Ching/Oxtoby, 164; *Rede*, 131–32). It is here that Wolff extended the role of the philosopher. Not only had he—Wolff and the figure of the sovereign philosopher—come between the texts, the concept of an individual human being cognizant of his environs had also entered the text, fully established as a physical entity. Put differently a new epistemology that was based on the body confronted the idea of a universal translatability of the divine text. However, as Wolff turned toward intellectual capacities that could seemingly transcend physiological symptoms and sensual perceptions, reason (via the soul) liberated itself from the body in its endless quest for virtue (165). Hence the ideal of individual human perfection through cognition became the center of Wolff's text.

As Wolff introduced ideas of virtue and vice, he arrived at a consequential reinterpretation of *cognitio historica*. He put forth a concept of temporality, an emergent sense of history and a teleology of cognition, regarding this mode of recognition in turn as linked to the lower and upper faculties of cognition, (sensual) perception, and reason, respectively: "While perceptions only show us the present," he wrote, "the future is disclosed only to reason" (Ching/Oxtoby, 166; *Rede*, 142–43). Perceptions and feelings were thought to represent something momentary; their immediacy assures us of self-certainty, while future actions remain at a distance and thus appear hidden, unpredictable, and disturbing. Confined by the probabilities of history, codified and preserved in annals, they appeared to allow people in turn to structure the same actions in accordance with past and present experiences:

> If one regards as thoughtless, foolhardy and perilous the task of assigning limits to the understanding in the quest of truth, one should judge likewise that attempt of those who would like to set limits to the strength with which nature is capable of directing itself to the good. A philosopher who has deepened the knowledge of his human mind could judge the progress of the Chinese by attentively reading their annals, where the deeds and acts of their ancient emperors and kings are celebrated. But since it is certain that they have not reached the highest goal, who would wish to say that one could not go beyond where they have stopped? Let us go back to our present theme, and, without asking how far one may go, go rather as far as one can. This is in accord with the custom of the ancient Chinese, who followed the examples of their ancestors not only in like cases but also in different circumstances, and who taught that one ought not stop till one has arrived at sovereign perfection, and that means never to stand still. (*Rede*, 154–76; cf. Ching/Oxtoby, 166; cf. Hsia, 54)

Here Wolff established a threshold in early eighteenth-century conceptualizations of *cognitio historica*. To be sure, as a mode of epistemological inquiry, it derived its legitimacy from a text, the annals of the Chinese emperors who were considered suitable to model behavior and predict capabilities, and who commanded a never-ending struggle for perfection. And these texts not only enabled derivation but offered mediation as well. Unlike the uncontrolled empiricism of senses and desires, the guiding force of texts channeled cognition and transformed it considerably. Though *cognitio historica* might still "lack the rigorous formulation of arguments or explanations according to principles," as Zammito puts it (*Birth*, 20), it opened a pathway toward a historical worldview. Wolff began to transform, rhetorically, the accounts of Chinese sagas from exegetic criticism to historical reading.

If reasonable action led to virtuous results, people had to confront the problem of time and temporality to acquire virtue. In other words, such action(s) might not yield immediate results, or actions might mask themselves as reasonable through deceptive appearances; the eternal good might very well seem elusive, while a fleeting deception might tempt through its immediacy: "This is why they perpetually confound passing objects with eternal things, preferring the apparent good to the true good. They even reject the true good because they only provide pleasures in the future, pleasures they cannot anticipate" (*Rede*, 143; cf. Ching/Oxtoby, 166; Hsia, 52). In identifying such a teleological configuration of reason, Wolff's text exhibits the main features of classical Enlightenment thought. By acknowledging inhibitions to human rationality and the possibility of deviant behavior, Wolff appeased the reader by positing a *future* state of reason. In a culture where philosophers, scholars, and teachers presented themselves as mediators of conflicting paradigms of knowledge, this turning to history was tentative at best. More than fifty years later, in essays on the limits and possibilities of the Enlightenment, the need for the mediating instance "vanished" and gave way to a self-reflexive individual and his or her intellectual competence.[2] It was only then philosophers fully articulated their sovereign subjectivity, producing texts that, detached from any relation to other texts and tradition, projected the individual in a continuum of time and link the present and future through an act of cognition and reflection.

In his time, however, Wolff assured himself of his own significance by pointing out the textual foundation of "the sovereign philosopher." He saw texts and Chinese texts most particularly as defining (and confining) the philosopher's projection of history. From them, Wolff deducted a model of individual sovereignty and reason to emulate. Since this individual was, after all, an intellectual whose independence evolved from his specialized interaction with texts, the resulting subject-position promoted cognitive superiority. It was the position of the philosopher, whose voice transformed the world into a form of knowledge that opposed the ordinary reader rather than linking texts to each other through translating and interpreting. In other words, the philosopher with his subjectivity, no longer enmeshed and merely reproduced in a universe of texts, had to conquer and possess knowledge.

Conversely, by abandoning the idea of universal translation, the figure of the philosopher destroyed a seamless texture of the world. As subjectivity constituted itself not only in deciphering the universal texture of transparent knowledge, but also supplemented this texture through the philosopher-subject's inventions, the claim to universality and the autostylization of the philosopher became rhetorically linked. The philosopher became universalism's new grounding principle. In making this assertion, Wolff took Confucius as his Chinese counterpart, mirroring himself and his dependence on texts and tradition; their rhetorical link signified the role of the individual reader and teacher, not the textual universe. Eerily, this representation reiterated the early Enlightenment's belief in a symmetrical design of the

Eastern and Western hemispheres, while foreshadowing a new epistemological configuration in constructing ethnic difference. Although this configuration of Eastern and Western counterparts must not be confused with Hegel's Self and Other, it anticipated the abstract notion of a sovereign subject eclipsing the material, historical, and geographical circumstances of people's ethnic existence. Whereas the Hegelian Self strives to completely sublate its Other in History, Wolff's mirror images of Western and Eastern philosophers subjected ethnic existence and its perception to the postulate of philosophical cognition.

DISCIPLINED STATE SUBJECTS

This elevated status of Confucius in early eighteenth-century culture was not confined to Wolff's writing; even his *Lecture* reveals the discursive realm where principles of Confucianism and its crucial element of social and intellectual hierarchies might take hold: schooling. Once Wolff's rhetoric had shifted to revolve around an individual human being, he enlisted various examples to illustrate virtue and reason and the corresponding stages of human recognition. To underscore intellectual differentiation among people, Wolff proposed a classification in accordance with the faculties of human understanding. Their distinction into upper and lower faculties reflected the various degrees of clarity and transparency in the signs that people use and produce and that proceed from obscure to distinct forms (*cognitio philosophica*). Correspondingly, people belong to a social class or group that best suits their capacity for reasoning (*Rede*, 180–82; Schulte-Sasse, *Briefwechsel*, 170–72; Wellbery, *Laokoon*, 15).

In order to show the universal validity of combining cognitive and social stratification in such a way, Wolff turned to China once more, using the Chinese school system to illustrate the attainability of a virtuous existence. Familiar with concepts proposed in Confucius' *Great Learning* and the Neo-Confucian *Elementary Learning*, he discussed two types of education that the Chinese had purportedly enjoyed during the empire's greatest perfection, two tiers that trained the respective parts of the human soul: "One was called the School for Children, which was founded upon the inferior part of the soul; the other was called the School of Adults, which regarded entirely the superior part of the soul" (*Rede*, 186–88; cf. Ching/Oxtoby, 170).[3] While every young boy could attend the former school, which trained them to use their *intuition*, only a few select young men would go on to the higher level where they perfected their *understanding* and ultimately reached the highest level of *abstract "clear" recognition* through intel-lectual reflection. These upper-level students possessed nobility: either a high social standing or great intellectual capacities. Whereas ties to the imperial families assured acceptance, common people had to dis-tinguish themselves through "better understanding, rather pointed judgment and more diligence" than everybody else. While the School for Children raised people to be subservient, the School of Adults educated people to rule (195).

Without doubt, Wolff used an image that is both complex and loaded. On one hand, schooling served to describe aspects of the epis-temological threshold defining Wolff's writing. It chronicled the shift in the understanding of transparency: from the transparent character and text to a transparent process, to the transparency of cognition itself. This state would lead to the individual production of transpar-ent signs, reflecting an identity of word and thing; institutionally, the realm of this achievement was the School of Adults. On the other hand, both Wolff's practical philosophy (and the thought that he reconstructed and reappropriated to its Eastern counterpart) sanc-tioned a model of human understanding that hinged upon and explained traits of personal evolution and codependency. Hence schooling marked the epitome of social differentiation. As Wolff con-cluded that only a few select and socially anonymous individuals could achieve distinct recognition, and that this stage could only be reached after a long period of learning, philosophical invention, and interpre-tation, he also laid out the social conditions for and ramifications of this process. While Wolff's idea of schooling emphasized the centrality of individuality in defining its method, its aim and purpose were the communal structures. Schooling, Wolff implied, would only be suc-cessful as long as it engaged the emotional, psychological, and social structures of the family, enabling it, in turn, to provide a model for the workings of a state through its subjects. As Wolff's imagery used schooling to link different forms of communal relationships to each other, it invoked an idea that from early Confucianism on had formed the core of filial piety, as well as a corresponding pattern of social appreciation, interaction, and engagement (Ivanhoe).

Further fleshing out this idea of filial piety, Wolff stated rather bluntly: "The duties most prescribed in the School for Children were *respect toward parents, elders, and superiors*, modesty, and submission to laws, which one sought to impress on these still tender souls" (Ching/Oxtoby, 171–72; *Rede*, 195; emphasis in Hsia, 60). In extending filial piety to the elders of society, education transferred the generational obligations of family relations onto sociological and political hierarchies where it was not so much a tool of "rational normalization" as a structure of empathy, perpetuating the supremacy of roles rather than of persons (John Schrecker; Whitlock). Because the emphasis was on positions, the emphatic structure could apply to all spheres of society. Furthermore, since Chinese teachings of filial piety presumed a concept of (economic) compensation for an abstract, nonpayable love of parents for their children, the idea became involved with sacrifice and suitable for circulation in larger, societal communities; compensation entailed sacrificing independence and egoism (Chow, 159). Discussing the sociological implications of filial piety, Max Weber points out the connections between piety as an element of "a doctrine of conventions" and social stability. Together with the ancestral cult, he claims, filial piety constitutes a universal basis for social subordination. In addition to the elimination of any manifestation of personal religion, the two elements form an "aesthetically attractive" doctrine, which, though evoking images of an ethnic community modeled on the wholeness of and mutual support within a family, supports power and privilege of the bureaucratic caste.[4]

The ideal of filial piety illuminates the structure of Enlightenment reality. It played a role in articulating Enlightenment social narrative, because it implied loyalty to tradition and religious teachings on one hand, while creating and legitimizing new systems of dependency (e.g., family, state bureaucracy, *ethnos*) on the other. Filial piety exposed the Enlightenment's inherent political tension that arose when individuals were torn between roles: as readers of a universal coherence and enactor of social hierarchies and an organism-like unity of communities (Mauser, 217). Whereas Leibniz made a distinction between the ideal of filial piety within the *political* community of Chinese philosophers and the universal force of reading and translating represented by the scholar-monarch, ultimately keeping the two models of subjectivity apart, Wolff abandoned this clear distinction. He created instead a sovereign whose patriarchal power paralleled that of a family's father. Just as a good parent would provide a stellar example to children, the monarch would to state subjects.

> The Chinese demanded that a man should learn to regulate his conduct and his life before making himself head of a family, that he should learn to govern his own house before being admitted to public government [. . .] [E]mperors and kings served as examples to their peoples, heads of families to their houses, fathers to their children, and they made themselves useful to those whom they were unable to subject to the rule of reason. (Ching/Oxtoby, 176–77; *Rede*, 243, 246–47)

Universal reason deduced from a text appeared lost and got replaced by functional roles. Just as parents and children complement each other to form a family, rulers and their subjects constituted the complementary elements of a state. They formed a reality through which the Enlightenment fictions of public and universal equality would be transmitted.[5]

The observance of filial piety affects people in ways that alter the distribution and structures of power within a society, much like the experience of the disciplined body which Foucault describes in "Docile Bodies," a chapter of *Discipline and Punish*. Foucault introduces seventeenth- and eighteenth-century disciplines as "general formulas of domination," different from "asceticism and 'disciplines' of a monastic type," for example. Filial piety certainly belongs to the latter type, as its "function [is] to obtain renunciations rather than increases of utility and which, although they involve obedience to others, [have] as their principal aim an increase in the mastery of each individual over his own body" (137). As discipline diminishes the forces of the body, it produces politically obedient subjects, not unlike ascetic types. Therefore, political obedience is the effect that filial piety and discipline share. These produced the paradoxical, conceptual entanglements during the Enlightenment that pitted the personal sovereignty of the individual against the community. Both filial piety and the disciplinary regimes of modern societies engender subjectivity by subjecting individual desires, energies, and bodies to a community, be it as small and personal as a family or as anonymous and unwieldy as a state, nation, or *Volk* (*ethnos*). Discipline and filial piety paved the way for functionally differentiated communities that could be imagined as naturally evolved; discursively, they gave rise to narratives that wove aspects of the Chinese cipher into the formulations of community in German lands.

One of these narratives is "The Chinese Morals Teacher," in *The Journal of Tiefurt*. Here we find a model for producing the ideal political subject of the Enlightenment state. While it promises to link figurations of filial piety to the concept's cultural and geographical origin, the text reflects an environment that had little in common with the actual or, for that matter, with the imagined China; instead it exposes the fate of an ideal—the enlightened monarchy—in the reality of the Weimar court in the 1770s and 1780s. "The Chinese Morals Teacher" illustrates an altered process of appropriating the geographically distant locale.

The short treatise must be understood within the confines of Duchess Anna Amalia's Weimar court society. During the court's prime, its members, including chamberlains and ladies-in-waiting, and prominent Weimar figures such as Herder and Wieland, spent summers in Tiefurt, near Weimar. There they began writing a journal, *The Journal of Tiefurt*, whose anonymous contributions—poems, dramatic fragments, fables, and essay contests—were distributed in handwritten form over the course of four years (1781–84). Angela Borchert has described how the *Journal* documented the "social and cultural experiment" that unfolded in Weimar at the time, noting a creative tension between the poetic conventions shaped by courtly etiquette and the emergent literary forms of a mixed culture that blended aristocratic and bourgeois elements. The situation was also rife with psychological and social tensions resulting from devotion, sacrifice, and expected (but not received) compensation (Seckendorff, *Letters*; Bode, 193–97; Bruford, 74–96), and gender tensions (Kord, "Hunchback," 233–45). Behavioral codes—moderation of affect and indifference, calm and restraint, and, last but not least, the ornaments of aristocratic distinction—tempered a clear and programmatic courtly life (Elias, 171). Members of the court cast themselves in theatrical roles that undermined and, on occasion, elevated their social role. Creating verbal and social plays that fostered lighthearted communication was part and parcel of the court society's interactions (Matuschek, 146–47, 156). Like Leibniz's allegory of an enlightened monarch which arose from reading and translating the divine text, and Wolff's vision of a public role for the philosopher, which he posited self-confidently, the verbal play simulated something innovative at the court: the fiction of Enlightenment shining through in *The Journal of Tiefurt*, "an enterprise devoted to the entertainment of a select society" (xi). Playing games—be they theatrical or verbal—established a counterpoint to the other learned society that existed in late eighteenth-century German lands and the academic discourse of the university, while reworking traditions of Italian and French academies (Borchert, 371). The Tiefurt court represented a microcosmic public sphere that alluded to some of Leibniz's and Wolff's ideas while creating another discursive locale, the journal.

Many relationships at this court conjured up the specter of filial piety. Goethe's attempt to educate the prince, Carl August, is but one example. Presenting us at once with devotion and surrender, his poem "Illmenau" (1776) chronicles the relatively fruitless joint efforts of Goethe, Knebel, and von Seckendorff to advance the young prince's education (*Werke* 1:107–12). A tale of personal sacrifice, the poem relates Goethe's goals as an educator, as well as the limited pedagogical and political impact he actually had on Duke Carl August. In reflecting the situation at the Weimar court, the poem refers to a broader social phenomenon at the core of eighteenth-century aristocratic societies, namely, the presence of private instructors at princely courts who often sought to advance the more secular, emancipating stance of the Enlightenment. Such educational efforts were effectively attempts to inculcate filial piety as a political program. For with respect to his social, economic, and political position the teacher was a subservient state-subject; philosophically and morally, however, he was the pupil's superior, ruler, and sovereign. The psychological complications involved in this inversion of a sacrificial structure defined the success and (more frequent) failure of princely education (*Fürstenerziehung*). Their representation provides us with the disillusioning counterpart to literary genres that sought to further such education through successful models of development, where rational pedagogy tamed aristocratic absolutism (Bersier, 2–4).

These tensions marked the discursive situation in which the anonymous author(s) wrote "The Chinese Morals Teacher," and they are reflected in the text itself. First of all, the six-page, two-part piece displays a tension between title and narrative. Though the title suggests that the reader is dealing with an exotic document conveying "ethnic wisdom," the body of the text belies this assumption. Its two parts instruct the reader about the necessity and appropriateness of social etiquette, arguing that proper behavior and communication in society—seemingly trivial outward appearances and mere exteriorities of human existence—reveal an inner core and the essence of individual subjectivity. As the argument progresses, it examines the workings of this relationship in the formation of communities and the state, though never allowing for direct inferences about the Weimar court itself. Thus the treatise combined two eighteenth-century ideals whose inmost differences give "The Chinese Morals Teacher" its twofold structure: whereas the "first lesson" reproduces an early Enlightenment ideal of infinite texture, the "second lesson" shifts the focus to hierarchical relationships among human beings through which they fully constitute themselves as subjects. Thus, on the surface, "The Chinese Morals Teacher" appears hollow, like decorum, but we shall see the traces of the early Enlightenment image of China in the text. The remnants of the ideal filial piety persist.

The treatise opens by calling polite behavior an ornament, a useless obligation of social etiquette lacking any deeper meaning, thus relegating polite manners to the status of exteriority. It maintains that though gestures reflect a universal order and translate it in diverse communicative situations, they say nothing about the person who interacts, nor do they influence the essence of being. At best, they represent a system of empty signs or signifiers of the court. And yet these signs establish social interaction and etiquette; they regulate the behavior of people toward each other as they signified "respect and dismay" (79). Verbal expressions that people use in conversations therefore reflect what they think about the people with whom they converse, but never what they think about themselves. They must hide the subject's passion and control emotions—or "affects" in eighteenth-century parlance. As gestures point to another person's inside, they must effectively conceal the speaking subject's inside:

> Even if these reasons are not sufficient motivation yet to pay attention to your outward appearance, so be aware that only those who both in private and public know how to seal their passions, to be in command of themselves, and only those who give more than they demand, can resourcefully master the trickiest situations. Only they will be able to expect glory. (79)

This ascetic model asked people to be modest and supportive in relation to others in order to find harmony in themselves. Only by observing the "conventions of exteriorities" in private as well as in public life could they attain a virtuous stage of existence. Paradoxically here, in complying with the communal codes lay people's potential to designate themselves as individual subjects.

Thomas Müller investigates this process of subject formation through rhetoric and language. Analyzing the styles, devices, and patterns that dominated in early eighteenth-century texts, he contends that people aspired to, and perhaps indeed achieved, equality in conversation. They accomplished this ideal state by suppressing instincts, emotions, and sentiments and by regulating speech, a behavioral code that not surprisingly reflected new scientific beliefs. The early Enlightenment treated affects, that is, emotions, as scientific (not as morally inflated) phenomena. To classify them scientifically contributed to a conceptualization of equality among people, allowing Enlightenment thinkers to neglect social, intellectual, and sexual characteristics when discussing their rational and psychological disposition. At the same time, they could demand the hiding of emotional predispositions while postulating the moral sovereignty of the individual subject (25).

Self-knowledge became a prerequisite for in-depth knowledge of other peoples' minds. Arguing that the control of emotions and instincts is an auto-induced process, not a response to exterior forces, Müller insinuates that the production of self corresponds to the creation of community. People transfer control onto other people by listening to them, judging them, and, ultimately, by speaking to them, and thus by classifying them. What we could describe as a secondary process of identity formation enforces the suppression of instincts, because the hidden desires, aggressions, and barely controlled emotions are further crippled once people realize that other people also watch and listen, talk and judge (69). The culture of repression stabilizes and innovates itself while propagating the importance of the individual. In this respect, Müller ascribes an importance to listening and speaking that resembles the role of speech in Foucault's analysis of confession, or the various regimes of disciplining the subject's body, not least among them education (*Discipline and Punish* 186).

Müller's essay appears then as the analytical inversion of the first part of "The Chinese Morals Teacher." Consideration for others evolves as the ultimate criterion for virtuous behavior. Individual subjects must obey the conventions of community, including its rhetorical and behavioral patterns; because they indicate at first the individual's opinion of other people and convey an emotional response to other people's behavior; thus exterior signs constitute the subject through speech. Evidently these signs no longer referred to God or a divine text, nor did they point to their chief interpreter, the sovereign; rather, they expressed people's affection for each other. Signs were no longer sole comments on divine creation, but reflected the intrinsic quality of the things that sign-users perceived, created, and chose to name. Thus "The Chinese Morals Teacher" no longer reflected an "unbroken surface" of the world, but projected the multiple surfaces of people as engendered by perception (of another person) and expression (in words).

Barely noticeable, though, this obscure little text reflected the contemporary cultural emphasis on scientifically inspired emotion control and its effects on communities. Aside from observing the proper conventions when interacting with others, the teacher informs us that an individual speaker must seek harmony in himself: "Be advised that every gesture that does not correspond to the will of the soul will expose you. You will appear as if you were dressed in a foreign garment. Because man cannot always do what he wants, but rarely ever what he does not want" (80). Any trace of inauthenticity intended to conceal inner disturbance will create an expression of disharmony, despite all one's efforts to accomplish the opposite through speaking. Ultimately, this disharmony between the speaker's inside and outside will destroy the harmonious community of people: "Beware, however, of becoming a nuisance to yourself and others when sticking to etiquette. If you have to pressure yourself into being decent and polite, you are by nature incapable of pure interaction" (80).

Having exposed the danger of deceptive speech and behavior, "the first lesson" in "The Chinese Morals Teacher" offered a corrective model for subjectivity that introduced filial piety directly and provided what so far appears to be a rhetorical decorum meant to accompany rather than advance the ideal behavioral pattern. The text consistently addresses the readers as "children," while simulating the Chinese teacher figure merely through the title and the form of address. But by simulating Confucius, this teacher-subject imparts morals; imitating Wolff, the subject projects himself as the educating philosopher. By signaling affection rather than possession ("my children"), the subject situates himself as a subject of relation and articulates—and indeed produces—his subjects/readers. "The Chinese Morals Teacher" is as much the text at hand as it is a personalized character in the text; the text gains an authoritative, directive function. Just as parents enforce their parental authority over children, the political subject of the text inflicts his authority over the citizens.

In conversation, the subject informs us, a speaker must seek harmony within himself. Any disharmony will destroy the harmonious community of people. Not only does this principle recall the harmony between the Chinese microcosms and macrocosm, a set of commonly held beliefs among early eighteenth century-thinkers, the text also engages concepts of filial piety directly. "Politeness, loyalty, and modesty" are seen as having the ability to correct an overreaching, disharmonious individual; "[d]iligent attention to truth, gentle nobility, and undivided sense of duty" assure personal and communal advancement (81). The text counters any notion of personal ambition or utilitarian thinking; instead, it criticizes their rampant prominence in society and then exposes their damaging effects: "the many connections, conspiracies and assurances to defend each other, to fight for the other 'til death [. . .] the pretense of importance, aspirations to be seen as merchants and profiteers, as confidants of nobility" (81). For although these ideas were typical of eighteenth-century utilitarian thinking, "The Chinese Morals Teacher" portrays them as obstacles to a civilized society: Those who fell for them, were merely "foolish children" (81). It is here that the text imparts a trace of a personified character: the Chinese morals teacher resided outside Weimar; he looked upon Europe and criticized European thought and virtues.

These instances of subjectivity bring out other associations with China, such as virtues attributed to quiet reading, contemplation, and meditation. Contemplation stirs people toward a concept that, according to Leibniz, we can find in Chinese philosophies and society: preestablished harmony. As humans turn from conversation to introspection and reflection, they find inner harmony as soon as they give up the desire for ornamental, superfluous exteriorities. Accepting the limitations of worldly existence, they recognize their corresponding place in the larger world (cf. 81). Simultaneously though, the concluding paragraph of "the first lesson" reiterates the particular rereading of the Chinese motif that informs the relationship between title and text: "Man's best mirror is man himself" (81). Rhetorically recapping (and augmenting) the mirror image in Wolff's text, this passage reflects how Europe situated itself in relation to the world. China's Confucius no longer authenticated the role of the sovereign philosopher who orchestrated the Enlightenment's public sphere; individual personhood did. China and Europe existed no longer in a "reading relationship," where each locale served as an expression of an underlying universal order. Instead, "China" had come to signify its own geographical alterity, namely, newly conceived ideals of the Enlightenment's public sphere in action, ideals that were distinctly European.[6] As European reality did not live up to the ideal, "China" had to criticize it.

CHINA AT THE LIMITS: AN EXTERIOR CRITIC OF THE WEIMAR COURT

We can expand on the ideas of conversation, reading of exterior signs, and relation, all of which "The Chinese Morals Teacher" depicts as foundational elements of individuality, and by comparing them with other texts produced at the court in Weimar. Faced with the elusiveness of their educational efforts at court, the authors held on to the ideal of an enlightened community and its administration, readily attributing it to or locating it in China. They used rhetorical figures to invoke a specific or obscure Asian location, a fictional Asian source, even an actual or rhetorical mirror associated with Asia. A case in point is Christoph Martin Wieland's *Der goldene Spiegel* (The Golden Mirror; 1774), a text that predated *The Journal of Tiefurt* and, in some respects, reworked an older model of enlightened monarchy and its "Chinese roots." A novel of princely education, *The Golden Mirror* is situated in a fictional oriental land and professes to be (not unusually) a translation and to have a "Chinese source" (see chapter 4 here). The tales of Scheschian, meant to function as an instructional tool for Schach Gebal, the novel's character in need of education, resemble of course the annals and classical texts of the Chinese which enabled their rulers to govern wisely and philosophically, harmoniously, and, ultimately, rationally. Wieland wanted his book to be read in the same way, expecting rulers to recognize the book's noble and altruistic truths and apply them toward the welfare of their respective nations, and expecting ordinary readers to see the parallels between the mythical Scheschian and their home country. The text was intended to provide the foundation and instrument for the personal influence Wieland, as a responsible intellectual, hoped to have not only on Carl August, whom he helped educate in the years after the book's publication, but also on Joseph II, whom he had allegedly portrayed in the novel (Wilson, "Intellekt," 483–85).

But not all writers in Weimar were concerned with reforming court society, even if they were or aspired to become members of it. Many were more interested in representing an altered ideal of an ethically egalitarian, tentatively bourgeois public sphere open to criticism, as was the case not only in "The Chinese Morals Teacher," but also in Jakob Michael Reinhold Lenz's comedy *Der neue Menoza* (The New Menoza; 1774). Lenz's drama reworked the figure of a reasonable, virtuous Eastern philosopher whose travels in Europe allowed him to comment upon both the moral decline of the aristocracy and the hypocrisy that had begun to prevail among the rising bourgeois class. Born in Europe and educated in Asia, the protagonist, Prince Tandi, embodies those traits of the early Enlightenment that emphasized the relationship, discernable through reading, between these geographical locales. Sure enough, through reading we uncover the character's genealogy: the equally weighted importance of his origin and his upbringing, their mutual influence in bringing about his rational judgment, his erudite and modest existence, and the purity of his character.

In this genealogy, the tradition of reading China intersected with Lenz's poetic theories. Tandi's position embodies not only elements of ideal China—à la Leibniz, Wolff, and *The Journal of Tiefurt*—but also a critique of Wieland's *Golden Mirror*, condensing a cultural history up to and including the moment when China becomes an empty signifier, detached from the material and perceptual situations of the Jesuit encounter and no longer meaningful. Since this earlier transparency of signification was lost, late eighteenth-century critics could not help but mock the character, accusing Tandi of "acting like a European" (Leidner/Wurst, 12). But to us, a critical and corrective role evolves from the character's dramatic function. As he becomes a commentator and revealer in the drama, Tandi reads the signs of his environment, and in the process, unmasks both potential and flaws.

He also reads the recent history of perceiving and representing ethnic alterity in German texts and, very importantly, joins a European tradition in the making, for Lenz's play reminds us of French literary examples of the motif of a sovereign Eastern philosopher who holds a mirror up to Europe's face—consider Montesquieu's *Persian Letters* (1721) and Voltaire's *Candide* (1759).

Other German-language texts have been nearly forgotten and, like "The Chinese Morals Teacher," have hardly been analyzed beyond their self-proclaimed attention to China. In this small corpus, Georg Christoph Lichtenberg's satire "Von den Kriegs- und Fast-Schulen der Schinesen" (On the Chinese Warfare and Fasting Schools; 1796) stands out, condemning the hitherto positive values of schooling, restraint, and asceticism as ridiculous. What all the different texts had in common, however, was their pronounced criticism of specific aspects of bourgeois Germany, its communities, social strata, group dynamics, and, especially, its *petit bourgeois* individuals. Thus these narratives parted from the "Chinese texts" published in *The Journal of Tiefurt* in that the latter attempted to salvage a model community.

Accordingly, "The Chinese Morals Teacher" sought to mend the rift between the reality of absolutist court and bourgeois ambition, between rationality and petty instincts. Glossing over any trace of disunity, this community helped to install the sovereign subject firmly and with a grand poetic gesture. The text's "second lesson" further develops this concept of individual subjectivity in relation to community, while holding on to the concept of a preestablished harmony: "Never bemoan your fate, my children! Because whatever it is, nature gave you the strength to endure it. Life's happiness springs not from what is outside of you, but from what is within you" (112). Without doubt, the "second lesson" touches upon an emergence of the body as the foundation of individual agency, and this image began to compete with reading exterior signs in an attempt to communicate community and predetermination. Nowhere is this competing epistemology more explicit than in the last part of the text, which refers to the journey of life, including birth, development, and death. But even here the preestablished order of existence prevails, manifest in the all-encompassing recommendation to reason: "[R]eason is your rudder, and experience your compass [. . .] [E]veryone's course is predetermined, as is the time in which to complete it" (112). The teacher asserts that everyone possesses innate reason, regardless of his or her intellectual capabilities and talents, so that as a result of rational living, people will accept the social position assigned them by universal harmony, including the social privilege and/or suffering. After all, no matter which position people occupy, "each one of them is important to the state." "Perfect harmony" must be society's highest ideal; deprivation and modest income are praised over wealth and indulgence. Consequently, the second lecture ends with a renewed appeal to give up all interest in material wealth, assuring the reader of the ultimate happiness and satisfaction that result from modesty and generosity. Thus "The Chinese Morals Teacher" agreed that nature imposes its universal coherence and judgment upon humans.

This universal, naturalized order, however, included individual limitations, that had to be imposed for the sake of community and that were no longer articulated through and in the name of a divine text but, curiously enough, through an appeal to individual responsibility and such texts as a diary: "There will be a moment in life, my children, where all that counts are memories of good and virtuous actions; in vain you will hide in golden palaces; nature's judgment will be upon you and will separate you from material possessions. Your long journey will be like an evil diary with every page contesting you, judging you" (113). Invoked in the last lines of the narrative, the diary marked of course the profound shift in grounding the rhetoric of universalism in eighteenth-century culture. On one hand, the diary recaptured the subjectivity attributed to reading during the early Enlightenment: by serving as a book for future generations, it taught people through example. Even if it detailed despicable or irresponsible behavior, the diary implicitly conveyed an ideal: like a mirror, it contained a model for outstanding behavior—similar to the ways in which the teaching of morals was modeled on ancient Chinese books. Thus, the end of the "second lesson" embraces the treatise's title by interpreting it: the text derives meaning from an ethical subject's relationship to (ancient Chinese) books.

Like any reading of these books, "The Chinese Morals Teacher" revealed and endorsed the authority it sought to understand and relate to others. But unlike the authority Leibniz discovered in the books—the world's innate reason, the sovereign monarch, the possibility of universal representation—this authority is revealed to be European. On the other hand, the genre of the diary advocated a model of subjectivity that was grounded in individuality and whose inside and outside referred not to a larger universe, but only to the person himself. No other eighteenth-century genre (with the exception of, perhaps, the letter) participated in the physical nature of humans in such an intense way, representing the outpourings of inner feelings and doing so strictly for private consumption. In this respect, reading a diary was predicated upon a notion of writing, for since the diary embodies a sign of life and individual authorship, it initiates a system of representation that endures beyond death.

"The Chinese Morals Teacher" left behind an ambiguous notion of subjectivity: subordinate to community, the subject had become self-assertive, with emphasis on the construction of an absent teacher looking on and criticizing from the geographically distant "China." Limited in its political scope, subjectivity had gained permanence in its survival as personal fiction whose future role was likened to the Chinese history books. In any case, subjectivity was stabilized through its reference to China. The writers' community at Tiefurt took up this reference in a curious pair of fragmentary texts with the same title—the treatise-like serial "The Wheel of Fate" published anonymously in *The Journal of Tiefurt*, and a two-volume novel by Carl Siegmund von Seckendorff, *The Wheel of Fate*, of which the second volume cannot be found. These texts not only present a puzzle in terms of authorship (see *Das Journal von Tiefurt*, 371), they also contain dense imagery, the exhaustive interpretation of which has eluded most commentators to date. I propose that to gain a fuller understanding, we regard both texts in relation to the writers' community and in the eighteenth-century context of perceiving China as a culture defined and stabilized by books. Picturing both communal settings and individual aspirations at the court in Weimar, the texts reveal political ambitions and ethical shortcomings, exposing political, historical, and aesthetic limits to Anna Amalia's court society and corroborating Daniel Wilson's contention that Weimar's enlightened monarchy was nothing but a fiction.

Because of stylistic similarities and recurrent motifs in serial and novel, Seckendorff (1744–85) has been presumed the author of both texts. A minor aristocrat, chamberlain, and princely confidante, he was an important figure in Weimar, considered by contemporaries and subsequent scholars alike to be "truly educated," the actual spiritual and intellectual center of the Weimar court, and a "great mind" (Suphan, xxiii; Borchert, 323). A talented composer—he wrote the music for several of Goethe's *Singspiele*—he wrote and copied many of the *Journal*'s contributions. And, as Angela Borchert demonstrates, he provided important insights into individual perceptions of daily life at the court. Like Goethe, Herder, and Wieland, Seckendorff complained of boredom because of the limited possibilities for unusual activities and fresh distractions. As boredom pervaded the days spent at Tiefurt, *The Journal* became a group effort to fend off collectively what Patricia Meyer Spacks describes as an "intensely personal experience" at the advent of individuality (20; see also *Das Journal*, 2, 8–16). In his novels, Seckendorff ridiculed the hypocritical attitudes that, perhaps in response to boredom, spread among members of the group: occupied with nothing but their own amusement, they nevertheless paid lip service to enlightened writing, journalism, and the celebration of the muses. Such empty play could hardly satisfy the ambitious Seckendorff, nor could the complicated personal relationships among members of the court society. In a letter to his brother Albrecht dated June 1, 1776, he complained about the impeding promotion of "entertainers to high ranks [. . .] among them that of privy secretary [. . .] making everybody else extras, literally automatons" (cf. Debon, 73; see also Bruford, 90–93). He had come to the court a year earlier in the hope of advancing his career, but he would be forever a chamberlain in Weimar, overshadowed, like many others, by Goethe—and, according to letters and documents, he was keenly aware of it. Nevertheless, Seckendorff played a pivotal role in Tiefurt's artistic life (Borchert, 329–31).

The three installments in *The Journal of Tiefurt* and the novel share title and main character, Tschoang-tse, but while the serial's subtitle promises "A Chinese Story," the novel's announces in straightforward manner "the story of Tschoang-tse," emphasizing the character. The novel contains passages (35–39, 40–49) that are identical to the three pieces of the fragment in the journal, making the latter seem like a condensed version of the former; however, this is misleading because overall the novel expands upon, revisits, and profoundly alters crucial aspects of the moralistic tale. Without much introduction it begins to narrate the experiences of the prominent but legendary Taoist Tschoang-tse on his journey to ultimate perfection (*Bildung*). In the most comprehensive reading of *The Wheel of Fate* to date, the Sinologist Günter Debon describes the novel as a typical representation of the master-pupil relationship, with Lao-tse releasing Tschoang-tse into life and instructing him to study the secrets of the Tao, the eternal law of predestination (Debon, 73). Though we will see that the influences of reading Taoism are strong and much more persistent here than in the serial, the allusion to the character of Chinese philosophy merely underscores the text's true purpose: to probe the construction of individual subjectivity through an educational journey (*Bildungsreise*). At the same time Seckendorff's new model for constructing subjectivity collides with the structural and developmental patterns of a story of salvation, going so far as to simulate, through Tschoang-tse's journey, the reception of Jesus Christ by the masses. Equally conflicting are the unduly elaborate, digressive passages that characterize the novel, detracting from the tale's erudite undercurrents and moving the writing toward extensive depictions of nature. Finally, the novel reworks what we might call a generic Chinese tale in that it resembles the rhetorical patterns of "The Chinese Morals Teacher." Meditative or contemplative passages figure prominently and function as a decorative element that literally enlarges the text. Consistent with the genre convention for eighteenth-century novels, especially their more popular representatives, these "gallant" stylistic elements resonated with the perception of the Chinese as a meditating people, an idea that persisted at the court (*Das Journal*, 28–29; see also 352–53).

The implications of this stylistic mix are complex. Not coincidentally, the text moves away from the erudite treatise and the mirror of Chinese philosophers and toward the innovative genre of the novel, but traces of the older model of "textualizing the universe" persist. Though I do not see here a pattern of retextualization in the sense of returning to the premodern, divine text, I do believe that the tale of Tschoang-tse's journey toward perfection supported and augmented the courtly philosophy of hoping to educate and edify Duke Carl August. Debon has suggested as much, emphasizing that Seckendorff often wore the mask of Du Fu (712–70) and took on the Chinese poet's role of public critic in order to express the chamberlain's feelings of being neglected and little appreciated by the young duke, for not only did the promotion to princely secretary elude him, leaving him in dire financial need and with a diminished reputation, Duke Carl August also kept his distance (67). The motif of a criticizing Chinese character, albeit masked, resembles the rhetorical structure of "The Chinese Morals Teacher."

Expanding on Debon's observation, I would like to propose a refined reading that pays particular attention to the writers' circle and the options for poetic influence these writers envisioned in *The Journal of Tiefurt*. In light of the letters, diary entries, and documents by contemporaries attesting to (not only) Seckendorff's frustration over *The Journal*'s failure and the loss of the novel's second volume, which—if it ever indeed existed—apparently culminated in the completion of Tschoang-tse's education, it is certainly difficult to make sense of the role the Tiefurt circle played in cultural genealogy and literary history.[7] The sense of incompleteness resonates with the other projects of the Tiefurt circle: the novel remains as unfinished as the project of princely education. Like the creation of the Enlightenment journal, the model of a mixed bourgeois-aristocratic public sphere open to debate and entertainment, Duke Carl August's education remained provisional and incomplete, if clearly set out; ultimately, however, the ambitious program fails. Like Tschoang-tse, the young

duke began the process (and pretended to complete it), only to surrender to bureaucrats and artistic enterprises. He never implemented
effective policy change, as Wilson has repeatedly demonstrated, emu-
lating instead the idea of an enlightened monarch that the writers
around him were all too ready to bestow upon him and for which they
easily bent the tentatively democratic rules of an enlightened public
sphere (Skeletons, 295; see also *Das Goethe Tabu*).

The larger network of the Weimar court also sheds new light upon
the character and story of the bonze, the figure of a secluded Buddhist
monk or priest and, at the same time, one corrupting the pillars of the
traditional Chinese civil service. The bonze takes on a prominent yet
failing role in *The Wheel of Fate*. Like Tschoang-tse, he undergoes a
journey that is complicated and full of obstacles. Though eventually
attaining redemption, he fails in his educational efforts. The implied
criticism was evident—even strikingly explicit—to an eighteenth-
century mind. As the image of philosophical China softened in the
eighteenth century, images of bonzes came to represent the opposite
of Mandarin erudition and allegiance to tradition (see Debon, 74).
They stood for pompousness and self-promotion derived from and
emulated in unprecedented access to the monarch's favor, power, and
attention. In the context of the Weimar court, the character certainly
seems indicative of Seckendorff's rivalry with Goethe. The criticism of
the overly ambitious, bourgeois civil servant who quickly made a career
as a member of the Weimar governing council, was hardly a Freudian
slip, but very likely a calculated slap at Goethe.

ROMANTIC SUBJECTS

The serial "Wheel of Fate" begins as an annal, situating a character—
"a famous philosopher, named Tschoang-tse"—in a dynasty, in an
intellectual tradition or school, and in a city, as well as by defining him
sociologically as a Mandarin (83). Throughout his life Tschoang-tse has
had a recurrent and very disturbing dream which, not unlike prophe-
cies, ends with physical injury to Tschoang-tse in that he always wakes
up when he falls out of his bed. He therefore turns to his teacher, "the
immortal Lao-tse, also called the old child since he was born with grey
hair," and asks for an explication of his dream. The latter character is of
course the mythical Lao-tse, who is said to have lived in the fourth century. He is sometimes considered an older contemporary of Confucius
(Needham, 35) and sometimes treated as an invented figure whose
purpose was to give authority to the *Tao-te-Ching*, the well-known

and otherwise anonymous compilation of texts by Taoist philosophers (von Glasenapp, 154).

Lao-tse interprets dreams as an indication of reincarnation and observes with respect to Tschoang-tse: "[Y]our immortal soul rushed to a higher destiny. Since then, it has inhabited many a body, but now it resides in yours" (84). Appropriating the textual tradition handed down in the *Tao-te-Ching*, Tschoang-tse takes the form of a butterfly in his dream, which Lao-tse regards as a sign of restlessness, symbolizing the efforts with which Tschoang-tse explores philosophical questions. Consequently, Lao-tse predicts that Tschoang-tse will have an addictive, insatiable desire to know, committing him to a never-ending quest for knowledge, to be achieved through indulgence and immoderation: "This tale reveals your outstanding talents for worldly wisdom ['Weltweisheit'], the flower of science and art, to which you are so strongly drawn. The more you absorb of them, the wiser you will become and the more able to approach new areas and respond to the desire to satisfy your quest" (84–85).

With regard to both knowledge and the imagination, Tschoang-tse is driven by the desires of Self. But within the microcosmic order of the world, he represents merely an enunciated subject that is thrown into this order by predestination. Even his talent for and interest in philosophy reflect his position and structure his activities, as Tschoang-tse needs to hear the interpreting and guiding voice of Lao-tse, the *Tao-te-ching*, in order to assume this position and follow the path of his life. Meanwhile, for the readers in the late eighteenth century and the Weimar court and their illustrious yet small circle of followers, Lao-tse's role underscored the importance of Chinese authority in public life: after all, Lao-tse's *Tao* was the source that modeled a series of events unfolding in Tschoang-tse's life. Lao-tse suggested for example that Tschoang-tse use his intellectual disposition to accumulate knowledge, enabling him better to pursue recognition continuously, rather than sporadically, as his intellectual capacities and curiosities grew. As Tschoang-tse's activities remained confined to theoretical occupations, his (as well as his teacher's) textual representation reiterated the early Enlightenment imagery of China as the realm of philosophers. However, the nature of Tschoang-tse's philosophical activities was profoundly altered. Although installed by the Tao, the character liberated his Self from interpreting texts, generating instead an ever-increasing desire to know himself and his environs. This Self-reflection went beyond the ramifications of teaching: the ethical prohibitions and social hierarchies that entrapped Confucius' circle of pupils had completely disappeared.

Out of this emancipation, a new subjectivity was born that would gradually evolve into the autopoetic subject of early Romanticism. At once creator and creation, poet and poetic work, origin and destiny, this subject exemplified the production and structure of knowledge and poetry—even the idea of itself—and in the process perpetually reproduced his own subjectivity. Autopoeisis generates text out of the variety, plenitude, and differences of perception, yet seeks to unite them in idealized images of wholeness. Stylistically, by resorting to new nature metaphors, this concept opposed the metaphors of divine text and worldly texture of the early Enlightenment. The result was a subject perceived as natural and genuine, a subject whose ontology Helmut Müller-Sievers appropriately calls "selfgeneration." At the same time—and somewhat paradoxically—the autopoetic subject transcended, as we shall see below, the dominant narrative of modernity and its foundational element as well as the integrity and wholeness of the human body.

But the formation of this new, Romantic subject was not yet complete. True, in "The Wheel of Fate," the order of nature creates possibilities for Tschoang-tse, yet it imposes restrictions upon him as well. Subjected to the cycle of day and night, Tschoang-tse reacts differently to these periods; his emotional patterns introduce him to new dimensions of his Self. Day signifies activity, recognition, and innovation, while night means peace, darkness, and stasis. Night suspends life, interrupting the activity of day and, thereby, providing much-needed rest: "Thus you experience joy when watching the sunrise; its heavenly fire weds the spark of your immortality and reawakens life in you. The calm appearance of the moon remains steady: it promises peace and tranquility, rest from daily business, and the separation of evening and morning" (85). Similarly, Lao-tse—the force of tradition—mediates Tschoang-tse's reach for nature, instructing Tschoang-tse to contemplate his teachings and assuring him that he will be back to share the rest of the story. A dutiful follower, Tschoang-tse complies and sleeps. The next morning he asks Lao-tse to predict his fate. The wise man refuses, since explaining the past or future would only disturb the young fellow's present state of mind, but Lao-tse recommends that Tschaong-tse remain true to himself, indicating that having self-knowledge is a prerequisite to acquiring world-knowledge. Enter a dominant cognitive construct of modern philosophy, consciousness versus self-consciousness. As the premise of recognition, development, and education to perfection, this construct takes the preestablished harmony of the Tao as its origin while shifting the authority of progress onto the Self: "You must first achieve the

Fate that awaits you; be wise in your ways, respect my advice, and let only your conscience, which the mother of creation gave you as orientation and guide, be your judge" (95). Such genuine truthfulness to conscience and consciousness implies of course the notion of an adamant identity, subjectivity that subsumes the subject's origin, movement, and destination into a unity. Henceforth, the aspiration to restore this unity structures Tschaong-tse's path, becoming an inner guide as he unfolds his subjectivity in a journey toward ultimate completion.

Tschaong-tse strolls away, his eyes closed, and sleepwalking, he climbs a mountain. Short of breath, he opens his mouth and his eyes and suddenly realizes that he has reached a beautiful, sun-flooded sanctuary where all creeks, rivers, and lakes reflect the light of the day. The vibrant imagery turns rolling hills into a golden, paradise-like landscape and overwhelms Tschaong-tse:

> A dazzling spectacle startled him, for an endless valley stretched before him surrounded by towering mountains, and the glowing sun had just risen above the horizon, gilding the blossoming fields. All creeks, all rivers, all streams reflected the sun's brilliance, flowing sparkling through the meadows and faintly murmuring that the friendly goddess was near. Humble and honored, Tschoang-tse bowed to the earth and prayed, hardly daring to look at this divine performance. (96)

Here for the first time in our discussion of China in eighteenth-century German texts we encounter the immanence and disruptive qualities of vision as the character responds sensually to his surroundings and the author attempts to convey his response. Tschaong-tse obviously experiences an illusion as he witnesses the *spectacle* of nature, for it seems to depart from "reality," producing an impression of a landscape instead. This powerful fictional image disturbs Tschaong-tse to a point where he is afraid of drowning in nature's deceit, something Lao-tse had cautioned against when he said: "Never allow yourself [. . .] to be deceived by illusion" (94).

Despite its seeming threat to Tschoang-tse's sense of reason, the passage has a centering effect on the narrative, for in a narratological sense the image arrests the story's progress, allowing for an inner-textual commentary on the nature of sense perception in Tschoang-tse's unveiling of the "false" nature of the imagery. Unlike other fictional characters and lyrical selves in late eighteenth-century literature, Tschoang-tse does not surrender to the image. Mesmerized for a brief second, he hopes for spiritual grounding in prayer, but when the illusionary beauty of vision overpowers the divine words that seek to speak through nature, he realizes that indulging in this moment of natural spectacle would impair his judgment and, ultimately, he turns away.

The manner in which "The Wheel of Fate" narrates this moment of perceiving nature reflects the difficulty of expressing visuality in words; moreover, it indicates a threshold in eighteenth-century theories of language and representation that entailed a substantial rearrangement of words and things. The clarity and transparency of early Enlightenment representation, where a sign conveyed the essence of a thing behind a word, gave way to a more opaque image that condensed the histories, material conditions, and perceptive situations that gave rise to the representation. "The Wheel of Fate" casts this epistemological transition in a problematic light. As the intensity of nature's play causes a moment of intuition, or of knowledge that is not mediated through artificial signs, image, representation of the image, and expression seem to coincide, rendering the essence of nature in its most transparent way, by creating a natural sign. Yet the text dismisses this mode of signification, for as the sensual intensity of the moment disguises the truth of nature, verbal language cannot adequately represent nature either. Instead, language becomes obscure: numerous hyperbolic constructions depict the "verbal" landscape. Interlaced with syntactical oxymora created by adjectives and static and dynamic verb forms, this use of hyperbole emphasizes the disturbing effects of vision which can only be dispelled by interpreting them as a divine articulation.

In other words, Tschoang-tse's reaction contains a critique of language and it is twofold. On one hand, if signs attempt to capture the essence of perception, they become self-reflective and deceptive, concealing their exterior referentiality and conveying an emotion to the perceiver instead. On the other hand, however, this signifying option remains elusive because the text's subject, Tschoang-tse, is entrapped by the "sacred text" of philosophical tradition. He must engage in philosophical reflection, relating what he sees to what he knows already, in order to achieve distinct cognition. Achieving the knowledge which Tschoang-tse desires and hopes to develop requires the mediation of language. Entrenched in the Chinese philosophical tradition, Tschoang-tse's knowledge appears alienated from any experience other than that of reading books—even though the books speak not through him, but through Lao-tse.

Overall, the sensual impact of seeing nature puts tradition at risk, as vision disrupts coherence and denies the truth of texts. Blinded by the landscape's beauty, Tschoang-tse becomes susceptible to emotions. Engaging in an inner dialogue, he doubts the wisdom of his teacher Lao-tse, who has urged him to cultivate his reasoning capacities and to tame his desires. Tschoang-tse even criticizes Lao-tse for his rigidity and lack of enjoyment: "Does your wisdom deny you all pleasure?" (94). The literary character is clearly a subject in crisis, but just when he is about to succumb to his blissful vision, an unexpected, moaning voice awakens him and restores his rational capacities. Rescuing him from drifting off into a delusion, the voice assures Tschoang-tse of his physical existence and his ultimate presence in that very moment—as had his falling out of bed at night. The voice marks dawn just as his falling did, and the onset of a new day brings renewed and clear recognition. It prays to the sun and to the ascending morning, asking for resurrection from the apathy and emotional starvation of the night. Simultaneously, the voice and the sense of hearing dissolve the collision between image and text.

As the voice pleads with nature and its images, it reveals its own relationship to nature. Unlike flora and fauna that revive daily and seasonally, this voice lacks energy and motivation. Unlike the murmuring of the divine goddess who permeated the blissful imagery of the landscape, the voice echoes—bodiless—from a wall. Having given up any hope that nature might animate it, give it a body, and lift its spirit, the voice sounds increasingly doubtful. Indeed, it could not be more removed from the intrinsic unity and harmony of nature that reincarnation promises. Eventually, as it bemoans its own demise, we recognize that the voice belongs to death: "But I, the outcast, the broken, the exiled! Who can raise me, preserve me? Who can quench my thirst? Who can animate me, bring me back to joyous life, me, the dead? Who? Who?" (97). Naturally, this is a voice with which Tschoang-tse is unfamiliar, inviting his empathy as well as his revulsion. But Tschoang-tse's curiosity makes him climb the wall from which the voice is coming, and he descends into the neighboring desert-like space. Searching for another human being, he ultimately realizes that nobody is there. Scared and dizzy, he rests, and then he hears the voice again, coming from a tiny hole in a stone, and suddenly threatening: "Why do you tempt me, enemy of my peace! Or rather, enemy of yourself! Beware of the *flame of truth*! Beware if you enter the struggle defenseless!" (141).

The recognition and representation of truth, perceived as the essence of Enlightenment philosophy and poetry, poses a concrete threat to Tschoang-tse's integrity. First and foremost, the voice insinuates that his quest for infinite knowledge and ultimate truth must remain unfulfilled, throwing him into the cycles of self-doubt and frustration and making him realize that his identity will never be unwavering. And yet in a far more literal sense, Tschoang-tse is forced to realize that the meaning of truth has changed as well; it reflects no longer the eternal order of an infinite universe waiting to be deciphered, but rather the finitude of human life. Death and finitude cannot be negotiated or overcome, a suggestion the voice might corroborate as it ultimately rejects any further exchange with Tschoang-tse. To modify Alice Kuzniar's thesis on early Romantic literature, the voice marks its own liminality, for it expresses the finitude of body even though it lacks body (1197). Accepting the limitations of physical existence means accepting the inevitability of death and, this in turn, represents the ultimate truth of existence.

Both the spectacle of nature and the encounter with death leave Tschoang-tse puzzled and aware of the limits of human existence, but also convinced that it is impossible to ignore these limitations. The first experience helps Tschoang-tse realize the constraints that traditional, book-based knowledge imposes on sensual experience and that are reflected in the inadequacy of language when it attempts to render perceptions in text. Lao-tse, as the carrier and transmitter of tradition, cannot help Tschoang-tse to read, represent, and translate his perceptions. And though texts can adequately represent spatial imagery, they cannot express the presence of the moment, the temporal coordinates of experience. The second experience teaches Tschoang-tse about the finitude of life, locating death in a space ("behind the wall") that can be entered but also left behind. Hearing the voice of death promises an exit from the limitations of knowledge, the ultimate transcendence. By climbing the wall, Tschoang-tse overcomes the obstacle that prevents him from knowing more, seeming to leave the realm of language that alienates him from sensuality and enter a space where he feels the presence of the infinite. Death constitutes a temptation, the place the subject ultimately wishes to be, if only because epistemological constraints cease to exist there. Ironically, representing the boundless absolute requires the image of a border, a defined, even confined space. The representational entanglement of fleeting voice and limit signifies a crisis of recognition inflicted upon the subject: understanding that there is neither a way to know (nor any "sense" or "meaning") beyond the limitations of life, and sensing also that this earthly knowledge is always limited, the subject inevitably becomes fractured.

This overall constellation anticipated the symbols of early Romanticism: night and day, voice and silence, life and death. Unlike in many Romantic texts, in "The Wheel of Fate" these pairings implied no gendered constellations; however, they did embody conflicting dynamics among concepts that eighteenth-century writers, as well as their Romantic successors, came to identify with the Eastern and Western hemispheres.[8] The Eastern world, or Orient, was thought to perceive the absolute, whereas the Western experience focused on constrictions. Lao-tse's tale produces a subject-position that, enunciated and enacted by Chinese philosophers, promised unity and wholesomeness of experience—human action in harmony with the macrocosm of world. Tschoang-tse represented, however tentatively, collusion between tradition and the immanence of experience. His struggle demonstrated that the promise of harmony was futile, that despite his striving for absolute knowledge, he had to acknowledge his limitations and yet seek to overcome them by constantly asking questions, by listening and reflecting. The subject constantly examined the possibility of reaching the absolute, blissful state it desired, asking what this state entailed and where it was situated, and the answer resided with death, a nonalienated stage of existence. As Tschoang-tse desired the nonalienation that death promised, the fear of death's finitude was kept at bay. Death—and the desert-like space behind the wall—represented a space that eliminated time and evinced characteristics that had prevailed in the literary imagery of China's history since the eighteenth century and that, by the time "The Wheel of Fate" was published, had gained great cultural currency (Schuster, 205–14). Loaded with geographical markers and ethnic histories of an existing earthly place, the tale's imagery resembled a heterotopia. In subsequent decades, writers would invest thus-constructed "Oriental locales" with ever more utopian thought, further depleting the space of any material reality that might have persisted in the Western imagination (Foucault, "Of other Spaces," 22–27).

Confused and angry, Tschaong-tse leaves the mysterious desert and continues his journey. On his way he begins to formulate his first thoughts on the purpose of life. He repeatedly questions the authority of his teacher, complaining that he has not received true guidance from Lao-tse and ignoring Lao-tse's advice to listen to the inner voice of his consciousness. Only then, Lao-tse had suggested, can Tschoang-tse make qualified choices in his life. Discounting such wisdom, Tschoang-tse insists on guidance for intellectuals like himself who no longer have transparent access to the world and to knowledge. Momentarily it appears as if Tschoang-tse's character devolves back into the tradition of Chinese texts and their European readers, but this is not so. By accusing Lao-tse of neglect, he detaches himself from the superior authority of the text (*Tao*) and experiences instead a merger between himself and nature: his thoughts and expressions correspond to nature, and both thought and nature bear the seeds of new life. At this moment, Tschoang-tse fully actualizes himself as a sovereign subject through autopoesis, reaching a stage of absolute bliss that henceforth structures his cognition: while realizing itself as the *origin* of absolute experience, the subject becomes aware of the alienating forces of life. Tschoang-tse listens to the voices of life that separate the subject from its absolute state; therefore, as it absorbs life in its movement toward absolute knowledge, the subject engages in a process of self-reflection. Reaching the highest form of cognition,[9] the subject becomes its own model, so to speak.

At the same time, the configuration of subjectivity in "The Wheel of Fate" announced what David Wellbery terms Romantic "metamorphosis," a notion of subjectivity that expresses the autopoetic process through a constant change of shape, contours, and perceptive fields and that would guide the poetics of early Romanticism. In "The Wheel of Fate," as well as in subsequent examples of Romantic texts by Wackenroder, Schlegel, and Günderrode, to name a few, the subject inhabits an Asian locale, and, in each of these texts, the capacity of subjectivity to transcend the physical limitations of the human body evolves as sensual experience—often hearing—confronts the textual tradition of reading Asia (Wellbery, *The Specular Moment*; von Mücke/Kelly, 1–22, 182; Tautz, "Autopoeisis," 67–68).

* * *

Although the question whether the novel or the serial came first remains open, the novel's target is clearly defined: a blunt critique of the court through a popular theatrical activity at Anna Amalia's court, the masquerade (see Kord, "Cult"). It also dissects the fundamental fiction of an erudite Enlightenment that has defined the image of Goethe's Weimar since the 1770s. In contrast, the ideas contained in the fragmentary "Wheel of Fate" were far more influential to the development of poetics. Taken together, novel and fragment illustrate a transitional moment at the Weimar Court and illuminate the lasting poetic, cultural, and political influence of a particular time and place in Germany—a time and place that still affect formulations of Germanness today, regardless of its questionable reliability. 1780s Weimar and its writers were about to experience a crisis of Enlightenment (and one of its correlating literary genres, the *Bildungsroman*) which would lead to the rise of early Romanticism, "exiled" to nearby Jena. *The Journal's* "Wheel of Fate"—only ten pages and "to be continued" (143)—reflected this process, demonstrating both the construction of sovereign subjectivity at the core of Enlightenment and identifying the signs and symptoms of this ideal falling apart, and making way for a poetic convention that was both troubling and appealing to Goethe: early Romanticism (see Hinderer; Wellbery, *The Specular Moment*).

The flirtation of *The Journal of Tiefurt*—and, by extension, the court society—with its own poetic alterity remained episodic and, perhaps, accidental. A persistent undercurrent, however, was the awareness of and engagement with "Chinese motifs." Though they fostered consideration of larger, enlightened communities, the writers' professed interest in a national community overall fell far short of their ideas about communal erudition and poetic production (50–52). Chinese ciphers indeed played a role in achieving the latter. When it came to critiquing boredom and shallowness, hierarchies and jockeying for position among writers, and reflecting on their own subjectivity, writers alluded to what they called Asian thought. Their allusions strike a positive, if playful and at times ironic tone, making it entirely conceivable that its contributors conceived *The Journal of Tiefurt* as a reference to or even imitation of the detailed nature of the Chinese.

The members of the Weimar court were not alone, neither among German principalities with their obsession for collecting Asian artifacts and building in Japanese or Chinese architectural styles, nor among their European contemporaries. Weimar was not the only court to possess a Chinese pavilion. But unlike English writers, for example, who discussed accounts of Chinese architecture and gardening as expressions of decorative detail and ultimate boredom, *The Journal* enlisted the Eastern hemisphere in its efforts to curb boredom. In parallel with play, puzzle, and rhetorical debate—all of which displayed the telltale signs of obsessive production, the antidote to boredom—*The Journal* also contained pieces on meditation and praised good meditative practices, a staple "in Buddha's religion," as an effective tool to channel one's contemplative energies (28–29, 31, 352–53). Similarly, "The Chinese Morals Teacher" and the two texts by Seckendorff presented positive models of communities that avoided the emptiness of distraction and ultimately fostered the Enlightenment project, while inadvertently exposing the alterity of failure and ideal subjectivity.

4

DETAILED ETHNICITY:
PERCEPTION AND GENDER
IN TRAVEL ACCOUNTS

In chapters 2 and 3 I discussed the manner in which representational coherence is established within a world that claims to espouse a universal worldview, identifying various processes that both demarcate and integrate difference as a symptom of universal reason and recognition. These processes are exemplified by Leibniz's use of translation and by Wolff's portrayal of Confucius and the Western philosopher as each other's mirror or counterpart. Decades later, the Weimar court society produced erudite essays, novels, and plays projecting China as a superior model testing the limits of European Enlightenment and its formulation of community. Finally, anticipating Romantic models of transcendence, Enlightenment accounts suggested "accepting" death as the ultimate representation of finitude—by way of Chinese authority. In any case, the texture embracing China and Europe evolved from *reading*, from the preoccupation with books, ancient philosophies, and their reinterpretation in a European framework.

But what happened to these models for reading among cultures when they collided with other powerful experiences such as actually seeing China? What happened to such a carefully cultivated image as it circulated in different social spaces, genres, and populations and saturated the emerging market of popular novels and lending libraries that caused book production to double between 1770 and 1800 (Zantop, 32)? What happened when expansive travelogues began to replace erudite philosophical tracts? Toward the end of the eighteenth century travel texts flooded German lands in the form of popular book series (e.g., *Magazine of Curious Travelogues*), installments in journals ("Mr. M**'s Journey"), and so did travelogues in multiple editions geared toward readers of different classes and often in competing versions (Zantop, 32; cf. Hentschel; also Griep, and Kutter). A case in point is *Des Herrn Sonnerat Reise nach Ostindien und China, in den Jahren 1774 bis 1781, nebst dessen Beobachtungen über Pegu, Madagascar, das Cap, die Inseln France und Bourbon, die Maldiven, Ceylon, Malacca, die Philippinen und Molucken, aus dem Französischen* (Sonnerat's Journey): a new translation and edition which appeared in 1783 listed readers' preferences, cost efficiency, and an altered knowledge base as reasons for the reissuing of the travelogue that had first become available to German readers only a few months earlier. Collectively, these accounts exemplified a literary situation that could not have been more different from the isolated, esoteric community at Tiefurt and its elusive goals of wider influence.

These travel accounts also attest to the phenomenon of authenticating ethnic imagery through vision. Aware of the long European tradition of praising China for its legal and moral codes, they began to focus on the current state of the empire, demanding that it pay attention to the observer and undergo renewed investigation by philosophers. As the author of *Sonnerat's Journey* makes these demands (259), he follows up with a long list of known facts about China, handed down by the textual tradition that had formed in the aftermath of Jesuit settlements and reports. While he confirms some aspects of the tradition through his illustrative account, he simply disputes others. But he also criticizes the Jesuits' philosophical foundation for reading China. When accusing the missionaries of having sought world domination and legitimacy for repressive regimes in Europe through their favorable reports on the Chinese, the author attacks reading and textuality as modes of perceiving alterity. Relentless in his critique, he blames "economists" for abusing the same textually manipulated accounts in their outspokenness against European monarchs (260–61). In the end though, not even he can spare the textual tradition, because his observation depends on the parameters set up in written accounts as well as on Chinese interpretations of their own tradition. Like the Jesuits and Leibniz before him, he relates information on the political and civil hierarchies of the Chinese empire, especially on the role of literati and mandarins. But unlike his predecessors, he interprets the empire's recourse to books and textual authorities as recipes for stagnation, arbitrariness, and corruption—though he cynically remarks that being stuck in old knowledge may actually have prevented the Chinese from migrating (260). Last but not least, the author does not fail to mention laziness and egotism, foot-binding and polygamy, all of which doubtlessly negated the image of China as Europe's ethical example.

Late eighteenth-century travel reports published in the *Magazine of Curious Travelogues* or in weekly installments also subverted the idealized construct of China by simultaneously alluding to traditional representations and recording the sight of new, conflicting phenomena. For example the expansive, epistolary "Journey of Mr. M** to China in 1773 and 1774" expresses this phenomenon particularly well: "The relations I established by trading with the most famous Chinese merchants disillusioned me. Hardly anything is left of the noble idea, of the excellence, which I had previously attributed to this nation" (254). As Mr. M** experiences China, he bemoans the loss of "model China," thereby affirming what I regard as a compelling moment of the Enlightenment discourse on ethnic difference: the fundamental discrepancies between what is *read* and what is *seen*. Experience destroyed the illusion of a correspondence between reality and representation; *things* behind *words* appeared hidden, distorted, and even manipulative rather than being made transparent through language. Experience disrupted the various practices of translating ethnic difference as an expression of universal order, as well as holding it up as a mirror in an effort to legitimize the new, particularizing European ideal of an enlightened public sphere.

This classical unity of representation vanished in the course of the eighteenth century—only to make its persistent return as a philosophical or aesthetic postulate (Foucault, *Archaeology*, 12; see also *Order*, 303–43). Accordingly, the image of the Chinese nation as a meticulously ordered society did not disappear. In fact, long before this representation of China entered (Hegel's) philosophy as the sign of an undifferentiated origin, it hibernated in narratives of experience. Thus an altered text remained on the horizon.[1] But the rich textual corpus of narrated voyages called attention to the newly established relevance of vision in yet another way. China began to appear in the context of other travel destinations. On their way to China, travelers circumnavigated Africa, and seeing new geographical locales appealed to both experience and metaphor. As travelers approached—literally as well as figuratively—a revised image of China, they confronted older accounts of Africa that, despite being contained in books, preserved all the traces of sensual perception: sound, fragrance, and sight. Thus, as travelers integrated them into their preconceived knowledge of the continent, the encounter with Africa seemed like a déjà vu. It certainly was represented as such.

Despite the representational challenges inflicted by vision, the claim of universalism continued to structure the text signifying China, but in a gendered version: as universal Woman, whose domesticated, beautiful ideal existed in Europe as well as in China. At the same time, ethnicity unfolded in many variations in the course of traveling, almost always bearing traces of immediacy and sense perception. Ethnic differences manifested themselves in observations on infrastructure and in cartographical writing, in accounts of mercantilism and trade, geography, and history. They pervaded the manner in which authors related accounts of race, cultural habits, and daily life in distant lands, as well as their spite toward fashion, luxury, and other vices. Consequently, the comparison between the imaginary idea of the Chinese nation and observed reality with regard to the basic structure of textual domination and perceptual subversion serves as the point of departure in this chapter. In what follows, I shall demonstrate how perceptual instances are traced in texts and how these textual effects, which I shall call "details," relate (to) expressions of ethnic difference and gender dynamics. I will suggest that the tension between instantaneous perception and textual tradition produces ethnicity in relation to gendered communities—underscoring the fact that in the late eighteenth century, "Germany" (in the sense of a modern nation-state) was very much a fantasy and fiction.

THE SUBJECT ON THE MOVE: TRAVELER, AUTHOR, READER

In 1775, *Der Teutsche Merkur* (The German Mercury), the most prominent among the many weekly and monthly journals that had saturated the print market in German lands, published the "Journey of Mr. M** to China in 1773 and 1774."[2] The serial account comprises three letters that chronicle the voyage from France via the Isle de France and Malac, along the Chinese coast to Macao, and finally to China (Wampu, Kantong) and back to Europe. The traveling merchant, M**, whose stories these sixty-plus pages narrate, identifies himself as the author of the letters. A footnote in the publication claims that the journal printed the text "based on the hitherto unpublished manuscript of [M**'s] letters)" and mentions a French original (60). Many passages in it resemble passages in *Sonnerat's Journey* in terms of content, routes taken, and references made.[3] Nevertheless, this epistolary account provides us with an ideal pathway into the untangling of the complex relations among authors, travelers, and readers. These relations expose an economy of writing and reading, narrative creation, and discursive deciphering that allows us to trace the nuances of detailed ethnicity evolving in the texts. Furthermore, they illustrate how *Woman* becomes a rhetorical placeholder of universalism.

Therefore, "Mr. M**'s Journey" serves as a core text in this chapter, read against the backdrop of numerous other travelogues from *Sonnerat's Journey* and the *Magazine of Curious Travelogues* to Georg Forster's *Voyage around the World*.

M** writes to his sister, the mother of a travel companion, and his brother, and the result is a cohesive story that unfolds as M** conveys geographical, economic, and cultural information. Yet he also (and repeatedly) attempts to define both the purpose of the journey and the traveler's expectations. Purely informational passages thus alternate with evaluations of whether or not goals have been realized and hopes fulfilled; in addition, reflections about the aesthetics of travel narratives and his self-image as a writer deter us from moving smoothly through the text. Overall though, this epistolary account demonstrates the autonomous subject on multiple levels: as a material condition and the narrative fiction of self-made individuals, as a subject of action and a subject of reflection. Or, as Elizabeth Heckendorn Cook puts it: "While reading, we are intended to imagine a scene of writing: behind the printed page is a manuscript bearing the traces of a bodily origin. Formally as well as thematically, then, the letter constructs the writing subject as corporeal and thus as an already existing knowledge that can be mapped by the transparent medium of print" ("Limping Woman," 23).

In other words, our modern understanding of subjectivity—as a concept intrinsically linked to and emanating from individual, discrete bodies—arises from the image of the writer's body shining through in the textual form of the letter. Reproduced through printing and therefore circulating publicly, this image can be endlessly reassembled in the process of reading. At once individual and prototypical, subjectivity takes "a textual form that articulates the ideologically loaded qualities of discreteness and autonomy assigned to each body/ subject" (23). Thus construed, the reading and writing processes happen simultaneously in the epistolary autobiography where the writer evolves into the page and, in tracing himself to the discrete body, projects himself as a sovereign subject. In the process, autonomous subjectivity produces and unites the private and public spheres, as well as the materiality and the discursively constructed historical moment (Cook, *Epistolary Bodies*, 6, 12, 29, 173). "Author-traveler" refers, then, to an autobiographical subject who not only reflected about himself while traveling, but also created himself as traveler in the process of writing. As a result, the story develops different subject positions and, though driven by attempts to reconcile them, continuously reasserts the tensions among these positions. Thus the text reveals the highly ambiguous way in which epistolary autobiography expresses an authenticity that simultaneously functions as the ultimate model of the sovereign subject and the evidence of its crisis; for we shall see that the author, while narrating his life, pursues an idea he cannot actualize.

Such contrived authenticity also characterized other travel genres (journals, questionnaires, reports, and novels), though the actual authorial involvement in the journeys appears more obscured here. This was especially true whenever the accounts sought to establish an objective distance, that is, to produce a factual truth rather than to convey the unfiltered impression, the immediacy of experience. Sometimes the authors did not even participate in the travel, especially when it was seafaring. They were hired after the journeys' successful completion and instructed to fashion the notes by scientists, merchants, and sailors into a book (Hentschel). When they were actually on board, the authors' vision was often limited to specific tasks, such as relating scientific information to both scholarly and lay community or compiling useful information for the merchants they accompanied.[4] Erudition even shaped the quality of observation, as we shall see in the case of Georg Forster's *Voyage*. Most frequently, however, authors of travelogues weighed their accounts against others, comparing, contrasting, and concluding in light of what seems like compilations of texts. In this respect they resembled an observing translator arranging, in an almost Leibnizian tradition, observations within a universe of texts.

These varying authorial positions are further complicated if we consider the relationship between author and translator. After all, many eighteenth-century German-language texts about travel to distant, overseas locations were either translated from other languages or, at the very least, were claimed to be translations. While these claims played an often underestimated role in forging a national community of readers—a role which I hope to clarify in this chapter—at this point the following will suffice: author-translators provided, in keeping with late eighteenth-century traditions, a linguistic and cultural translation of distant objects, lands, and people modeled according to the expectations of their readers (Zantop, 32–34; Tautz, "Cutting"). Hence no matter how disparate in genre, style, and genesis, these accounts share one subject matter: travel, always invoking a human being in motion, whose dislocation in territory and progress through narrative space causes psychological disarray and density. Travel literature, evolving around transformations of and in territorial space, appears to have been a primary site for empirical subjects to clash with linguistic and aesthetic ones. Since it was also the site where the individuality (of the traveler) met the collectivity (of readers), the multifaceted corpus of travel literature exposes, just as autobiographical and epistolary genres do, the intricate processes of modern subject formation.

In all the travelogues, perceived opposing forces counter the desire for autonomous subjectivity and the traveler's goal-oriented motion through space. These instances of subjectivity evolve in response to perceptions and representations linking other bodies and texts to the travelogue. Consequently, traveler-authors appear as an effect of multiple causes or origins: as an effect of the conflicting psychosocial spheres that shaped the production and circulation of texts, as an effect of traditions of travel practice, travel fiction, and reading ethnic difference. Furthermore, the traveler-author is produced in relation to a truly elusive reader. In *Sonnerat's Journey*, however, he arises as an effect of the gender, family role, and public function of the reader-subjects to whom he writes his letters. Ultimately, a thus-traversed subject eclipses the fiction of sovereign subjectivity whose different models—the sovereign philosopher, the obedient state-subject, the dutiful *filius*, and the subject at the verge of crisis— have introduced in the previous chapter; captured by the epistolary travel account, the sovereign subject literally appears to "travel restlessly" (see Van den Abbeele, xiii–xxx).

* * *

The genealogy of the modern subject and its expression through models of narrative identification are intrinsically linked to strategies and effects of spatial transformation. Aesthetic spaces establish and negotiate the relationship between author and reader, and the perception of empirical space and its aesthetic transformation are at the core of travel literature. Critics have argued persuasively that as an experiential realm of eighteenth-century subjectivity, neither travel nor storytelling suffices, whereas domesticity and reading do. Jay Caplan, for example, characterizes subjectivity as a sacrificial and compensatory relation among author, reader, and literary representations. Nancy Armstrong demonstrates that the experiential loss of political authority and societal contract established domestic authority and gender contract in fiction. Zantop focuses on the prenational implications of domesticated reading, arguing that colonial fantasies, the confinement of the reader to fictional exploration of imperial space, created a German community that saw itself as both morally superior and politically and economically inferior in relation to its European peers.

Finally, Berman wrestles the concept of a national subjectivity away from readers and relocates it firmly in the sphere of authorial intention.

Both Zantop and Berman draw on Mary Louise Pratt's *Imperial Eyes*, a book that articulates what is missing from other critiques, namely an inclusion of *empirical genres*, genres that do not aspire to substitute empirical reality for aesthetic experience, but preserve the tension between "reality" and "fiction" as their very foundation (4). Linking the genealogy of the European imperial subject to the functional distinction between geographical (public) and perceptual (private) spaces of experience, Pratt defines these spaces through the cultural practices of writing and reading. By engaging numerous people in an imaginary way in a journey, the writing of travel books creates the illusion that geographical discoveries are of broader social concern, concealing the fact that only a few people have gained public respect or economic advantage through travel. However, reading functions in a reciprocal manner. Though sharing the ideals and desires of public experience, for which travel becomes the metaphor, people read as individuals and mostly in privacy. Accordingly, geographical and political expansion through travel, the writing of travel books, and the intensity of reading share a purpose within the formation of bourgeois identity: they endow private existence with public relevance.

The distinct relation between foreign and domestic space structures Pratt's argument. I would like to suggest, however, that we rethink the textual manifestations of the relations among traveler, author, and reader in terms of "contact zones," a central and influential notion Pratt proposes. While she defines them geographically and anthropologically as "social spaces where disparate cultures meet, clash, and grapple with each other, often in highly asymmetrical relations of domination and subordination" (4), I believe that contact zones constitute a locale where one can grasp the relation between geographical and perceptual space. In a text they function both as a point of reference and as a descriptive tool for the traveler-author's examination of sensations and perceptions. Thus, contact zones become a means of describing the rhetorical discrepancy between what the traveler sees and what the author expresses. But they also form the textual space that engages the domestic subject of reading in the perception of ethnic difference, while at the same time preserving the textual tradition with which the newly perceived impression collides.

Taking this understanding of contact zones even further, I contend that they constitute the discursive or psychosocial complement of what Naomi Schor calls the detail in narrative. The detail marks a

visual or textual presence that, for all its apparently superfluous, ornamental, or unduly prosaic nature, becomes associated with femininity
and its numerous connotations. Cultural history and philosophy have
rendered the detail a formal imperfection and deviation *per se* in any
narrative of modern culture that preserves, in a paradoxical twist, the
memory of undefined materialities prior to their signification and unifying form (cf. also Foucault, *Discipline*, 141). I propose that as details
capture constructions of subjectivity and immanence, travel accounts
tend to conceal such instances by resorting to distancing objectivity.
They profess to reach objectivity either by describing precisely the
geographic coordinates of the journey, weather patterns, nature, etc.—
all clearly with the intention of producing utilitarian, even cartographic knowledge—or by picking narrative insufficiencies as a central
theme. Conversely, in order to make sense out of their own insufficiencies, the narratives rely on innovative positions of narrative identification. Like the imagery, these innovations evolve out of the clash
between textual tradition and perceptual presence or experience. In the
end, the detail affords us access to the materialities and perceptions it
conceals, especially those connoting and designating the ethnic.
Furthermore, although sensual perceptions of alterity cannot be
equated with textual inscriptions of femininity, I believe that gender difference influences narrative constructions of ethnicity. Consequently,
detail helps to map the interrelations between constructions of ethnic
difference and gender.

*   *   *

In "Mr. M**'s Journey," Mr. M** begins the letter to his sister with
elaborate reflections on the limitations of experience and narration.
He wants to share his travel adventures with the reader by telling his
story; he wants to report on the high sea, torrential rivers, and
thrilling boat rides. Disillusioned about the reality of travel, which for
him means boredom instead of adventure, and disappointment
instead of bliss, he disguises his own desire by misconstruing it as the
desire of the reader: "These empty images of horror may affect the
fearful people in your dioceses, but not me. No little storm, no high
sea, no blustery little gale—nothing to enhance my boring travelogue" (67). Though M** firmly believes that lack of experience must
ultimately result in insufficient narration of his own Self, he insists on
the uniqueness of his experience when emphasizing the limits of the
sister's domestic realm: "Considering how moderate the climate is
where you are, you cannot even imagine the kind of storm that is

unfortunately all too common here!" (67). Eventually overwhelmed by boredom after days at sea, he forsakes his initial intention to turn the voyage into a shared experience through writing, but only after describing the effects his depiction of violent storms would have on his sister—"a hair-raising image for you" (72). Ultimately, he resigns himself to the fact that adventure is a fantasy that can only survive in the domestic realm.

Overall, the traveler-author assures himself of his narrative authority in a rather paradoxical way. While the traveler preserves his vision of adventure by placing it in the aesthetic realm of purposeful story-telling, the author subordinates this vision by dismissing it as a fantasy of the domestic reader. Informative and expository writing—a norm and expectation in travel reports—is completely suppressed, and a strange combination of indulgence, erudition, and entertainment becomes the narrative intention. Though this intention fails, the transposition of authority evolves into narrative innovation; by pro-ducing details, it anchors reading. The implied reader pauses; reflect-ing upon her being different from the author, she also relates herself to the traditional ideal and purpose of travel, that is, to adventure and self-assertion. Thus M**'s reflections on traveling, narrating, and reading create both gender boundaries and bonds when addressing the reader. His text, along with the many mass-produced travelogues on the contemporary German literary market, reflects the many ten-sions that accompanied the rise of the (gendered) sovereign subject. I shall examine these tensions in instances of detailed ethnicity that geographically take us en route to China.

EN ROUTE: CREATING ETHNIC SUBJECTS, READING ALONG GENDER LINES

The travel accounts considered here make use of a well-defined reper-toire of scenes, routes, and destinations, frequently recycling tropes, observations, and even entire passages. Voyages from Europe to Asia and to the Pacific routinely detail landings in Madeira, at the Cape of Good Hope, and on Isle de France (Mauritius). Traveler-authors invoke a reservoir of images and criteria of normative gender behavior. En route to destination and narration, they labor to tame, literally and figuratively, the distracting sight of land. They seek to minimize the unnerving effects the blinding visions have on their individual psychoemotional stability as well as on the coherence of their stories. But once they succeed in managing the initial sensual perceptions in their texts, the traveler-authors freely turn to constructing ethnic subjects out of the dispersing effects of what strikes them as unmediated alterity. Viewed in relation to their imaginary readers, the images become a means of relating ethnic alterity, organizing it, and mediating it as new information. Conversely, this textual alterity serves to construct, or at least reinforce, ideal subjectivity at home.

In all of these travelogues the first sight of land reflects the larger structural properties of the genre, namely the tension between textual knowledge and momentary impression. When M** arrives at Isle de France, he is struck by the view of the island: he absorbs it in detail, and, dazzled by its beauty, gives a minute description of what he sees: "It was with drunken delight that our eyes devoured the sight of land, something we had missed for so long. The dry, sunburned rocks enclosing the port looked to us like the shores of a magic land, and never have the valleys of our home smiled at me so charmingly as the view of this island, which a really objective first glance would surely find sad and objectionable" (73). To the reader's eye a corresponding landscape emerges, giving her the impression of actually participating in the journey.

This passage constitutes a so-called arrival scene, describing the traveler's initial encounter with another people, country, landscape, or unknown geographical region. Arrival scenes are typical of the travel genre because they "frame," as Pratt maintains, "the relations of contact and set the terms for its representation" (78). In "Mr. M**'s Journey" several passages—not just the crew's arrival at Isle de France, but also the arrival of a young black woman aboard ship and visits to a governor's house—share the relations or conditions of contact, reflecting a common element in representing contact in texts. The scenes capture another culture, preserving and reinforcing the initial construct of alterity as something unknown and new, to be depicted and to be read. But equally significant is what the passages reveal about the traveler-author. The texts communicate the relations of physically encountering alterity in a highly gendered, even sexual way (Weigel, 121; Agnew, 88; also Pelz, 1–45). At the same time these passages mark sharp distinctions from another form of contact, namely the collusion of the present account with a textual tradition and the proliferation of images and clichés through texts.

Metaphors and images of digestion ("our eyes devoured") linguistically interrelate the passage above and another scene where the author speaks of the sexual appetites rampant among the male crew ("made us even hungrier," 70) and which they seek to indulge with a sexually unrestrained black woman ("who [. . .] willingly succumbed to us on board"). The metaphors establish figurative links between the captivation of women and the exploration of land. Yet while the author portrays the black woman as an unruly force—a depiction to which I shall return shortly—the personification of the island ("smiled at me") surely passes for a sensual arousal that is defined by the gaze. The immanence of the sensual-perceptual field structures the traveler's encounter with the island and subsequently contributes to the conflation of the traveler's perception with the author's description and the image's reception by the reader. Here, physical (non)contact is replaced by a sensation, a gaze that ultimately suspends the distancing and dissociating effects of the glance. The former obscures the empirical act of seeing, focusing instead on the product or image, on that which is being perceived. In contrast, the latter describes the economy of viewing that the author seeks to establish through the metanarrative passages (Bal, 149–53), where the traveler-author appears keenly aware of his engagement in the act of looking that he ultimately defines as an act of representing and constructing. In this arrival scene, however, the traveler-viewer is merely affected. He perceives the island as a powerful image that causes hallucinatory effects when meeting his eye. The hallucination thus produced in him assures him of his subjective perception, its relevance, and his corporeal identity (Haas, 4). Through the impact of this image, the traveler appears as "the subject in place" and as "the subject in the face of another" (Bartkowski, 9). With his rapt gaze at the island, the traveler marks an instance of autonomous subjectivity. However, a corrective glance creeps back in, accompanying, though not dominating, this process of subject formation when the traveler reflects on the unrestrained visual indulgence and surreal, hallucinatory appearance of the island. M** recognizes himself as the instance of seeing. Thus the glance momentarily opposes the perceived image and ultimately corrects the initial impression by invoking the imperative of objectivity. Accordingly, the island offers a repulsive view.

Such corrections were frequently made in travelogues, usually before the impressions were captured in writing and always in response to contact with an all-pervasive textual tradition. Carpentier de Cossigny, the traveler-author of *The Voyage to China and Bengal*, was keenly aware of this tradition when speaking about his initial view of the Cape of Good Hope. Though he immediately leaps into linking his account to those recorded earlier, he attributes his tale's validity to his unique sight: "So many writers have described the Cape of Good Hope that it may seem entirely superfluous to speak about it again. But my way of seeing is so different from anyone else's that I will not hesitate to share at least a few of my observations" (9). Other writers, such as the author of *Thunberg's Travels*, refrained from any description of the Cape area because accounts exist elsewhere in abundance (iv). Still others struck a middle ground. Georg Forster, whose *Voyage around the World*—his account of his participation in Cook's second voyage—first appeared in English in 1777 and in German in 1784, relates sense impressions; however, he was careful to set them apart from "collecting, describing, and drawing the objects of natural history" (19), the actual purpose and task of his writing. In fact the conceptual underpinnings of his task, which Forster poignantly expressed in the German version by calling himself a *Gelehrter* (*Reise*, 7), appear in close alliance with the sublimation of the gaze in moments of arrival or the sight of land. Berman describes such textual management of sensual immediacy as "integration of emotion," "aesthetic experience," and "stirring of the soul" (26), all of which are critical elements of his argument for different national perspectives among European writers as they engaged and represented cultural alterity (cf. Tautz, "Cutting").

Forster's first view of Africa conjures up a narrative economy very similar to M**'s letter writing. On October 29, 1773, Forster notes the interplay of "clouds and fog," "blowing wind," and uncanny, erratic movements in the water, changing from "agitation" to "gradual subsiding" and back (*Voyage*, 48). He ultimately concludes: "There was a singularity, and a grandeur in the display of this phenomenon, which could not fail of giving occupation to the mind, and striking with a reverential awe, due to Omnipotence" (49). Securely containing immanence in an evaluation of these effects on the reader, he reestablishes the differences between the image, the rendering of the image by him, the traveler-author, and the readers' expectations: "[. . .] I hope I shall not have formed too favorable an opinion of my readers, if I expect that the generality will sympathize with me in these feelings, and that none will be found ignorant or depraved enough to despise them" (49). The sublimation of the gaze is experientially aligned with a desire for stability and firm grounding: Forster introduces his metanarrative reflection only when his shipmates see land. "Soil" ultimately provides more stability than the transitory stage of a voyage. In moments like this, Forster feels the need to explain his digression, his momentary lapse from "objectivity," just as he openly and in detail wonders whether any additional descriptive passages of Madeira will be of use to anyone. "I am aware indeed, that an account of Madeira may by some be looked upon as a superfluous work," he states, "but if, upon a candid perusal, it is found to contain such observations as have not yet appeared in the numerous journals of navigators, I hope I shall not need a farther apology" (25). At times, what could easily turn into a digression propels the narrative forward, as do Forster's reflections on his arrival on Pacific islands (154–55). To him, details are not acceptable merely as spaces for identification, but only if they supply new information. He is swept up in a textual tradition of utilitarian travel reports, natural history, and ethnic images that were shaped and proliferated by this tradition (see Hentschel; Kutter). What he seeks to impart, and perhaps to imitate, is actually a product of the textual culture he is immersed in.

The contrast to epistolary accounts could not be more obvious. Unlike Forster's reflection on observation and travel, metanarrative passages in epistolary fiction do not contribute to a utilitarian textual economy but subvert it. They are an effect of idealized reading and are intended to provide spaces of identification. By capturing his emotional response to the view of the island, these details add an inner dimension (*Innerlichkeit*) to the narrative. As the reader engages in the travel illusion, the traveler-author experiences momentary bliss as the hallucination appeals to another side of his self. Feeling and emotion defeat the traveler's utilitarian, self-mastering personality. This identification compensates for the experience of loss—an effect of the individual's interaction with the outside world—by assuring him of inner emotional stability and wealth. The narrative acquires an inner dimension by absorbing the ethnographic information on Isle de France the author wants to convey. This dimension opposes the exteriorized, utilitarian purpose of travel, which only a disinterested, objective glance at the island could restore. In ways similar to (de)gendered domestic reading, the traveler-author accepts "on the one hand, the claim to innocence and disinterestedness, and on the other, the vocabulary of ego-centered lust and desire. On one hand, there is a demanding (masculine) self with needs to be met, and, on the other, a receptive (feminine) self penetrated by sentiments" (Pratt, 57). Therefore, the detail establishes a sentimental pattern of identification at the level of storytelling, a pattern whose sensuous and emotional qualities have not only been associated with femininity, but become symptomatic for narrative renewal (Chow, 85).

After endless torment about his (in)sufficiency as a storyteller, M** speaks about the other people who boarded the ship to Isle de France en route to China, and on the ship, the women among his travel companions arouse his sexual fantasies. He specifically discusses the sexual submissiveness of a "Negro woman"—the aforementioned arrival of a black woman on board—assuming that his sister will be full of disgust as she reads the account: "However, the lady who at first intended to travel with us realized that her virtue would be at stake in the company of young, hot-blooded fellows grown even hungrier at sea, so she left the day before our ship departed. In her place remained a young Negro woman who all the more willingly succumbed to us on board" (70). Woman, the rhetorical figure through which the traveler-author narrates his desire, multiplies here: women no longer merely occupy the position of the reader-subject, but also act in the narrated story. The black woman enters a structural and interpretive relationship to the European lady: by taking the latter's place, she presumably becomes her substitute. Besides that, both women are indeed constructed through the lens of the domestic reader, so that several women are placed in relation to each other.

The European lady, though (or because she is) absent from the community of male travelers, lives up to the bourgeois ideal of a woman. Concerned about her reputation, she leaves the ship and signals that she is not available. Moreover, since relinquishing her travel plans means staying away from any public activity, she maintains her role as guardian of domesticity and restores thereby social spaces violated by the "Negro woman." The latter is a *public woman* entering male space as she boards the ship. Lacking *virtue*, the eighteenth-century word for chastity, modesty, and fidelity, she willingly submits to sex—at least according to the author's account and the beliefs circulating among the late eighteenth-century European populace.[5] Elsewhere in the text, M** suggests that the black woman may cause feelings of revulsion in his sister because she does not live up to the European ideal of beauty. But here, neither shape nor skin color, neither beauty nor ugliness is at issue. What is supposed to repel the sister is not even primarily the woman's sexual generosity, but the action that precedes this generosity: the black woman's transgression into the public space constitutes the discursive ground for the sister's revulsion, whereas the European lady, who shares the domesticity of the reader, functions as a model for identification.

The *Magazine of Curious Travelogues* features comparable accounts of "public women" who regularly work as prostitutes or can be persuaded to prostitute themselves for Western goods, or who lack a domicile and family, the realms that would define them as equals in the eyes of European, bourgeois women. Public women often congregate in the vicinity of ships, such as in Macao's port, where travelers observe "girls who sell their favors" ([Beniowski], 341). Travelers express surprise if luxurious sheets, clothes, and other European objects fail to entice women into offering their services. One author compares them to gypsies and, when asked his meaning, suggests that the ignorant have a gander at the first band of gypsies he can find behind a hedge in Essex (*Verstreute Nachrichten*, 249).

Hence the underlying gender dynamics produce ethnic difference. The representation of the black woman indicates—in a "de-tailed" (originally meaning "cut-off") manner—a disruption of any narrative economy geared toward a communal European unity of those traveling and those left behind at home, of the author and his readers, of traveling non-German Europeans and reading Germans. (This unity revolves, of course, around the complementary duo of public exploration and conquest on one hand and domestic resilience on the other.) Furthermore, by being subjected to the binary matrix of gender and to the respective identification with European bourgeois men and women, the representation of the black woman marks a transgressive subject-position beyond the scope of the particular narrative. Submerged in the binary matrix of heterosexuality, this position coincides with sex as a form of transgression. So ethnicity marks the locus of "sex," just as "sex" marks the locus of the ethnic. By introducing it as the sensual impact of the black woman, "sex" is discursively produced; by being eliminated from the ideal of bourgeois subjectivity and arrested as an aspect of otherness, "sex" becomes discursively regulated (cf. Foucault, *History*; Butler).

This alignment of ethnicity and gender has had profound and often contradictory effects on our understanding of subjectivity and community; their interrelation is at best of a fractured nature. Apparently the distribution of bourgeois gender identities confirmed the illusion of a subject whose ideal of sovereignty coincided with his bourgeois experience in the aesthetic realm of reading. The domestic sphere constituted the realm where this subject appeared as a sovereign force whose ethical and philosophical narratives of selfhood had liberating effects. At the same time, the domestic sphere produced the ideal subject as an oppressive force that banned desire and pleasure. This subject depended on gender complementarities and the conjugal family as places where sexual repression could be initiated and stabilized, the latter often through economic, legal, and social dependencies (Foucault, *History*, 108–14; Hull, 194, 229–56, 294–95; Gray, *Productive Men*).

Simultaneously, depictions of trangressive femininity expressed the danger in which European males found themselves when pursuing widely respected activities that defined the idealized late eighteenth-century male subject and that can be circumscribed as productive, useful, and public: seafaring, marine mercantilism, and the natural explorations of the time. The texts produced images exposing the more pervasive dangers inherent in these activities, showing what treacherous undertakings they could become, and alluding to the transient nature of such idealized masculinity. While the activities bore the potential to constitute sovereign, utilitarian subjectivity, they also entailed temptation along the way. As these images were detailed in narrative, they signaled the traveling subject's desires while forcing the author to tame these desires. The resulting details, rather than being augmented and offered as models for identificatory consumption, had to be suppressed or sublimated, cut out, or, better yet, never penned to paper. If they appeared nevertheless, they needed to be softened for the female reader at home and presented in a way that would respect her sensitivities; more generally, they could render nothing but "thought experiments."[6]

Conversely, in depicting the black woman, the traveler-author's rhetorical gesture pinpointed a racial other whose transsocial and sexual economies differed categorically from European bourgeois values, thereby shifting attention away from the gendered relationship between letter writer and reader. This is yet another way of reflecting this dichotomy and its sublimation in fiction. The author focuses on the unmediated physicality of the body but returns to the gendered social spheres and the way they relate to the emergence of modern subjectivity in order to underscore the centrality of the "black body." Though I will focus on the biological and aesthetic delineation of race in the next chapter, an examination of the depictions of Creoles proves instructive here, because they shed light on the social imagery at work in delineating racial identities. Pitting them against diligence, charity, and continence, the eminent virtues of European women, the traveler-author in "Mr. M**'s Journey" paints Creole women as lazy, lustful, and harsh to their inferiors. Bourgeois women's work meets the needs of the family, which is expressed in the text through a metaphorical recourse to manual labor ("hand," "needle,"), and the house as workplace (77). For Creole women spatial and functional correlates shape social expectations, which they do not fulfill. Physical and social deformation point to these insufficiencies; the worst among them, according to the author, being the women's practice of punishing their black maidservants for any perceived infraction by beating them. Such behavior went against the basic principles of modern bourgeois society, where punishment was to be adjusted to the nature and effects of the offense and guided by the "juridical and moral value placed on property relations" and the respect paid to the integrity of the individual human being (Foucault, *Discipline*, 74). One recourse (e.g., monetary penalties or the death sentence) came to represent both punishment and offense (e.g., theft and murder, respectively). Accordingly, a fine would be the appropriate punishment if the maidservant's "crime" somehow damaged property, but Creole women disobeyed this rule, resorting instead to corporeal punishment, which the author construes as sign of their inhumanity. Thus "Creole women" are discursively constructed, evaluated, and ultimately denounced in this text. Their European side expresses itself only in negativity, while their body drives the behavior toward non-Europeans. For, when referring to their physical nature, the author associates Creoles with blacks.

I have attributed such a crucial role to depictions of Creoles because they are indicative of a transitional moment in travel literature's representations of cultural alterity: increasingly they gave way to representations where social differentiation and nondifferentiation were juxtaposed—and simultaneously aligned—with whiteness and blackness, respectively; and the racial opposition was then often couched in terms of beauty and ugliness. In a parallel development, scientific writings about race began to flourish, all of which reflects increasing anxiety over what could not be classified (e.g., "mixed races").[7] In "Mr. M**'S Journey" the description of street scenes separates "Negroes" from blacks, the former indicating here (and elsewhere) the social status of slaves.[8] Similarly, Forster's accounts of landing places, islands, nations, and cities along the African coast give far more room to the composition of Christian communities on Madeira, the general differences between rural and city populations, and the diverse society at the Cape of Good Hope, than to distinctions among various black peoples. Frequently, his narrative moves toward descriptions along the lines of aesthetic division: beauty versus ugliness.

Other travel texts often maintained nondifferentiation in an effort to transform the immanence of visuality into a lasting image. In *Verstreute Nachrichten von einer Reise in die Südsee—Unternehmungen der Gesellschaft zur Beförderung der Entdeckungen im Inneren Afrikas* (Various Report on a Voyage to the South Sea—Contributions of the Society for Furthering Knowledge of Inner Africa), an ambitious collection of several travelogues in the *Magazine of Curious New Travelogues*, the author goes so far as to erase the visual signatures of individuality and ethnic alterity that existed among non-Europeans. While acknowledging a wide range of facial features and skin color among the peoples he sees, he lumps individuals of different genders and ethnicities together: "I saw an Abyssinian woman and a Bengali man. They were alike in color, facial features, and build" (153). He concludes that all Africans must be identical, "namely black," even if their social and tribal organizations, customs, and participation in trade differ sharply. Though, as he condescendingly remarks, "the natives of Bornu display a more civilized nature in some respects" (316), skin color overrides any perceived alterity and differentiation among Africans, South Asians, and islanders. As the author goes on to compare and establish similarities between various African ethnicities and other non-European people, he indeed forges a homogenous black Other while portraying whites, in contrast, in a highly differentiating manner. The careful distinctions among "inhabitants," who are most likely European—perhaps also Creole—men, women, and slave guards impart social differentiation; they reflect ethical, gender, and organizational hierarchies among the white community. As these distinctions delineate the disciplinary mechanisms of the society represented here, they also affirm the defining power of any culture or agent that undertook the description. While they remind us of the incongruent moments and competing strategies in defining alterity, of the traces from which radical narratives could emerge, these distinctions document, albeit in a mediated way, the full force of vision.

As we shall see in the next chapter, the process of racial, ethnic, and cultural homogenization became increasingly filtered through aesthetic discourse, which in fact completed the process of stripping alterity of its inherent manifold diversity. Henceforth alterity's persistence outside the homogenizing narrative of "the Other" would seem impossible. At the same time, "discipline" shaped late eighteenth-century society, preserving "the political dream of a pure community" which motivated a "massive, binary division of one set of people and another," such as, for instance, the separation of blacks from whites (Foucault, *Discipline*, 198–99). Constant supervision, enslavement, and being ranked lowest in the social hierarchy placed blacks correspondingly in a position where they perpetuated the referential structure of an undifferentiated, completely exteriorized Otherness or, as Foucault maintains, they were left in "a mass among which it was useless to differentiate." Blacks were culturally produced as "subjected and practiced bodies, docile bodies," made under the gaze of the disembodied "imperial eye," which "increases the forces of the body (in economic terms of utility) and diminishes these same forces (in political terms of obedience)" (138). But in addition to being disciplined, the black body was also marked as Other through the all-encompassing act of seeing.[9]

This strategy of representing subjugation emanated from a position of European superiority on a real level and was constantly reaffirmed through the proliferation of images in texts. The socioeconomic dominance of Europeans has enabled them to articulate a corresponding notion of Self in texts: the resulting act of subjugating alterity defines a textual dynamic that proliferates such superiority while attempting to conceal it (Musgrave, "Justification").[10] After all, in the epistolary account, the voice of the author condemns slavery by calling guards "inhuman." Stating that he merely records what he observes, the author implies that there is such a phenomenon as objectivity of sight, an uninvolved or objective way of looking. By speaking against the inhuman slave guards, he assumes an outsider-position for himself and everyone who merely sees and records.

Many eighteenth-century travel writers carried out what Pratt calls an "anti-conquest." In rhetoric and content the writers denounce slavery and, in general, overt practices of racial subjugation. In its effects, anticonquest resembles the detailing of nature through an objective glance: it assured the traveler-author of his innocence. They spoke with the authority of the philosopher whose voice asserted universal truth and knowledge. Yet unlike Wolff's figure of the philosopher, whose sole function was to authenticate knowledge as emanating from one creative intellect, the traveler-philosopher also held up the ethical figures of man and humanism. The author's ethical dimension—the respect of individuality, corporeal integrity, and, ultimately, historical freedom—became the principle of all action, "without any definite meaning being given to this principle" (Foucault, *Discipline*, 75). Consequently slavery—in gross violation of these ethical principles—is condemned in "Mr. M**'s Journey." Africans, however, are denied representation as individuals once they are represented as blacks; they have no access to a community formed according to the principles of utilitarian, mercantile societies. Their lifestyle and looks seem incommensurable with that of the other inhabitants of Isle de France.

*   *   *

Both the second and third letters of "Mr. M**'s Journey" describe efforts to tame social transgression while offering strategies on how to curb distracting perceptions and thus restore narrative unity. In terms of content and locale, the first letter simply conveys M**'s encounter with the Cape of Good Hope and his experiences on Isle de France, while the other two letters literally complete the journey to China. Their aesthetic function is equally significant. Errors in perception are successfully banned as several narrative patterns of the first letter become points of reference for the second (whereas cartographic intentions define the traveler-author's writing in the last letter).

Indeed, he regards the second letter as a detail of or supplement to the entire travel account. Unlike the first letter, which evolves from the tense relationship among various subject positions—traveler, author, and reader—and which positioned autonomous subjectivity at the point of their intersection, the second letter finds its impulse in absent letters that M**'s travel companion allegedly sent to his mother, in addition to M**'s letter to his sister, and comes across as a simple variation of the first.

Ironically, this formal deviation lends a new authority to the author as traveler, because the letter's authenticity can be assured from the outset through the comparison of information. Even in its distinctness the letter recalls sentimental passages in the first letter. But now, to narrate no longer means to mediate instantaneous perception and traditional forms of expression, but rather to negotiate textual variation and repetition. Eliminating the immediacy of travel experience, the author refers to his own reservoir of stylistic means and narrative intents, as well as to his self-image as a writer. As a result, he produces an account that is informative, erudite, and precise, thus fully corresponding to the longstanding cultural expectations and purposes of eighteenth-century travel that, of course, infused the author's narrative intention. Many of the *Magazine*'s travelogues, *Sonnerat's Journey*, and Forster's *Voyage* treat detail similarly. By placing their texts in relation to older accounts and using this relation as a point of departure for selections, cuts, additions, and fictionalizations, they install themselves as authors. They create new works by inventing themselves as original voices in presenting travel, whose originality consists in departing from an existing account while preserving the reference to the other text as a sign of authentic travel.

This technique sheds new light on late eighteenth-century evaluations of Peter Kolb's widely discussed and referenced *Description of the Cape of Good Hope and the Hottentots Living There* (ca. 1720), many of which we find in the *Magazine*, as well as in Forster's *Voyage*. Kolb's *Description* influenced many subsequent eighteenth-century representations of blacks. In it he not only documented his observations, but also evaluated earlier accounts of the indigenous people. On one hand, he was the first recorder to regard the Khoikhoi as "cultural, political, religious, and social beings" (Pratt, 49), which led him to evaluate their government, trade, family structure, warfare and so on—all elements basic to a society, at least in Europeans' view— and to attribute a relational meaning to his observations, saying that these social structures arose from the particular circumstances of the Khoikhoi and thus fulfill their needs. On the other hand, he maintained and therefore affirmed the perceptual criteria his predecessors had used in their descriptions of the same people. Kolb's observations were much like those of his predecessors: that the Khoikhoi were unclean, constantly drunk, and rather primitive; that they stank, were perpetually lazy, and expressed their needs in wild dances; that although they could understand Dutch, French, and Portuguese, they could not articulate any of these languages properly since their "horrible accent" turned everything they said into an incomprehensible "noise."

In this respect, Kolb's book participated in a larger textual tradition that, grounded in perception, shaped concepts of ethnicity according to sensual and physical impressions (see Pratt, 41–49). Subsequent assessments usually exaggerated these perceptions, some offering corrections but most tending toward historicization and statements questioning the human nature of the Khoikhoi. Forster's *Voyage*, while invoking depictions of people as beautiful and ugly, contains detailed descriptions of social differentiation that remain outside the aesthetic discourse, especially in the description of the Cape region. Forster distinguished between "the [extensive] number of white people" and "various nations of Hottentots [that] surround" them, estimating the ratio of white people to slaves, "chiefly brought from Madagascar," and assessing the military, political, and social interaction among these various groups. Finally, he described the sometimes conflict-ridden interactions between Hottentots and Bushmen, their occupations and habits, but he never resorted to aesthetic description; on the contrary, heterogeneity among both blacks and whites dominates his account (58–61). It is, I believe, the relationship to the textual tradition, and especially to Kolb's account, that defined Forster's observational stance in describing the Cape. The older text provides a foil against which Forster's objective view can be judged.

But Kolb's account of the Khoikhoi people can also be traced in the travel letters' representations of African people, as well as in the various volumes of the *Magazine of Curious Travelogues*. Where Forster reaffirmed Kolb's accounts, the travel letters abandoned the premise of relative meaning and anthropological inquiry that guided Kolb's argument. They generalize the account of a particular people by applying it to the population of an island situated in the vicinity, thus appropriating a textual tradition without adherence to its discursive origin. They constitute one of many instances of writing that began to associate blackness, and indeed the entire African continent, with sensation; henceforth, smell, color, taste, and even digestion were used to describe African blackness. The travelogues frequently devalued the

state systems of blacks, claiming that their political assembly functioned according to irrational mechanisms and sensual criteria; more
often than not, these accounts assert an animalistic state of existence
(*Verstreute Nachrichten*, 341; Cossigny, 14–18, 21).

At the same time, the culture of travel and its documentation offers
glimpses into the contested nature of representation. The German
translator of *Thunberg's Travels* eliminated the depiction of the Cape
region, claiming that the author proliferated a false, inhuman, and dis-
respectful account and suggesting instead that the reader consult
alternatives that encouraged "our pity for the nation" (v). Sometimes
contradictory strategies persisted simultaneously in one text.
Cossigny, the author of *Voyage to Bengal and China*, refuses, for
example, to comment on the accuracy of the textual tradition because
he neither spent sufficient time among the Khoikhoi nor understood
their language well enough to assess the accounts' validity; at the same
time, he does not shy away from correcting older accounts, justifying
his representation by exposing colonial intentions and affirming the
relevance of observation. While asserting that the Dutch colonizers
labored to prevent readers, fellow scientists, naturalists, and merchants from getting any reliable information, he declares flat out that
Kolb was mistaken in his account of Khoikhoi women and corrects it
with his own observations. Overall, he steers toward a derogatory
image of the people, remarking that "a few hordes of Hottentots
became civilized, or better: they became humans, [. . .] while others
remained wild" (63). This statement eloquently sums up the vast corpus of eighteenth-century accounts of the Khoikhoi people and the
transformation these accounts underwent in the course of the century.
They would lead, of course, to a new way of seeing that found its
culmination in Hegel's narrative of history.

Because they identify sources and lines of transmission and explain
textual proliferations and inaccuracies of description, some details
assume a crucial role in reorganizing archival textuality of alterity in
the eighteenth century. They also alter the narrative economy. I contend that in generating unique dynamics through reflections on the
authors' and readers' subjectivities—that is, in the metanarrative passages and details—travel texts created their own structural super-
fluities that underlined their reputation as trivial or fashionable
literature.[11] Among such details, those dealing with dress and cosmetics
stand out. They not only duplicate the metanarrative reflection, but
also add to the reservoir of representing ethnic difference.

First of all, these details often express a general discontent with
fashion. If impractical, fashionable attire certainly does more harm to

the traveler than being useful to him, causing mockery and ridicule and undermining his status, influence, and reception in the distant land. The social flaw of improper attire impedes the fulfillment of economic tasks and, equally often, the corresponding narrative. The discourse of "fashion" saturates travel accounts and postpones purposeful enterprise, utilitarian intent, and progressing structure in "Mr. M**'s Journey," *Sonnerat's Journey,* and the *Magazine*'s travelogues, as well as in Forster's *Voyage around the World.* No matter where the travelers are at any given point, dress and costume, uniform and accessories— their mere sight and the elaborate transactions involved in acquiring these material objects—provide a distraction. Detailing fashionable objects takes up narrative space.

At times welcomed but often frowned upon, the status of these objects points to less innocent aspects of cultural encounter than the evaluation of practicality in Forster's accounts of Madeira and the Cape region. On one end of the spectrum stands the author, to whom the sale of animal skins and fur in Macao gauges the degree to which the larger region can be successfully colonized and be profitable in further enterprise; he reads such mercantile interest as a desire to become European. On the other hand, there are the accounts that portray dress codes as the ultimate sign of exoticism and cultural alterity. For example, in constructing blackness, the travelogues not only erase traces of individuality and heterogeneity that exist in ethnic alterity, but also suppress the distracting and multiplying effects of fashion as observations lump together the tattooed chins of blacks and Bengalis, nail polishes used by Chinese and Tartars, and the veils of Haitian priests—all in order to construct a holistic image of Coptic and Abyssinian people. Often traveler-authors assert racial commonalities based on observations about hair care and hair fashion, and all in an effort to equalize visual impressions.[12] At the same time, banning them to seemingly superfluous and merely decorative details of storytelling disguises their defining effects.

But ultimately, fashionable details signaled not only distance from but also closeness to the traditional imagery of ethnic locales, harboring, as we shall see, the images of idealized, cross-cultural femininity, a place where China persisted as the locale of universality. Thus, another capacity for narrating fashion surfaces as well: the enactment of gender-specific representation and communities. Overall, whereas men and superfluous, ornamental fashion seem incompatible, even disastrous, women become the *media* of fashion in narrative because they simultaneously expose the signifying potential of fashion and are subject to fashion's signifying regime. Accordingly, fashion itself signals instability, expressed in the epistolary account through the author-subject's fears and insecurities when dealing with women: "Maybe I err in my opinion about women here," states the writer, "however, even in light of such danger, I shall depict them just as I saw them" (76). Conversely, fashion tracks the fundamental (in)security arising from vision. Just like unruly perceptions, fashion circulated in texts, often running the risk of destabilizing discursively defined gender norms. This effect is especially manifest in the more elaborate genre of travelogue: unlike accounts of flora, fauna, and culture, which stabilized the new classifications revolving around the authority of sight, depictions of fashionable women evaded categorization and classification within one of the domains of a meaningful bourgeois existence.

WOMEN'S BEAUTY: PRESERVING UNIVERSALISM AS A CHINESE CIPHER

The semiotics of female beauty combined the diverse traits of fashion: its instability and desirability, its innovation and, possibly, cultural purity and relevance; and it reinforced the new status of vision. Attractiveness indeed passed for a natural sign of bourgeois virtue, corresponding to an ideal of beauty that presumed the expression of inner harmony through face and dress. Throughout the travelogues, however, fashion and beauty also serve to distinguish and valorize geographical regions and their respective cultures. Disguising, unreadable fashions signify Africa's blackness—an ultimately impenetrable Otherness—while fashion and cosmetics also symbolize Asia's universal readability.

This configuration set images of Asian beauty apart from the rare instances where travelogues described black women as beautiful, albeit not without likening them to idealized sculptures that just happened to be black (Cossigny, 5; Purdy, "Whiteness," 87–88, 91). In "Mr. M**'s Journey," the author indirectly introduces such a contradictory understanding of beauty when he describes Bengali women: "The most slender and harmonious build, the brightest teeth, eyes that some European faces would exhibit, a silky skin and the most sophisticated purity—all these characteristics easily make up for the white complexion and the blush they lack" (78). Though frequently reiterating his devotion to European beauty, he does not forget to voice his concern, remembering his suspicion of fashion's deception. Ridiculing the red and white skin tones of European women, he expresses doubt that virtue is indeed expressed through appearance (76). When mocking virtue's natural paleness with merely a hint of a blush, the author questions the principle of a Eurocentric signifying regime, suggesting that all too often make-up replaces natural blush as the sign of innate virtue, turning complexion into a skillful artifact that covers moral falseness. Of course this recognition parallels the comments about vision. The act of seeing the signs of virtue cannot completely unveil women's personality. Their interior remains hidden from the stranger's look. Visible are only the effects of their actions. In this respect, *Woman*, previously the locus of bourgeois subjectivity and a bridge between the imperial and the domestic self, became the symbol of the intrinsic instability between what was "seen" and what was "said," between perception and representation.

Below the ideological and epistemological effects, the text reveals material conditions: the author's fear reflected the status of cosmetics, and more generally, of fashion in the late eighteenth century. They were viewed as having truly transformative effects when it came to concealing age and class differences among women, at the same time having undeniable limits when used to hide the foolishness of a person's character. Cosmetics played an ambiguous role in designating culture. If artificial colors simultaneously mystified and enhanced natural qualities, cosmetics might become a representational strategy that both enforced and unsettled discursive functions such as ethnicity, race, and femaleness (Gwilliam, 144, 155). Cosmetics and fashion could be read either as attachments—that is, ornaments that "reflect underlying social transformations not yet directly visible to the observer"—or as a veil concealing differences induced by power (Purdy, "Discipline," 1; see also his *Tyranny*, 77–78, 123–24). In the first capacity they signaled the falseness or deceptive character of bourgeois virtue, anticipating racism as a cultural phenomenon. Regarded as veils, cosmetics and fashion suggested that virtuous women could no longer be distinguished from the nonvirtuous. But cosmetics and fashion could also be viewed as a "site in the application and rejection of power [itself]" (Purdy, "Discipline," 1) since, after all, ideals of bourgeois virtue caused this application of cosmetics to become popular. Here, fashion operated as a signifying regime, playing an important role in the fiction of Enlightenment universalism; so while cultural difference inevitably seemed to surface in physical features (racial difference), cosmetics could conceal this difference and thus support the fiction of universalism by exposing its texture-like nature.

Nevertheless the ways in which fashion was imposed upon and circulated in colonies reveal Europe's imperial strategies. "Mr. M**'s Journey" describes in great detail how the wife of a Portuguese arbitrator in Asia persistently questions the traveler about the latest European fashions. Typical of a European woman living in the colonies, this lady, though apparently out of touch with European reality, holds onto the cultural ideal of European superiority. The traveler-author, on the other hand, sees himself as a cultural authority, a status we find throughout travel literature. Acquired through interactions with both the European colonizers and the Asian colonized, it points to patterns of acceptance and assimilation that were typical and that resulted from reciprocal seeing (Pratt, 69–70). Therefore, the traveler presents himself as the ultimate arbiter of taste. He indeed decides what is fashionable, thus opening a cycle of repetition and mimetic behavior. "Mrs. Schabanderin, the only European lady in the colony," follows whatever he tells her in order to be fashionable. In turn, he can certainly expect that she will be accepted as an authority on European fashion. He fully expects that his outrageous suggestions will ensure his lasting legacy (138).

Fashion thus became a metaphor for the functioning and stabilizing of colonial power. In the larger discourse on travel, fashion was preserved in details that—though merely decorative with respect to storytelling and narrative progression—could assess cultural assimilation, for both fashion and cultural colonialism depended on imitation. Kant, for example, saw fashion as an expression of the human disposition to compare oneself with and eventually to imitate superiors (*Anthropology*, 112–13). Cultural colonialism succeeds, as Pratt points out, when elements of its structure are imitated by and integrated into the behavioral patterns of the colonized, even though processes of cultural assimilation must be regarded as instances of transculturation. After all, colonialized people always actively select, adapt, and alter the structure of colonializing power (6). At the same time, colonial power becomes inferior since it is a poor imitation of the domestic center. The colonial impact of fashion is pitted against superior taste; empty, exterior forms (the hairdo) stand against inner value (see also Forster, *Voyage*, 59). If tied to inferior aesthetics, however, colonialism appears less desirable than the ideal home, the domestic sphere in which the ideal bourgeois self survives.

Though fashion ornaments such as an overdone hairdo allegedly defy absolute ideas, such as taste and beauty, they may perpetuate structures that reassure the narrative authority of the sovereign subject. Still other images preserved traditional European accounts of Chinese culture:

> The heads of Chinese women would also be acceptable in France. Small
> yet lively eyes à la chinoise, beautiful red mouths, and milky-white skin
> add up to a neat whole. The latter charm, namely their milky-white
> skin, they do not come by naturally: the fashion which makes you
> redden your cheeks teaches them to coat their faces with a plaster-like
> mask. (143)

On one hand, the whiteness of face clearly defined the ideal of
female virtue, purity, and innocence, giving rise to the discursive
juxtaposition with blackness that for centuries to come would
underscore obscurity and animalistic passion and cement the expression of ethnic and racial difference in visual terms (see Haehnel, 178;
Gilroy). On the other hand, this passage seems highly redundant,
resembling in part M**'s account of Bengali women. Chinese
women simply comprise another layer in M**'s tale of Asian beauty,
and blushing, once considered a natural sign of virtue, has become
an artificial phenomenon, an effect of the fashion regime. So this
quotation calls into question the idea of natural beauty, instead
viewing it as a product of cosmetics that were used by Chinese and
European women alike.

The discursive role of cosmetics and its universalizing outcome were
furthermore reinforced by accounts of a designated female space. As
several travelogues praise the domesticity of Chinese women, they
reveal their authors' true obsession: the beauty and virtue of female
domesticity. When discussing foot-binding, M** insists that this habit
is a means for Chinese men to keep the beauty of their wives for themselves by limiting their mobility (142). Other authors complain that
they never saw women once they reached the Chinese coast, claiming
that their husbands locked them up at home to shield them from
temptation and the admiring and lustful looks of deprived sailors; still
others praise the nurturing and healing power of women, who, on
more than one occasion nursed them back from injury and food and
water deprivation—in short, from near death (*Verstreute Nachrichten*,
269). Sonnerat comments on foot-binding and, as we can safely infer
from the context and tone of his account, criticizes the practice as part
of what he considers despicable, uniquely Chinese practices not in correspondence with the idealized image handed down by tradition. He
obviously had no problem with the gender differentiation inherent in
Eastern as well as Western societies; after all, the idealized European
woman also inhabited confined domestic spaces.

These images sought to sustain early Enlightenment ideas of universalism which portrayed China, with its advanced philosophy and model institutions in government and schooling, as the ideal state to which Europeans should aspire. As chapters 2 and 3 have demonstrated, numerous Enlightenment writers understood the ethnic differences between China and Europe as varied expressions of the same reasonable order of the world, and consequently regarded them as surface phenomena. In travelogues, phenomena such as cosmetics and domestic seclusion functioned in similar ways. Following the cultural conventions, both served to express universal female virtue. Cosmetics concealed then not only (non)correspondences between inside and outside, virtue and outer beauty, but repeatedly covered the signs of ethnic difference. Yet while masking ethnic difference, cosmetics certainly emphasized another dichotomy of modern society, namely, gender difference. By underscoring gender difference as a virtue, cosmetics became a representational system endowed with its own meaning; designating ideals of femaleness and femininity, cosmetics emerged as a true asset for women while constituting a threat and empty ornament for men.

Similarly, the domestic realm developed as the sphere in which ideals could survive. In the Chinese woman, in the similarity of her appearance and beauty to that of European women, the traditional image of China was still present: the meticulous order, the ethical purity, the persuasiveness of character, and the spiritual balance among all parts of a whole. Although the content of the imagination was altered and although it was fractured along perceptual and gender lines, the image of the Chinese woman still perpetuated the idea that China and Europe were complementary parts within of an ideal whole. The location and quality of this image changed, however, and was no longer linked to the ideal Enlightenment state, but to Woman.

COGNITIVE MAPS, CARTOGRAPHICAL WRITING, AND EXCHANGE: RESTORING THE UNITY OF THE SUBJECT

Apart from domesticity as the universal ideal of Woman, other aspects of traditional representations of China remained associated with its geographical location. Not just in Weimar and Tiefurt, but also throughout Europe aristocrats were fascinated with Chinoiserie and collected its artifacts. The Chinese language was still debated in texts though its reputation declined sharply. Criticizing the idleness of wealthy Chinese, Sonnerat mocks their language, insisting that they never tended the land—that is, engaged in practical, useful activities— but wasted their lives instead, first in studying the language, and second by obsessing about their palaces (279). Not coincidentally, the duality of language and architecture shaped the image of China. The language continued to embrace the world, but it was no longer thought to contain the signs of transparent reason. The new signifiers were foolish cosmetics and architectural detail.

Barely visible to readers today, these altered systems of representation preserved semantic properties of the older accounts. Glamorized for their mystery, textual expressions of Chinoiserie depended, according to David Porter, on the formal beauty and aesthetic ideal that earlier generations had seen in the written Chinese character. In other words, these new systems of representation stood for the signifier, by now an empty decorum or detail. They constituted, writes Porter, "an explicit rejection, in the aesthetic domain, of the very principle of substantiality that had been ascribed to China by those who had sought there a privileged site of linguistic or theological legitimacy" (135). While Porter points out that the increasing popularity of Chinoiserie went hand in hand with "the progressive delegitimization of Chinese imperial power"—both actual and imagined—a slightly different assertion holds true as well: whereas reading the philosophical texts and characters had produced the universal textures of the early Enlightenment, reading women now produced the universal texture of gender idealism. In other words, Chinese beauty entailed more than "surface clutter," if it correlated with European female beauty (164).

Other strategies of representation consistent with what Forster describes as the principles of natural history structure M**'s final letter in its pursuit of textual stability, coherence, and "objectivity." Noting images of ethnicity that have persisted over time, we realize that they were indeed aligned with idealized male communities of readers and the mercantile, utilitarian interests that defined them in the public eye. For example, the last part of the second and the entire third letter of "Mr M**'s Journey" represent China in a manner that appropriates strategies of reading and writing and revolves on reading about China rather than actually seeing it. These sections reduce the living image to a category or part of a classification system by evaluating mercantile practices, infrastructure, and demographics. Transcending seeing and perception, they map the travel space cartographically. In the larger discourse on travel, such representations of the journey often resembled a geographical account as they recast the exact travel routes. Often professing to be so accurate in their descriptions that maps could be furnished upon arrival back home, writers provided navigational details that helped to correct older maps. They shared information on passages and mercantile seafaring routes. In return—and without so intending—travelogues either directly positioned themselves in relation to prior voyages, often in prefaces amounting to histories of maritime exploration, or they simultaneously concealed and unveiled the traveler-author's familiarity with previously written stories about the Asian and African continents and Pacific islands. Without doubt the traveler-authors' ways of seeing were influenced by exposure to texts and the knowledge contained therein: they set out to confirm the many reports they had read prior to traveling.

These correlations between anticipated and actual experience, between what the traveler read, saw, and finally recorded—or passed on to be recorded by others—reflected a travel practice that constituted itself as variation (in the sense of what Leibniz described as "different translation" or subjectivity). Travel oriented itself within a universe of past routes, enterprises, and journeys, but it also marked a crucial innovation, which again was documented through a correlating philosophical discourse. Seventy years after Leibniz, Kant established a correlation between travel and cognition that was based on reading. He not only described travel as a practical activity supporting a theory of universal progress through cognition, but also declared: "One of the ways of extending the range of anthropology is traveling, or at least reading travelogues" (*Anthropology*, 4). Anthropological studies at home enabled humans to uphold and strengthen their cognitive autonomy when traveling and to come up with a cognitive map that they could use as their means of orientation. Without such cognitive maps, cosmopolitanism was limited, if possible at all, and observation remained chaotic, unstructured, and thus unproductive (20). In this respect the idea of a cognitive map, which Kant introduced in his preface, symbolized the merger of travel and theories of knowledge. Cognitive maps form a loose correlation to sovereign subjectivity, encompassing the *telos* and work of a traveling subject. Based on books as a medium and reading as the relation of constituting subjectivity, the concept precedes perception and travel experience; it provides order, guidance, and a model before eventually giving way to ideas of creation, narrative, and storytelling that are solely derived from the personhood of the author.[13]

M** relies on such cognitive maps when positioning himself as traveling and writing subject, when attempting to achieve a formal correspondence between the epistemological tradition—what he read prior to his journey—and his actual experience. The account seemingly bans perception, and there is no longer any indication that the author actually experienced the journey; he may as well have used the information provided by a typical eighteenth-century travel questionnaire, a map, or another travel report to create his story. But just as cognitive maps may guide travel writing, details preserved in texts assist in recognizing ethnicity. As the travelogues provide depictions of landscapes that resemble the image created by maps, they archive older accounts of ethnicity, while rendering the viewer—the bearer of immanence and experience—superfluous:

> We took on a Chinese pilot to guide us to Wampu while we sailed up the so-called Yellow River. I have never seen anything more impressive than the shores of this river. Immense pastures and rice fields crisscrossed by a thousand waterways and strewn with cities, market-towns, and villages; here and there high towers in the Chinese style, with the help of which the court of Nanking, though more than 400 miles away, can learn within a few hours what is happening in the remote parts of the empire; costly tombs decorated with pyramids, and mansions in the most sophisticated taste—fill the traveler's vision and make for an unbelievably beautiful landscape. Small boats which pass you everywhere on the river make the country seem pleasantly active and alive. (139–40)

Centered on the lifeless, static components of architectural detail and decorum which define space, the description resurrects an important element of the traditional imagery of China, the meticulously ordered and smoothly functioning Chinese state. An information system reaching even the most remote areas places all parts of the country under perfect surveillance by the Chinese court and its bureaucratic caste of mandarins. Infrastructural markers such as the Chinese Wall, rivers, castles, and mausoleums—not the eye of the beholder—frame the field of vision and give it a static character. Contact, it turns out, presents itself as an imposition of Chinoiserie: details, frozen in time, yet drawing on a mysterious and bygone meaning, shape the perception and representation of China. Its culture, the image insinuates, could be depicted and represented, but cannot really be known if knowledge entailed personal, self-involved experience. By focusing on details of the landscape and architecture, though, the passage initiates what I propose to call cartographic writing. Though establishing borders resembling physical boundaries, this type of writing is highly desensualized and therefore transcends physicality. As a result, in late eighteenth-century travelogues, China comes across as a space where any possible transcendence, including that of one's own physical desires and impressions, has already been achieved.

Similarly, large portions of travel texts depict commercial sea routes, describing the geography and passages of the ocean, while conveniently suppressing kinetic and visual experiences as long as the sea is quiet and no islands are in sight. They comment on the architecture of cities and towns, defense installations, roads, and demography which, on one hand, connect cartographic writing to my earlier readings of social partitioning and racial homogenization. On the other hand, by focusing on administrative and organizational units, they perpetuate the ambiguous image of Enlightenment and empire formation. Travel texts were particularly prone to expose the dual outcome of Enlightenment, its paradoxical manifestation as both knowledge expansion and imperial conquest. They illustrated, as Berman has argued, the nexus of nation-building, Enlightenment intention, and imperial outcome, or showed, as Greg Laugero demonstrates, how eighteenth-century road-construction became an important tool for literally extending Enlightenment to other regions, and for envisioning the universal, all-comprising effects of this psychological and territorial expansion. Laugero examines the relation between the "material and conceptual event of 'unification' through 'fragmentation' in relation to the making of roads and the emergence of literature in the eighteenth and nineteenth centuries" (45). Using roads literally as a geographical point of departure, he sketches the "making of the modern individual," a process that relied heavily on structures and elements of communication, exchange of goods and information, and access to minds and uncharted territory. He presumes that the material conquest of and access to space provided the foundation for a reconceptualization of society on the figurative level, a contention that others have reiterated when delineating the nexus of epistemology and spatial metaphors (see Goetschel, 329–31).

These spatial appropriations of experience played a major role in adjusting the travelogues' narrative. Before finally achieving a prototypical travel story where expectations would coincide with experience, sensations had to be successfully suppressed and ideas born. Sensual responses had to be successfully eliminated and replaced with useful demographic information, together with statements on occupation, assessments of economy, and comments on political power. In "M**'s Journey," the author uses these details to describe Macao's contact zone between the cultures, the quarter of the city in part inhabited by "six thousand men who call themselves Portuguese mestizos" (247). Contrary to his sensual description of Creole women, the author emphasizes the public status and business reputation of these men. They are part of a mercantile society, an economy mediated by abstract, desensualized values (e.g., profit, exchange, and equality). Accordingly, their reputation depends both on their resistance within a system that suppresses them economically and on their acceptance of a society obsessed with the ideology of economic and political freedom.

Similarly, in other accounts evidence of a purposeful maritime and agrarian use, along with a natural equilibrium, "creates the idea that the land [China] must have been occupied by a civilized nation, a large and diligent people" (*Verstreute Nachrichten*, 51). When authors observed a discrepancy between the traditional images of China and the reality they found, they frequently circumvented the problem arising from the two colliding modes of perception. Speaking of "ethical decay" among the Chinese, they reiterated the trustworthiness of the ancient books and the models propagated by them. Any departure from historical norms, they asserted, continued to be criticized by the wise old men among the Chinese, who were the rare, noncorruptible exceptions among their contemporaries ("M**'s Journey," 255). In the end the idea of an infrastructure-based society preserved and cultivated the traditional representation of China. Furthermore, the author relied on Chinese sources when evaluating the relationship between fictional accounts and the factual reality of China. They constituted cut-off ("de-tailed") threads of the universal texture, which had, decades earlier, embraced China and Europe , and whose remains were conserved through the exchange of information and stories.

Because of the fusion of mental and territorial space, cartographical writing can easily be construed as advocating colonization and latent imperialism. Texts published in the *Magazine* reflect openly on the economic, geographical, and cultural conditions of setting up a colony. Such shrewd practicality provides a sharp contrast to the reflections on fashion and imitation that figured so prominently in scrutinizing both colonial intent and failure of acculturation. Similarly, the novels created an interested, self-motivated, and utilitarian counterpart to Forster's descriptions of colonies, in which he labored to assert an objective view that prided itself on personal innocence and the professed disinterest of the scholar. Furthermore, they contrast discussions of colonizing Asia with reflections on the colonization of Africa; we find both often—and not incidentally—in the same accounts. Whereas the latter focus on the habits of the native inhabitants, the transformations such habits have undergone since coming in contact with Europeans, and the implicit, unintended delineations of race in the ensuing discourse, the former, that is, accounts of colonization in Asia, and China in particular, evolve from an assessment of administration, social hierarchies, military situation and protection, mercantile tradition, demography and infrastructure, agriculture and urbanization, and the existence of natural resources, potential export markets, and, on occasion, religion. The texts envision a voluntary "surrender" among inhabitants, as well as adaptability and nonviolence among Europeans—an exchange that Pratt has described as assimilation and reciprocity—and favor, in keeping with tendencies among Dutch and Danish contemporaries, the establishment of trade companies rather than actual settlement by Europeans ([Beniowski], 333–35). Most accounts come to the conclusion that, despite an open resistance on the part of their government, the Chinese, while growing into "the only trading nation" on the Asian continent, kept access to their ports restricted and prevented their nationals from venturing outside the empire's borders. This in turn forced Europeans to come to peaceful arrangements and show mutual respect if they wished to trade with the Chinese.

Forster's précis "On Asia" provides a case in point. Drafted in French (around 1792) as an outline of a larger geographical paper, it contains a few passages on China. These emphasize the large territory and hint at its isolation. Though Forster mentions China's (literally central) position in Asian trade, he viewed the country within the larger network of Asian commerce and could not help but notice the competition among European nations, especially the Dutch and the English. The remaining European powers, Forster observed, came in a distant third; however, as he pointed to Russia's influence, he inevitably constructed an image that involved the geographical enclosure, confinement, and definition of Asia through others (*Werke*, 5:600–14; see also Cossigny, 53; Sonnerat, 262–76).

Commercial exchange thus played an important role in reworking the image of China. While Forster's *Voyage* mentions China only in passing, as the crew awaits a ship to supply them with food and the flair of "hearty hospitality" brought along from China, other accounts participate in the textual alterations of model China. On his way from Kamchatka back to Europe, one traveler-author negotiated his arrival in Macao with a Chinese mandarin who recorded his intentions and restricted his access to the city, as well as his purchase of food and essential supplies. Moreover, their initial exchange offers insights into the products that late eighteenth-century merchants associated with China—porcelain and tea—as well as into the products they considered an extension of their self-image—fur and leather for warm attire. These products symbolized the traveler's intentions also: his hope that the Chinese bureaucrats might have a preference for essential products, raising the stakes for a productive export relation, and his realization that the mandarin wanted to acquire these products for his own benefit and profit. Though the latter benefited the European merchant as well, he used the experience to revise the traditional account of Chinese ethics, perpetuating instead an image of corruption among the bureaucrats ([Beniowski], 340–43).

This imagery began to circulate widely in travel texts (and was often conflated with that of the priestly bonzes); it was increasingly interpreted as a strategy that paralleled, paradoxically, the widely praised order and strict public morals in China. The mandarins abused their power in many ways, the traveler-authors insinuate, namely, by becoming wealthy through exchange with foreign travelers while suppressing the people through arbitrary legal and policy decisions that further confined them in their actual and intellectual movement (Sonnerat, 285–87). It was at this juncture that stagnation, Chinese lack of interest in migration, and the territorial stability of the country began to be regarded negatively, and these documentations of direct contact produced the context in which Sonnerat expressed his cynical contentment with Chinese nonmigration. The state system and ethics that for many decades had served as a model for Europe had finally become a hindrance to Europe's utilitarian enterprise.

The same utilitarian exchange defined not only the *actions* the traveler-author revealed in the last letter of "Mr. M**'s Journey," but also his *writing*. Rather than exposing the ambivalent psychic and experiential positions of the bourgeois subject, or repeating and imitating the formalities of writing as his letters to his sister and mother did, respectively, his last letter to his brother recaptures the traditional purpose of bourgeois travel. Information is exchanged between M** and his brother, mapping not only the mercantile character of their relationship, but also establishing the letter's basic function as a means of communication. While M** happily imparts information, he expects equally *valuable news* about Europe in return. Considering the questions his brother has asked him, M** appears to be working through a catalogue of his brother's interests. He composes his own fictional but accurate map, struggling to recapture the fantasies of sovereign subjectivity. Fortuitously, the letter ends with a passage that asserts the unity of expression and experience and that could easily sum up the vast corpus of late eighteenth-century travel literature. It symbolizes the intentions and machinations of encountering alterity through travel: experiencing and seeing other cultures but transposing the experience into the text of utilitarian, bourgeois existence.

This pattern appears in "Mr. M**'s Journey" in the account of a pilot, who—though he speaks another language—assures M** of the success of his enterprise, to which M** adds: "We see land, dearest brother. The pilot is on board, and as far as I can understand him—his cant is barely comprehensible—it looks as if my hope of a good market for my goods was right on the mark" (269). Of course, he sells more than material goods; he also sells his story. As he fulfills his potential as a utilitarian subject, his story ends. M** restores the unity between his bourgeois reality and his aesthetic ideal. In its narrative closure, expectation and experience merge and traveler-subject, author-subject, and reader-subject coincide. Sovereign subjectivity is reestablished.

*   *   *

Far from being uncontested, this quest for sovereign subjectivity unfolds through a series of narrative delays: it engages disruptions and passages chronicling the immediacy of sensual affect; it positions itself by appealing to different communities of readers and by taking recourse to a textual tradition of representing ethnic alterity. Often the reader's desires prefigured the author's intention; anticipating a psychological response on the part of the reader, the authors fashioned their accounts at the threshold of textual knowledge and handed them down to readers in what sometimes seems like a century-old tradition and vision, authenticated by the immediacy of experience. Thus, as subjectivity formed as the contact between cultures, it also seized the moments where reading and seeing, text and image collided. Narratives, and travelogues in particular, captured all of the above in what I have chosen to call "details."

Whether they are metanarrative or descriptive in nature, in many of the details a mediating and constructing role of subjectivity comes to the fore. Subjectivity involves the authors' public task of shaping a public sphere. While writing they create a well-defined space of publicly restrained subjectivity with its stabilizing correlate of European domesticity. In this respect, details mark the innovative spaces of narrative identification, and they point to domestic reading as the sphere where the ideal of sovereign subjectivity arises. The reading situation allows the detail—and the images the detail summons—to create bliss and to mark the beginnings of modern fiction, which, in turn, is inevitably associated with domesticity and women. However, it also opens up paths for scrutinizing more elusively defined communities of readers.

In instances that Daniel Purdy has called "identificatory reading" or consumption (*Tyranny*, 22–50, esp. 32, 41), the detail loses, momentarily, its aura of empty decorum and disruptive femininity. It becomes instead a centering space through which alternate perceptions can be retained and channeled toward succinct narrative meaning. Thus, by locating the ideal subject of travel in the domestic realm and in the process of reading, the detail creates an aesthetic space of identification that transcends gender boundaries. Here we can witness the formation of "armchair conquistadors," a poignant term Susanne Zantop uses to describe the paradoxical situation of the German reading public vis-à-vis the colonial enterprises of the eighteenth century (17). German infatuation with travelogues, or "travel mania," Zantop suggests, simulated an obsessive imaginary colonization; more importantly, this confinement to the imaginary took on an ambiguous, dual role (32). It was both a compensation for and an elevated ethical stance against actual imperial involvement in acquisition of territory, economic exploitation, and slavery, to name a few facets of classical colonialism.

As Germans read the translations of English and French travelogues, they remained a safe distance from actual contacts of imperial power, while nevertheless partaking of the authentic experience. Whereas Forster may indeed have been a representative of "radical Enlightenment" as Berman claims, and as such committed to objective viewing and new representations of knowledge and alterity (21–64), the reading public willingly followed English and French, Dutch and Danish authorities and texts and used the travelogues to indulge in the consumption of ethnic subjects. Not participating in actual travel and enterprise allowed readers to preserve their innocence as German women and men. Ever since then reading has constituted the realm in which ideals can be consumed while experience becomes synonymous with loss—of gender, communal and national ideals, and self-image.

The overall dynamics of writing and reading intersected with the tradition of reading China and produced new ways of seeing it. In chronicling these intersections, we sense the continuous attempts to decipher China and Asia within the old paradigm of reading that wove together universalism and bourgeois ethics in a universalizing texture. Perhaps ironically, these attempts arrived at the last reservoir where those ideals persisted: women and domesticity. Nevertheless, seeing and the sensual dimension in general created a new epistemological paradigm: the colors of ethnic difference. Geographically centered in Africa, this paradigm began to rival the older story. Together, however, the two paradigms began to gravitate toward an epistemology that would firmly establish "identity" and "difference" as cognitive figures of modernity.

Bodies on Stage: Late Eighteenth-Century Aesthetics of Blackness

Late eighteenth-century travel and its exposition in scientific reports, travelogues, novels, and letters are full of turmoil: contested perceptions simultaneously enact, threaten, and efface autonomous subjectivity. Eager to tame dazzling visions, distracting scents, and a general surplus of new impressions, the authors labored to restore the unity of the subject while holding up the alleged "truth" of traditional accounts as an imperative of representation. Showing that such an objective was nothing but a fiction, the accounts expose the gendered nature of traveling, writing, and reading. Thus, travel texts reflect—in a much more pronounced way than, for example, Wolff's notions of the sovereign philosopher and the enlightened community—the nexus of a self-proclaimed authority (the author-traveler) and the community of domestic subjects (readers excluded from the experience of travel).

Projecting images of ethnicity, traveling subjects depicted China and Africa as instances of ethnic alterity and Otherness while fantasizing about Germanness. In the process, the textually transmitted ideal of ethical and political perfection attributed to China faded into the background; vision, sensuality, and experience gained new prominence. This altered epistemological constellation was expressed in a proliferation of colorful speech and attempts to render impressions graphically. The corresponding representations of Africa frequently resorted to descriptions of scents, sounds, and skin color, while showing the first signs of the dichotomous distinction between beauty and ugliness, identity and difference.

And yet private, domestic reading could not truly create public ideas, no matter how pertinent it might be to the formation of national or ethnic communities. While fantasizing in their armchairs, private individuals could neither confront the inconsistencies of what they knew and what they saw—because they "only" read—nor reconcile the conflicting images with which they were presented. Though readers could deduce characteristics of the ideal German community, they could not enact it privately. Readers and writers had to engage in an actual communal setting, for example the theater. I therefore move my discussion from the metaphorical armchair of the domestic reader to the stage of eighteenth-century drama, where we witness the increasing tendency to aesthetic delineations of racial, ethnic, and national communities.

SEEING BODIES, IMAGINING COMMUNITIES

A text that helps us delve into the complex tangle of drama, aesthetics, and community is Friedrich Schiller's paradigmatic essay "The Stage as Moral Institution" (1784), on the role of aesthetics in human thought and action. Here Schiller (1759–1805) outlined his ideas on the dialogue between theater and life, contending that it culminates in an aesthetic experience of unity: the actions represented on stage coincide with the moral reality of the audience who no longer form a community of mere spectators, but perform a role in the play of life. He states: "Sulzer has remarked that the stage has arisen from a universal, irresistible longing for the new and extraordinary, from a desire to reach a stage of passion" (*Works*, 4:339). By regarding the audience as part of a *tableau mouvant*, Schiller proposed a constellation similar to the relationship between travel text and its emphatic reader as discussed here in chapter 4. Just as reading travelogues allows people the phantasmagoric experience of indulging in exploration of distant lands, theater simulates a communal unity on stage that resonates with the community of spectators off stage. As the boundaries between art and life collapse, people feel the pleasure that originally called theater into existence. Watching the stage enables people to experience themselves *as selves* or, in Schiller's terms, evoke the human experience *per se* (cf. "Schaubühne," 100). Just like the immanence of perception in travel texts, this communal experience is re-organized and developed into a successful defense against the disrupting nature of novelty: like the frame of a painting, the edge of the stage and the body of spectators delineate boundaries. The image belongs to a different realm of experience; it reaffirms the self without being the self.

In Schiller's aesthetic thinking, "The Stage as Moral Institution" marks a transition from "life imitating art" to a compensatory relationship between the two spheres of human existence. Its rhetoric conveys a deeper order of knowledge, namely, historically specific ways that human beings look at themselves. To be an individual means feeling or enjoying the other's sensibilities as well as seeing one's own, singular experience repeating itself within the community of individual spectators. Their gaze mirrors and intensifies the feeling of individuality, turning it into a beautiful ideal of humanity which seizes the spectators and upon which they eventually agree. Alternatively, though individuals share perceptive capacities such as the senses of touch and hearing and therefore surmount the limits that physical boundaries impose, certain perceptive capacities also act as separators. Unlike other senses, the sense of sight acquires a strictly defining, even constrictive role. The eye demarcates other bodies, thus keeping the spectators at a distance from each other. Thus by training the eye, late eighteenth-century theater became the space where people first practiced the modern mastery of vision through the intellect, rather than succumbing to visual dispersions and distractions. Modern visual culture took hold in the realm of theater, simultaneously creating and sustaining processes that stifle the pleasures involved in seeing. Rather than simply enjoying the sensuality of vision, people began to successfully enslave the visual to rational interpretation (see Stafford).

Schiller's essay points to this altered mode of seeing, which in turn evoked a revised understanding of the modern construction of race as a subset of ethnic difference. To understand race visually—that is, aesthetically—not only addresses the underlying metaphors of community and embodiment running through Schiller's text, but adds an important dimension to the burgeoning field of anthropological, historical, philosophical, and literary, in short, cultural, studies of race in that they seek to counter monolithic approaches to race as a construct defined exclusively biologically or sociologically and have attempted to elucidate the complexity and formidable appeal of the construct of race in modern societies (e.g., Stoler; Wheeler; Gilroy). My premise is that anthropocentric and racial constructs represent indeed what could be called "aesthetic symptoms" of modernity, because they are based on principles that entwine universality and teleology.[1]

The implication is that race, despite its deeply political and contested nature, shares major characteristics with the allegedly apolitical and harmonizing figures of aesthetics. However, cultural criticism has undertaken to demystify aesthetics and unveil its deeply political and ideological character, seeking, in the words of Marc Redfield, "to demonstrate that aesthetics not only fails to transcend the purposeful machinations of power, but reinforces these machinations through its very pretense to transcend them" (15–16). Moreover, "aesthetic formalizations," as well as the concept of race and its critique, reflect the paradoxical nature of "man," appealing to his transcendental nature (as an ethical imperative), while revealing the discursive powers producing "man" and prescriptive universality of the concept. (The latter involves most commonly exposure of the deceptive nature of "aesthetic formalization," since "man" is envisioned as white.) Race, it turns out, is constructed (or constitutes itself) in relation rather than in opposition to aesthetics. Thus, Redfield not only recasts the modern symbiosis between politics and aesthetics as a codependent relationship, but, in building on the work of Michel Foucault, points to the intrinsic relation between aesthetics and the body that structures this codependency. It is symptomatic of the episteme that Foucault has described as the Age of Man (and alternatively as the Age of History), with its "twin figures of anthropology and humanism" (see p. 37 here, and Foucault, *Archaeology*, 12). Their relationship manifests itself more profoundly in the actual presence of bodies on stage (or the subsequent subjection of bodies to aesthetic debate). Aesthetics, which emerged in the second half of the eighteenth century as a discipline, centered on the body.

Understood in this historically refined manner, aesthetics appears detached from the prevalent usage of the word "aesthetic," referring to the general characteristics of art (e.g., aesthetic quality) and the qualities of the artistic object (e.g., aesthetic field, work of art). Enlightenment culture, for instance, privileged aesthetic objects with the highest degree of transparency. Such aesthetic theories become ultimately reductive when our epistemological interest shifts—that is, when we attempt to aestheticize human existence. We then turn away from the relation between subjects and their representation and the respective quality of aesthetic objects and instead turn to the experience of human beings, an experience that is not exclusively cognitive but struggles with the material concreteness of surroundings, "this flux of sensation and [bodily] imagination" (Wellbery, *Laokoon*, 20). Experience includes the perceptions of the body and embraces the processes through which humans construct their relationships to their surroundings, or, as Redfield has it, "the political production of 'man' in the world" (16).[2]

This chapter maps the emergence of race as an aesthetic symptom. In juxtaposing the performative rhetoric of Camper's tract on anatomy, *Lecture on the Origin and Color of Blacks*, with Schiller's drama *Fiesco*, I explore the then dominant perceptions of skin color as a material threat that would become a defining element of "race." These perceptions structured literary representations of blackness throughout the eighteenth century, as the portrayals of the "young Negro woman," of Creole ladies, and of "ugly Hottentots" in travel texts demonstrate and as my argument in the present chapter will underscore. Camper's tract and Schiller's play mark a threshold moment. Revolving around a black body on a stage, they treat blackness as the epitome of innovation that made people long for the theater—no matter whether the performance happened on the surgical stage of the anatomical theater or on the artistic stage of the municipal theater. The texts illuminate how medical and aesthetic writings were allied in disseminating beliefs and knowledge about skin color, and how the stage became a visual space and metaphor that could demonstrate this alliance linguistically and institutionally. Public dissections of (not only) blacks on the anatomical stage served the renewed interest in comparative science and helped to establish the aforementioned notion of man scientifically, often by appealing to aesthetic effects (Grimm/Grimm 14: 2302; see also Utz, "Schillers Dramaturgie," 63–64). A number of black characters appeared in eighteenth-century plays in roles as diverse as representing the abolitionist cause, personifying exoticism, and incorporating dark evilness, thus contributing to an aesthetic and ethical understanding of human emancipation (see Sadji, *Mohr*; Sutherland). Nevertheless, both Camper's and Schiller's texts staged earlier theories of skin color that were challenged around 1770. Bracketing the transition at either end, they did not shy away from evoking superstitious beliefs and resorting to imagery that—though not part of the "new scientific knowledge"—circulated widely and was proliferated and "proofed" through travelers' experience. Schiller's evocative use of "Hottentot eyes" in his composite figure of Franz Moor in *The Robbers* (1781) is but one example; it forged an image of a dramatic character that defined the limits of humanity.

Using these theories yielded great artistic effects and contributed to the perception of race as an epistemologically mysterious, complex notion. The persistent fear that there might be a threatening, material element infiltrating the body structured eighteenth-century efforts to discern the body's essence, especially to explain blackness. Ultimately, to the eighteenth-century mind, the notion of race must have seemed in dire need of clarification, classification, and simplification. By placing conflicting epistemologies in the framework of viewing and community, I suggest how an aesthetic foundation of race and racism was "invented" to cope with these perceived threats. As this approach emphasizes the role of perception in representation, it seeks to explain how the construction of race came about. In the process, my discussion sheds further light on the semioticization of skin color, that is, the fixation of black and white as aesthetic, anthropological, and historical opposites. It illustrates how a Hegelian way of thinking entails an understanding of race as the developmental stage within "man's coming to consciousness," and hints at the ways in which such an under-standing obliterates alterity.[3]

Understanding race as a compensatory notion that results directly from an altered way of viewing one's surroundings resonates with Barbara Duden's study on early eighteenth-century perceptions of the body. Duden asserts that, in the course of the eighteenth century, the classical notion of the "osmotic body" was gradually replaced with the modern notion of the "organic body." Not only can this episte-mological shift in body perception account for changing views on skin color, notably the conviction that skin color was a result of climate as opposed to an anatomical feature, it also finds its correlation in a pro-foundly altered understanding of aesthetics and artistic production. Whereas the permeability of the osmotic body indicates a constant material exchange between inside and outside, the organic body is a self-sufficient mechanism "[kept together] by the sensibility of the nerves and the sympathy of all its parts" (14, 11–12).

Osmosis is inextricably related to a bodily perception in which physical symptoms account for the body's exchange with the outside world. These symptoms mark the literal impressions of the out-side world, indicating a seamless transition between the inside and outside of bodies and signaling that the imaginary boundary separating the inside from the outside did not exist in premodern times. In con-trast, once people began to think of the body as an organism closed off from its surroundings, they began to interpret physical symptoms as reflecting the state of the inside, an inside which was controlled and securely contained. Any exchange with the outside, then, was either mediated through the senses and not material in nature, or a violation of the body's boundaries (see Figlio; Lacquer). Skin and nervous sys-tem acquired a structural function that constituted human beings as individuals. In the proverbial possession of their body, individuals were increasingly seen as asserting themselves sensually, beyond the Wolffian rationality of a speaking "I." Although "the human soul (which he understands as the self-reflexive centering principle of the nervous system) holds the body together" through its imaginative capacity, this capacity of the soul is a function derived from the body (Schulte-Sasse, "From the Body," 16; see also Figlio). Accordingly, the individualized, "organic" body as which human beings began to perceive themselves on the level of their material existence enabled them to refer to themselves as entities and to imagine themselves as wholeness—in short, to "represent" themselves as ideal. Because of its perceptual wholeness, that is, its perceived self-containment as well as its capacity to perceive sensually, the individual body became able to model aesthetics as a practical mode of human existence.

It is exactly this moment in the history of the body that inspired Schiller's theory of aesthetic experience and political ideals in his essay on the theater as a moral institution. Only when human beings feel, when they perceive their physical organism, can they imagine their "political organicity [to be] necessary for a nation to present and recognize itself" (Lacoue-Labarthe, 69; see also Redfield, 16). Only when they *see*, when they perceive other human beings as individuals, can they reassure themselves of their completeness and wholeness, of their individuality in the original sense of the word. At the same time, they detach the image of the individual from their own physical presence, freeing imagination from its material or corporeal origin and constituting the sovereign subject as an abstract ideal of human agency (see Duden, 26–31, 37–44; Mattenklott, 190; Schulte-Sasse, "From Body," 10; von Mücke/Kelly). Once "decorporealized," the modern notion of the body became the basis for all kinds of imaginary ideals of unity, personal identities as well as collective fantasies (e.g., "nation," "community").

Despite the prevalence of the imaginary body, the material body remained the shifting threat underneath: the residue of a bygone culture, present in the ways the circulation of and interaction among bodies and their environment was perceived. Consequently, the coexistence of two modes of perceiving the body structured numerous eighteenth-century texts. On one hand, we find these modes in texts detailing the numerous variations of climate theories, explaining black skin color as a direct result of a human being's interaction with the natural environment, heat, sun, and humidity, while regarding whiteness either as the absence of such interaction or a reflection of moderate surroundings. On the other hand, there were texts that attested to both actual and fictional relationships between white and black people, represented scientific efforts to develop racial norms, and/or imparted eighteenth-century mechanistic theories of color.

DISSECTION, AFFECTION, NORMALIZATION: EXPLAINING BLACKNESS

The Leiden anatomist Peter Camper (1722–1789) has been discussed as a decisive figure "in giving race the aura of an exact science"

(Bindman, 201), especially because of his comparative examination of the human skull (Bindman; Meijer). His interest in anatomical observation, comparison, and visual representation—exemplified in the title of his collected works on *The Connexion between the Sciences of Anatomy and The Arts of Drawing, Painting, Statuary* (1794)—has received considerable attention, and his work has been correctly positioned at the intersection of anatomy and aesthetics (Bindman, 202–09; Meijer 87–166; see also Honegger, 169). But while this positioning understands aesthetics as the quality of the perceived object, the skull, I propose to examine the inherent dynamics of viewing, traces of older epistemologies, and new knowledge conveyed in Camper's *Lecture*, a milestone in the development of (not only his) thought on race.

Like numerous contemporary sources, Camper asserted that heat and sunlight, by constantly penetrating the body, alter its texture and color, its vessels and nerves (Meijer, 184–87; see also Smith; Maupertius; Wassermann; Woodruff). He believed that heat is not only deposited into the body but, transformed into sexual energy, circulates among bodies. Similarly, heat stimulates the production of bile, which "is augmented and shed through the whole mass of body" (Smith, 25), and when exposed to the sun, bile was thought to turn black and cause a dark skin color. Though he never pursued these theories in detail, Camper cited two contemporary sources that interpreted black skin color accordingly. Meckel, a pupil of the then famous physician von Haller and a well-known anatomist himself, and Santorin, an anatomist, claimed that "Negroes were a different kind of human being whose blood and brain, for being black, colored their skin," or that "the liver secreted this black color" (Meijer, 186). Evidently these physiological theories of skin color, paired with the popular beliefs in "black bile" as a cause of melancholia and viciousness, enforced racial images (Müller; Schings).[4] Regarded as an imprint of the environment onto bodies, the blackness of skin was thought to permeate other bodies. Thus, the black body delineated the presence of an organic body in the collective imagination— implied in the concept of mutually "affected bodies"—while preserving the traces of osmosis. By configuring the body in such a paradoxical way, black skin color derived a semantic function: it signified the ultimate bodily threat. This status may explain the attributes of blackness that have infiltrated the cultural unconscious since then: in constant exchange with their environs, black bodies allegedly stored heat, transformed heat into sexual energy, and circulated it in altered form among bodies, even without contact in the physical sense. As a result, the oversexualized, hotheaded black character entered German literature, often as a mediating reference to the rare presence of blacks in German lands (Meijer, 59; Schiebinger, 388; Buck-Morss, 338–40).

This imaginary constellation subverted the understanding of ethnic difference as an expression of universalism and began to dominate in literature and culture, as the example of Antonius Guilielmus Amo Afer (1703–c.1759) shows. Two competing ideas of what blackness meant in a predominantly white environment cross in Amo's biography. As a child, he was traded by Dutch and West Indian colonialists and sent to the court of Wolfenbüttel-Brunswick, where he was baptized in 1707. His owner was Duke Anton Ulrich, who also happened to be Leibniz's benefactor and was outwardly a champion of educating others (Brentjes, *Anton Wilhelm Amo*, 29). Amo attended the universities in Halle and Wittenberg and later taught philosophy at both schools. He was a well-respected scholar whose writings perpetuated the Enlightenment's claim of universalism and whose first (now lost) public lecture, *De iure Maurorum in Europe*, probably supported this universal claim explicitly. After twenty years of successful public life, Amo's name was brought into disrepute in 1747 through two anonymously published poems that poked fun at him.

The poems' release was well orchestrated: they were widely announced; and they were probably read by a significant number of people, and they took hold in the public mind. They turned Amo into a threatening, promiscuous human being whose *body* affected the (female) community. The first poem, allegedly authored by a "love-stricken Moor" named Rosantes, shows knowledge and mastery of baroque *topoi*, thus identifying the author as an educated person. Calling himself a philosopher, he expresses sovereignty, pride, and self-confidence and proposes to a white woman, "Madame Astrine." The second poem, intended as her response, constructs Rosantes as a lust-driven creature belonging to a community of equally sensuous people—"the order of the Moors, [. . .] a lust-stricken people"—longing for physical satisfaction. Astrine, in contrast, describes herself as a virtuous woman, a representative of an equally honorable community. She is assured of her virtue through a dream in which she observes Rosantes and his black lover, who anticipates that Rosantes' attempts will not only be ill-fated because "a Moor is completely unknown to German maidens," but also devastating for Astrine, who instantly wakes up and concurs with the lover. She agrees that her soul could never love a black man; moreover, she resorts to a higher force, namely Venus as the goddess of love, who prophesies that Rosantes cannot be happy in this world (nor anywhere else with Astrine) precisely because he is a Moor. Astrine expresses her fear, begging and pleading with him to suppress his untamed desire, and the poem ends with a vague promise of appreciation and respect, provided "the Moor" obeys Astrine's wishes (Brentjes, *Antonius Guilielmus Amo Afer*, 293).

Parallels in his personal life, public reaction to the poems, and his departure from Wittenberg soon after the publication suggest that Amo served as a model for the male protagonist. In him, the conflicting perceptions of blackness were expressed through the body of a philosopher who nevertheless preserved the legacy of the early Enlightenment. The body functioned as the site where the primary manifestations of ethnic difference intersect. Amo participated in the Republic of Scholars where he not only *read* and perpetuated the symptoms of Enlightenment universalism, but he was also *seen*—an ideal fell apart once it faced the physicality and sensuality of perception.

Fear and threat, virtue and untamed bodies produced a cognitive figure that linked the awareness of selfhood and assertions of sovereign subjectivity to the persistent belief in the permeability of bodies. Not confined to fiction, this belief defined the beginnings of modern science as well, where it was buried in patients' protocols as well as in early anatomical classifications of race and gender (Duden; Lacqueur; Schiebinger, 394),[5] and especially in efforts to define racial norms in pseudoscientific newspaper and journal articles. Cataloguing race through prominent features, these articles also noted deviations within races. As counterparts to numerous fictional representations, the essays responded to the phantom of permeable blackness and the fear it generated. Indeed, defining and delineating racial norms went hand in hand with this fear, for classification represented an attempt at confronting and averting unregulated interaction and the free flow of material realities.

In 1787, several articles on skin color were published in the journal *Der Naturforscher* (The Natural Scientist), among them "Beytrag zur Geschichte der ungewöhnlichen Farben des Menschen" (Essay on the History of the Strange Skin Colors of Humans), in which the author, "Professor Loschge," was clearly torn between the belief that different skin colors among humans are coincidental and growing confidence in the accuracy of racial classification based entirely on the aura of scientific proof attached to classifying systems. Reporting on a man who, despite black and white racial features, seemed to originate from neither race and whose skin color could not be explained as a result of social and environmental influences, Loschge concluded that the man must be unique: representing his own type of human being, he eluded classification and remained a shifting threat amidst people of different, neatly classified races (227). Other essays observed "rare and strange deviations of skin color" that engendered abnormalities within the otherwise systematic classification of races and that the author could only reproduce textually by depicting all body parts with the accuracy of anatomical drawings (C.J.W., 123). Such arguments presume the existence of the concept of an individualized body which texts invoked by judging observed instances against racial norms, meanwhile alerting readers to possibilities of osmosis and fluidity capable of softening the carefully delineated boundaries of racial classification and persistently present.

Creating a detailed image of an organic body, even if it harbors the traces of osmosis, points us to the dubious epistemological role that visuality played in the aesthetic definition of race. Though conceptually enriched in the two hundred years that would follow, these examples of popular literature and natural science represent material roots of late twentieth-century theories of cultural hybridity. Scientific attempts at representing race visually in the eighteenth century complemented contemporary aesthetic writings by Edmund Burke and Moses Mendelssohn which, by taking recourse to Newton's mechanistic color theory, speak of the terror people felt when they saw black skin (131 and 248–49, respectively; see also Heimendahl; Gilman). Moreover, self-contained images of bodies and their "fluid" opposites correlate with ideas of expert and public ways of seeing that structure Camper's lecture as well as with the references to the two concepts of the human body. By revealing the conflicting structures of knowledge production through the nexus of skin color, visual authenticity, and community, Camper's text represented a milestone in the formation of aesthetic communities that are also, and predominantly, racial.

Staging the Black Body

Because of his training in anatomy and illustration, Camper possessed unique intuition for including visuality in the development of his social and natural scientific thought. His *Lecture* therefore conveys an understanding of anatomical theater more profound than the mere location of dissections. By placing a black corpse and body parts of whites and blacks next to each other, he confronted the older paradigms of scientific and popular knowledge through material display, rereading of texts, and the mediation of public and expert view.

Camper adhered in his writing to a rhetoric that preserves traces of the divine texture, opening the *Lecture* with an exposition retaining the biblical story:

> However, with the exception of the school of Theology, where does
> one give a stronger, more solemn evidence of the great wisdom, provi-
> dence, and unlimited power of God than in this Lecture Hall, where
> the beauty and perfection of our ingenious and excellent constitution
> are researched and displayed through the art of Dissection? Particularly
> because not everyone can be convinced by the bare force of reasoning,
> but all without exception are convinced by the very sight of this
> wonderful Masterpiece—that the Divine Creator of this Treasure must
> be an infinitely wise, powerful, and merciful Being! (Meijer, 183)

Aware of the schism between rational and biblical explanations of
natural phenomena, and the public controversy surrounding the privileging of human reason over divine creation, he embraced the role of
mediator.[6] He fulfilled a unique task as a medical expert at a time
when the medical profession had yet to establish itself and when popular medical opinion and expert knowledge were competing. He no
longer resembled the doctor who merely helped his patients by reading the signs and symptoms of their environs that they noticed in and
on their bodies. Instead, as an anatomist, Camper chronicled a transition in the role of the public viewing of the human body: whereas
anatomy in the early eighteenth century had been a ritual follow-up to
the punishment of an executed person, a continuation of the spectacle
and exposure of his mortality, it now served the exposure of human
essence and organic unity, before moving on to the "closed dissection
chamber where doctors acquired professional knowledge" (Duden,
Women, 9). In other words, Camper was an expert mediating the
public's view.

The distinction between public and expert view was intrinsically
linked to the emerging notion of an organic body on one hand, and
to the changing, yet paradoxically stable, role of publicly displaying
bodies on the other. Throughout history, writes Ian Adnan Burney,
"the dead body [has functioned] as a mark of authentication," serving, for example, as legal evidence in the British inquest practice (42).
Even as dissections became more and more removed from the public,
the body retained its cultural significance in offering visual proof. This
significance continued even as experts moved in to replace the unrestrained, immediate, and consequently confused "misreadings" of the
lay public, who, as "visual interpreters of the body [had the] tendency
to fix the meaningless external signs reflect[ing] an external order of
knowledge" (40). Even as the notion of the osmotic body and reading its external signs gave way to the body as an organic unity to be

examined away from the public, the importance of the public, or sight, and community persisted. What changed, of course, was the image the public developed of their own bodies: how individuals *saw* themselves.

The language of the body remained intact, though the signifier now signified something else. In the Classical Age, the osmotic body had been a transparent sign that made a larger order visible: Camper referred to this pattern of signification when conceding that those who could not "be convinced by the bare force of reasoning" would trust the display of God's sign, the corpse of the human body. In the modern age, by contrast, the organic body has become self-referential. Rather than establishing links to the entire texture of the world by reflecting external signs, the body has come to designate its own origin and have symbolic meanings, such as the ideal of sovereign subjectivity. Therefore, the body cannot disappear from the public view. When the human gaze is directed at a body on stage, it always induces a look at one's own body, confirming and controlling the making of the individual in the self-disciplining process that Foucault describes in *Discipline and Punish*. The body's new status no longer reflects the position of a particular human being in the divine order of the world, but corresponds to human (self-)perception, which is caught between *seeing* the other and "feeling" for oneself. Experts are there, whenever mediation is needed, when spectators—caught in premodern moral codes—consider visual engagement beguiling and lustful, and therefore unacceptable. Scientific experts help make the public view an aesthetic experience, transforming sensual, visual indulgence into an imaginary vision of self-identity and community. For example, experts appeal to the spectator's vision when their scientific interest revolves around the invisible, miniscule structures buried inside the body by redirecting the audience's interest to the "moral feeling of equality."

Thus, by performing the dissection of a black corpse, Camper developed his theory of skin color through the scientific method of comparative anatomy. He insisted on the equality of all humans when arguing that, no matter what color, the skin of different human beings has the same anatomical structure. Consequently, he concluded, they are of the same moral fabric and potential. The *Lecture* indicates the shift toward the new epistemology of seeing, because Camper attributed the ultimate persuasiveness of his argument to the public display of a body. His argument, moving from the perceptive register of reading "God's work of Creation" to actual visual proof (Honegger, 85), buries this shift in its rhetorical structure. Throughout, two themes contrast with an otherwise conclusive argument for anatomical and moral equality: the recourse to biblical metaphors and the constant appeal to the hitherto diffuse perceptions and feelings of the audience.

Camper distinguished between the cause and the effect of blackness and the physical location of color pigments in the skin's epidermis. In accordance with psychological explanations common in the eighteenth century, he attributed skin color to the imprint of the climate onto the body: "From what I have just noted in general, it seems obvious that the heat of the region where we live is the cause of the color" (188). The more light and sun affect the human body, the darker the skin, he concluded. Eventually, over the course of generations, the color would be innate: "In my opinion, it is likely that our descendants there [East or West Indies] would become pitch black if they lived there continually for a thousand years, and that the Angolese Negroes will turn white after a similar stay among us in Europe" (188).

We might interpret this explanation as referring to the still circulating premodern belief in an osmotic body. Turning to anatomical structure, however, Camper established anatomical identity between whites and blacks, claiming universal whiteness of the skin proper and leaving open the question of whether the normative color of the second layer of skin, the epidermis, is black or white. In the end he dismissed any efforts to set up anatomical norms aside from the ethics of "human" normativity (190). Camper proceeded to discuss "the location of blackness" in the epidermis, the physical embedding of color pigments; by comparing skin samples from white and black people through anatomical dissection, he proved that the structure of their skin is identical and consists of three layers, only one of which determines the color: "When this second layer is completely without color, then we are very white and pale: that is to say, we are white Moors, or rather, we are people similar to Blacks in every way except that we have this middle layer that is less tanned" (190). Though implying that the default or original color of skin may be black—and thus contradicting his earlier statement—Camper did not establish any explicit link between *cause* and *anatomy* of skin color. (In at least one instance his choice of words—"tanned"—suggests that he had not discarded the possible influence of climate.) Mostly he maintained a fairly strict separation between the two characteristics.

In this respect Camper's performative strategy reflects a transitional moment in theorizing skin color. By displaying the body, he provided an explication of the organic nature of individual human bodies. By reading and interpreting alternate sources, he, the anatomist, engaged a persistent cultural belief in the free exchange of bodily fluids in the universe. Similarly, he acknowledged the power of unmediated sight when referring to Newton's mechanistic theory of color perception and the premise that color is nothing but the reflection of light. He cited an example that circulated widely in European culture of the eighteenth century concerning the first encounter between white and black people. Like Burke, Mendelssohn, and Haller before him, Camper described seeing black skin color as a terrifying experience for people who do not see blacks daily: "The strangeness of seeing a Moor must have surely inspired him [Burke] with hatred and fear of their color" (185). Conversely, the claim that the anatomical structure of the skin, the vehicle of closure and containment, is identical for white and black people gave Camper enough evidence to claim moral equality and tie his scientific argument back into the larger cultural fabric of Divine Creation.

This also allowed Camper to account for the "terror of experience." His lecture brought to life a visual space that preserved the immanence of sight at a safe distance while nevertheless affirming the authority of visual proof. Here he had to resort to older aesthetic ideals, because the rhetoric of the opening portion, for all its ambivalence about epistemological paradigms, places the human body, to be dissected and seen, literally in front of the eye.[7] The audience had to recognize God's superiority while appreciating the body as a work of art: as an aesthetic object of great transparency, the human body must instantly convince the spectator of humans' superior qualities. Through the immediacy of the visual impression ("anschauende Erkenntnis"), the spectator acquires knowledge consistent with the language of universal order evident in the instance of an individual human being (von Mücke, *Virtue*, 18–61). The individual body thus becomes the benchmark for imagining the subject's sovereignty, unity, identity, and equality.

In this moment of cultural history, individuality was also clarified by its opposite, community, because the text runs counter to the dominance of individual cognition. Affirming distinctness of the individual subject—through vision and dissection—the argument defines the audience as contained within a sense of community whose perceptive capacities unite the individual spectators, creating a common feeling that presumably assures a collective reaction ("all without exception") to what they see. This imaginary construct of harmony not only employs metaphoric associations to corporeality, but is also based on the presence of individual bodies that can actually enter these harmonious relationships. In turn, these individual subjects constitute themselves by dissecting the wholeness of the communal body, that is, by visually distinguishing and thus distancing one body (i.e., subject) from another.

In light of this imaginary interplay between embodiment and dissection, community is constituted and preserved by placing the communal body at a visual distance from another, noncommunal body, be it an outcast individual, a person of a different race, or an alienating piece of theater or art. The interplay evolves as a guiding principle of Camper's demonstration, where the distinct presence of the black body on stage constructs the spectator-subject "as a private, absorbed consumer" (von Mücke, *Virtue*, 19). And, in assuming an egalitarian visual relation in which everybody can partake and ultimately become a member of the (white) community, the cognitive figure of producing communal identity by exhibiting difference also structures Schiller's essay on the aesthetics of theater.

The authority of modern knowledge production resides in this visual relation, defined by the omnipresent gaze of the watching individual and the sense of being watched. Because of this panoptical structure, the authority of knowledge emanates from the objects of investigation themselves, namely, from different individual bodies placed in a field of vision, and from their "insides as such" (Duden, *Women*, 9). The focus on the human inside "proves" anatomical sameness among all human beings; nevertheless, this proof cannot conceal exterior differences that are visible to the naked eye such as skin color. The individual human being arises as the new epistemological authority through self-perception; however, more than ever experts are necessary to translate such perception into knowledge.

In other words, experts must restore the "identity of representation," a representation of what is "seen" with what is "said." Ultimately, moments of mediation and identification discursively introduce "the figure of Man," a rhetoric that literally embodies the thinking of identity and that, as the eighteenth century progressed, gradually replaced the story of Creation in popular consciousness.[8] The effect of mutually intersecting powers, this rhetorical figure evolved out of the diffuse perceptions that reflect both premodern and modern ways of seeing and talking about the body. Henceforth, the figure of Man has absorbed the political and ideological connotations of individuality and developed into a philosophical and aesthetic idea whose detachment from material conditions and subsequent claim to universality have, ever since, structured debates.

Quite obviously this aesthetic turn was contested. Camper advanced his theory of skin color and human identity by exhibiting evidence from biological aspects of "man," yet he continued to express his brand of universalism by resorting to the Christian claim of moral equality. Other writers pursued equally conflicting strategies of representation. Best-selling playwrights and theater directors promoted abolitionist drama insisting on the moral equality of all human races, often despite and against the dramatic characters' aesthetic and ethical representations. August von Kotzebue, the prolific writer in Goethe's Weimar theater, is but one example. His plays (e.g., *The Negro Slaves*) advocated racial equality while naturalizing conquest through marriage and purporting precolonial fantasies. Suggestions of "holy communions" of cultures, universal family models, and "the brotherhood of humans" resembled a language inspired by older epistemological models while barely concealing the uneven power relations (Zantop, 132–40). In scientific writing, experts used an "anatomical atlas" to convey the idea of individuality grounded in the organic body and contained by a skin that safely conceals its inside; but even here, only the reference to the universal text of Divine Creation could truly animate the image that anatomy provided (Duden, 9; Eigen).

However, correspondingly, when scrutinizing the perceptions of skin color throughout the eighteenth century, one uncovers a triptych of cause, location, and effect, notable not only for its threefold manifestation, but also for the interaction of its parts. Camper himself labored to suspend effect throughout his lecture, constantly guarding against the return of the material body in order to sustain a "feeling of equality." It was precisely in this moment that Camper's rhetoric of scientific argumentation resembled the discussion of the beautiful and the sublime in Immanuel Kant's *Critique of Judgment* (1790), suggesting yet another dimension to the role of aesthetics in envisioning racial difference and uncannily anticipating, in practice, the theory that Kant would launch decades later without experiment or worldly knowledge and in complete isolation.

Aesthetics of Blackness at Work

Indeed Camper appealed to community and sensation by invoking what Kant called "the moral feeling," a notion based on an intersubjective agreement on what it means to be morally good and equal. Kant suggested that beauty is a symbol of such morality, claiming that our attraction to the beautiful predisposes us to be good. But what then is the beautiful, and how does Camper's *Lecture* reflect its symbolic qualities? Kant wrote pointedly about the beautiful as a judgment of taste: "Beautiful is what, without a concept, is liked universally" (64). Beauty is not intrinsic to an object but rather constitutes the relationship humans enter into when judging an object through an act of contemplation. This act arouses contentment and pleasure within us, the perceiving subject (63). Though the individual's judgment provides pleasure while experiencing the harmony of senses and faculties, the common validity of pleasurable experiences grows out of a universal principle *shared* by the individual subjects. Since it is "valid for everyone," this principle for judging the beautiful summons an image of community that is grounded in the perception of sensations. Kant called this interplay of understanding and imagination a common sense, a *sensus communis* (157–62; cf. Lyotard, 232; Hess, 205–30).

As this reflection is anchored in the material entity of the human body, it adds to a series of paradoxical constructions in Kant's philosophy which Hartmut and Gernot Böhme have called *Das Andere der Vernunft* (The Other of Reason; cf. Meg Armstrong; Goetschel). On one hand, since the beautiful is only a *presentation in us* produced by the interplay of our sensation, understanding, and imagination, it remains confined to our limited, subjective individuality. Therefore, this interplay simultaneously designates the individual through formal reflection. On the other hand, its representation depends on a material ground, a substance of individuality. An understanding of bodily integrity—based upon the image of wholeness, the organism of the human body, and the sensibility of its parts, including its physiological reflexes—provides such a grounding and foundation.

In this respect, Kant's theory on the judgment of taste, especially the beautiful, contains cognitive figures that remind us of formulations of community in Schiller's essay "The Stage as Moral Institution" and Camper's *Lecture*. In Schiller's rendering, humans, torn between instinct and reason, have to find a middle ground, a stage which can indeed be attained through the beautiful: "Aesthetics, or the sense of beauty, supplies this state for them" (339). In Camper's *Lecture* the symbolism of the figure of Man fuses aesthetics and morality when suggesting that the perception of a human organism recalls the perception of the beautiful, and that the aesthetic experience of community can indeed stand in for human equality.

This harmonizing unity is frequently disrupted when coping with the perception of color difference. Camper inserted "morality" into his rhetoric when faced with the possibility that the blackness of the body disturbs the spectators' contemplative distance: blackness ultimately remained excluded from beauty. However, the disturbing effects of seeing blackness and the efforts to submerge these effects resemble Kant's analysis of the sublime: "For what is sublime, in the proper meaning of the term, cannot be contained in any sensible form but concerns only ideas of reason, which, though they cannot be exhibited adequately, are aroused and called to mind by this very inadequacy, which can be exhibited in sensibility" (*Critique*, 99). He regarded the sublime, like the beautiful, as reflection without concept, strictly formal and not related to an object except through the experience that seeing the object arouses. Like the beautiful, it demands a means of representation to relay the qualities of this aesthetic experience in a distinct way—even though—Kant reminds us, this representation must never reconcile substance, experience, and expression. The sublime experience demands, then, a figure of representation that alludes to, yet nevertheless escapes, identity.

Thus we can imagine the transformation of blackness in Camper's *Lecture*—from a diffuse material threat to the category of race. In his argument Camper alluded to the figure of Man in conceptualizing blackness; however, he never identified one with the other. Such a conceptualization would only be intelligible in an epistemological moment when people retained a sense of permeable bodies while becoming aware of their corporeal identity. Though the black body evoked an image of sameness to which the community of white viewers could relate, whenever Camper spoke of anatomical structure, the permeating effects of blackness would destroy the universal subject of "humankind" that Camper tried to conjure up. Alternatively, this (beautiful) subject "humankind," whose identity would mirror individuality, could only be imagined as an abstract idea: through the "becoming colorless" of its actual constituents, who, forsaking their substance, desires, and materialities in the process of community formation, would be completely decorporealized and reorganized as a philosophical and aesthetic idea. Race, by contrast, is the idea produced through the transformation of a sensual experience that Kant would call sublime, precisely because it cannot be contained in any other form but as an idea or category involving difference. Put differently: the perception of skin color as a material threat set "race" apart from the anthropocentric origin and, at the same time, helped to establish the illusion of whiteness as "non-race."

In this respect, the category of race engaged what Martha Helfer has called "negative representation" (*Retreat*, 45–47), a quality that came to the fore in the concept's structural dependence on the figure of Man, as whose Other it appeared, but also in the ongoing efforts to fill the notion positively. Since its inception at the threshold between premodern and modern cultures, race has alluded to and been identified with a community consolidated by the sameness of the individuals who comprise it, while simultaneously distinguishing itself radically from other communities, usually by being placed in binary opposition. Though racial identity is based on the social, historical, and political dynamics within a community, it also constituted in relation to others, thus representing an attempt to achieve an identity of Self and suppress otherness. Aesthetically speaking, racial (self-)identification in modernity often engages the same symbolic modes as the figure of Man. Interracial perception, however, recalls the fundamentally differentiating structure of the sublime, and therefore, posits a distinction that goes back to the historically enacted opposition between the figure of Man and race.

In its complexity, race was produced discursively and aesthetically on the late eighteenth-century stage—where the parameters of subjective aesthetic perception were at times underscored by "scientific measurements" of racialized bodies—adding a new dimension to Schiller's thoughts on theater as an institution whose intended moral impact derived from both the aesthetic experience of community it enabled and the struggles it faced in coping with alterity. Not coincidentally, then, producing race according to the matrix of identity and difference inevitably recalled the separating effects of the theater: race, like the daily life of people outside the theater, conveys the reality of experience, whereas the figure of Man upholds the beautiful ideal and promise of human equality on the idealized stage of history.

*　　*　　*

Schiller explored such a teleological model of history, culminating in his *Aesthetic Education* (1795), where he negotiated the relationship between individual and communal perception and attributed a unique status to it, believing that aesthetic judgment becomes most powerful when epistemology and politics reach their limits, and probing the ramifications of elevating aesthetics to politics and vice versa. Equally significant are Schiller's "experiments" in which the symbiosis of political and aesthetic emancipation falls apart. Especially in his early plays—including *The Robbers* and *Fiesco*, and also *Love and Intrigue* (1783) and *Don Carlos* (1787–88)—we find a "physical presence of terror" that signals subtle doubt in both art's imitating and its emancipating power (*Werke*, 2:991; see also Wertheim). Written during the rebellious, radical period of Schiller's life, the plays reflect the author's belief in an aesthetic revolution while hinting—very much like his concurrent essay on the stage as a moral institution—at profound consequences, including terrorizing experiences, for individuality and community. *Fiesco*, Schiller's second play, represents in no way an exception; it radicalized the expressive, physical attributes of Franz Moor that conveyed such aesthetics in *The Robbers* to the extent that Hassan, "a Moor," functions as the catalyst and channel for aesthetic terror.

A revolt of Genoa's republican citizens against the tyrannical dictatorship of Gianettino Doria forms the play's central theme, and the uprising, as the title suggests, is led by Fiesco, a conspiring count. However, the revolt threatens to fail precisely because of Fiesco's dubious actions and intentions. Rumored to have betrayed his wife, Leonora, by having an affair with Julia Imperiali, Doria's sister, Fiesco abandons his republican ideas in the course of the play, striving instead for absolute and totalitarian power. After his wife dies by his sword in the chaos of the rebellion, Fiesco presents himself completely depleted of emotion, pleasure, and pain. Ready to be Genoa's new tyrant, he is confronted by Verrina, the devoted republican leader, who reveals Fiesco's betrayal and drowns him. Several subplots, such as the tense interaction between Fiesco and Verrina, Doria's rape of Verrina's daughter, Bertha, and Hassan's mysterious involvement in the political actions add additional twists to the drama.

Hassan is central to the play, conspiring with both Fiesco and Doria. Even the list of *dramatis personae* introduces Hassan in a pronounced manner, namely as "Mulai Hassan, a Moor" (cf. also Martin, 83–85). His skin color constitutes an important vehicle for structuring processes of aesthetic identification, at times undermining the racial attributions that the drama produces in the first place. As *Fiesco* complicated aesthetic identification for both the fictional community on stage and for the play's intended audience, it chronicled the genealogy of an aesthetic foundation of race.

Several critics have delineated racial differentiations within Schiller's theory of terror, pointing to the infamous "Hottentot eyes" and remarking here and there on Schiller's latent racism (Mielke, 216–18; Sadji, 187); however, critical accounts of how race was *produced* aesthetically on stage remain rare in the historiography of German literature and culture. For example, when Andreas Mielke writes that not even Schiller, as a proponent of the universal morality of aesthetic education and freedom, could refrain from perpetuating the eighteenth-century stereotype of Hottentot people, overlooking the fact that aesthetic education *is* deeply racialized (254). Schiller's ideal constructions of individuality and community propagated universalism yet presupposed a homogenous racial identity of a white Self and an oppositional Other modeled on this Self. When Uta Sadji criticizes Schiller for racializing aesthetic theory whenever he described terror as an aesthetic quality of blackness, she presumes an underlying ontology of race existing in dichotomies. As most critics take Schiller's demand for aesthetic communities at face value, they describe aesthetics as an aracial realm and ignore the fact that he offered aesthetic compensation for a political problem: his rhetoric of humankind and race was a construct meant to smooth over the disruptive perception of alterity. In that sense, Schiller's aesthetic writings are woven together as a metatext offering critical reflection on both (racial) differentiation and a heterogeneous conglomerate of individual identities and differences and capturing the intuition that alterity is not only an obstacle to aesthetic communities, but also a productive element in the drama of politics.

Against this background I treat Hassan as a contributing element to Schiller's aesthetic theory rather than a product of the theory's application. In the play, Hassan adopts neither the antitheatrical authentic presentation of self, which characterizes Verrina, nor Fiesco's symbolic recourse to language and societal and behavioral codes in enacting his self. Hassan is far from simply signifying the metaphysical presence of Nemesis, but he is equally distant from carrying the "blind violence of affect," whose presence eradicates any distance between on-stage and off-stage communities (Sautermeister, 182). Rather, he remains a liminal character unique for his transgressive effects, through which he comes to embody blackness and, as a dramatic character, accomplishes more than engendering a racial confrontation.

Embodiment revolved around, and simultaneously challenged, the competing perceptions of the body that existed in eighteenth-century culture, and body perceptions become a focus of *Fiesco*'s first act, when the apparent love triangle of Fiesco, his wife, and Julia Imperiali is set up. Throughout the act, the art of silhouettes, allusions to the eighteenth-century "science" of physiognomy, and the corresponding notions of embodiment are found to construct the relationship not only among these three characters but also between Hassan and Fiesco.[9] These entanglements produce aesthetic strategies as performative roles, that is, characters modulating their actions, their dramatic identities, and their reactions in each scene depending on context (Krimmer, 109–15). Characters put on or tear off masks (1.1 and 9) and indeed show their different colors (1.2 and 4). Performative roles emerge particularly starkly in act 2, scene 4, during a heated conversation between Fiesco and Julia Imperiali:

> *Julia:* A great and courtly falsehood, paraded upon stilts! While his tongue deifies me, his heart beats beneath the picture of another.
> *Fiesco:* Rather say it beats indignantly against it, and would shake off the odious burden. (*taking the picture of Leonora, which is suspended by a sky-blue ribbon from his breast, and delivering it to Julia*) Place your own image on that altar and you will instantly annihilate this idol.
> *Julia:* (*pleased, puts by the picture hastily*) A great sacrifice, by my honor, and which deserves my thanks. (*hangs her own picture about his neck*) So, my slave, henceforth bear your badge of service.
>
> (*Exit*) (178–79)

Throughout the play, *words* and *pictures* will retain the great power assigned to them here: if one believes his *words*, Fiesco loves Julia Imperiali; he worships, however, (the *picture* of) another woman, namely his wife Leonora. As Julia successfully attempts to restore the missing unity between speech and action, she exchanges the pictures, replacing Leonora's with her own. Henceforth, Julia occupies the most important position in Fiesco's life. After all, the pictures he wears on his body influence Fiesco's decisions and actions. Julia's picture even determines his faith. Fiesco becomes her "slave" and, because he "wears the color of his Master," almost a part of her; Julia imprints herself, via her picture, onto Fiesco's body. The characters' performative roles depend on changing notions of the body in the eighteenth century.

Julia's way of attaching herself to Fiesco reflects the popular belief of the time that a person's pleasurable engagement in an image, such as the repeated watching of a portrait or seeing a favorable person frequently, left a material trace in the watcher; the seen image imprinted itself onto the body of the viewer. This belief in the materiality of imagination was not only recorded in medical and court reports, but also documented in literary history, with Goethe's novel *Elective Affinities* as a prominent example: Charlotte and Eduard's child Otto does not resemble his parents but rather their respective soulmates, the captain and Ottilie, whom they imagined during conception (*Werke*, 6:321, 421). Such ideas about the physical imprint of images through extensive watching and exuberant fantasies reflect the notion of an osmotic, permeable body whose alleged effects on people and society were handed down through stories, anecdotes, and "authentic reports."

But this older knowledge is already mediated through the awareness of an organic body since the idea of individuality structures people's perception of themselves. This phase is reflected in the particular art form of the images Fiesco carries: silhouettes. They attest directly to the transitional body perception. Silhouettes had become popular in conjunction with eighteenth-century physiognomy, the art of interpreting the face as the expression of the body's inside. As a medium, silhouettes seemed perfectly suited to reduce complex individual traits to a quantifiable set of a particular type (Gray, *About Face*). I would suggest, however, that despite the transparency, scientific logic, and Enlightenment purpose of the medium, silhouettes also resonated with popular beliefs. Similarly, physiognomy stood not only for Christian anthropomorphism and its belief in a soul that expresses itself through individual bodies, but for the scholarly ambition to continue to weave the early Enlightenment text of clarity, transparency, and universal expression. The extraordinary popularity of physiognomy marked a moment in the history of body perception in which ideas of both the "osmotic" and the "organic" body blended (see Lavater; Gray, *About Face*, 1–27).[10] The interior traits of a character—personality, temper, and morals—were thought to produce correlating expressions, thus indicating a stage of direct reciprocity or exchange between inside and out.[11] But the art of physiognomy also depended on distinction, because people could only read the body's limit or boundary by comparing the facial expressions of their fellow humans to their own inner state. They interpreted and judged by a new measure: awareness of individuality and self-reflexivity. Physiognomy and its artistic representation in silhouettes helped people to set themselves apart from other people, groups, and classes and became important means for classifying late eighteenth-century societies (Bindman, esp.118–22).

Physiognomy's impact and conflicting body perceptions surface throughout the play. The latter manifest themselves also in concepts of femininity and an imaginary link between blackness and permeability. Just as Julia's image encodes permeability and her influence upon Fiesco, making him, in her words, her "slave," Hassan later appears as the "slave" of a political cause: when asked by Fiesco who he is, Hassan responds, "A slave of the Republic" (1.9; 187). The use of "slave" in both scenes assures Hassan's imaginary presence in scene 4, despite his physical absence from the stage. His "presence" resembles a detached *signified* (as opposed to *signifier*)—a metonym of permeability—whose meaning results from the idea that bodies may imprint themselves onto others. He embodies the essence of physiognomy: as physiognomy takes the role of "a visible mark for the invisible analogy," Hassan, by being another sign of this analogy, maintains a palpable presence on stage (Foucault, *Order*, 26). Just as pictures influence the people wearing them, Hassan's body affects the action on-stage, but he also constitutes a detached *signifier* whose role in the drama, as seen by characters and critics alike, "embraces a plurality of meanings: a plethora of the 'signified' in relation to a single 'signifier' " (Foucault, *Archaeology*, 118).

Hassan's self-identification as a "slave of the republic" points to the play's social and historical context, especially to the Western European involvement in slave trade at the end of the eighteenth century, which was rampant and often contrary to public declarations of abolitionist ideals. In fact, Hassan's use of the word "slave" is highly ambiguous as it may allude to African blacks who had fallen victim to European traders as well as to former slaves' loyalty to republican ideals (Wheeler, " 'Betrayed,' " 18–19; Buck-Morris, 837). But it implicated the audience as well. It allowed the German spectators to set themselves apart from the negative associations that came with slave trade and colonialism and that many European nations could not shed. It gains a metaphorical tone by drawing an analogy between the inferior societal position of the slave and the inferiority felt by the nonexistent German nation. It also points to the peculiarity of the national stage: though theater had emancipated itself from the French model, it relied—just like the emergent market for popular travelogues—on foreign information about distant cultures, on information that was usually provided by France and England. Therefore, as the playwright was becoming an advocate of abolition and nation, Hassan's use of the word "slave" veiled a complex political statement in the guise of aesthetics (Sadji, 83; Sutherland, "Black Skin," 81).[12]

As part of a conversation with Fiesco, Hassan's utterance comments on the drama as it has unfolded up to this point. When Fiesco responds, "Slavery is a wretched craft!" (187), he speaks not only espousing the abolitionist cause but, first and foremost, rejecting the role that Julia Imperiali assigned to him when giving him her picture. Thus, by reacting to Hassan's self-description, Fiesco articulates his own subjectivity—he is a sovereign individual who neither hides behind the representational power of codes, symbols, or masks, nor enacts the wishes of others. On one hand, he criticizes the politically performative role of slavery and thwarts the material danger of osmotic bodies; on the other, he tears off his (metaphorical) mask of deception and double-dealing and achieves authenticity. Creating an identity between politics and aesthetic performance, Fiesco thus steps ahead of the dramatic action. His words foreshadow the actions he will eventually take and prepare us especially for the aesthetic vision he develops in a soliloquy and in which he anticipates his totalitarian power as the ruler of Genoa. In this respect, even Fiesco steps outside the drama, for through his action, Schiller wove into the play a commentary on the stage's potential, thus anticipating political freedom through the power of theater.

Hassan too gains dramatic agency. Caught before he can kill Fiesco, Hassan dictates the use of language and continually labors to express his identity under Fiesco's defining, watchful eye:

> Fiesco: (*fixing his eye on him sharply*). What wouldst though here? Who art thou?
> Moor: (*as above*). A slave of the republic.
> Fiesco: (*keeping his eye sharply on him*). Slavery is a wretched craft. What dost thou seek?
> Moor: Sir, I am an honest man.
> Fiesco: Wear then that label on thy visage, it will not be superfluous—but what wouldst thou have?
> Moor: (*approaching him; Fiesco draws back*) Sir, I am no villain.
>
> (186–87)

Once exposed as a potential murderer, though, Hassan conjures up an image of the devil: "Damnation—your pardon—sire" (188).[13] By taking recourse to this rhetoric, Hassan embodies the centuries-old association of blackness with the devil (Martin, 20; see also Gilman, *On Blackness*, 20); however, in drawing on the ethical dichotomy of good versus evil, Hassan adheres to the moral code of good Christians: his faith and loyalty, he insists, distinguish him from common violent criminals.

It seems as if Schiller favored a one-dimensional, semiotic function of skin color—precisely by perpetuating an almost mythical stereotype and cliché—rather than addressing the complex genealogy of modern racial concepts. But Hassan's insistence on ethics signals that he, like Fiesco, possesses self-awareness and the individual sovereignty of reason. Fiesco *sees* Hassan's sovereignty in assuming that Hassan, too, dissembles and hides, not unlike Fiesco himself, his true motives for conspiring both with and against Fiesco. Nevertheless, the latter senses a greater threat coming from Hassan. Discursively, it depends on the images that a permeable body brings to Fiesco's mind: he considers Hassan's presence a foreboding of the challenges that his quest for power may face and is convinced that restraining Hassan helps thwart future adversaries. At the same time, he interprets his mistrust as a projection of his own innate fear that someone might mistrust him. Someone might sense his impending betrayal of the republican ideals. Stage directions indicate Fiesco's heightened despair as he seeks to capture, in vain, Hassan's essence through a defining gaze. He fails to identify the Moor and so, just as the image of an osmotic body signals the fear of unrestrained exchanges among individuals and their environs, Hassan denotes a profound instability—an otherness—in Fiesco's sense of self. (By extension, just as Hassan destabilizes Fiesco, Fiesco threatens to tear apart Genoa's republican identity.) Imagining the characters' symbiosis in such subtle and, simultaneously, culturally complex ways alters the monolithic reading of Hassan as Fiesco's oppositional Other. Hassan appears as the symbol of the obstacles Fiesco faces (Stern) or as Fiesco's helper and voice (Sadji, *Moor*, 187). Hence, the dynamics of Schiller's drama rest not in reading race; rather, race is produced as a fragile, shifting category to cope with the profound instabilities produced through perception.

However, Fiesco also reclaims discursive power by reducing Hassan to his physical qualities. Trying to unmask the origin of the assassination attempt, Fiesco shouts: "The scheme was too politic to be of *thy* own contrivance" (188). The possessive pronoun inserts the materiality of the black body into the discourse of betrayal, replacing the metaphors of good and evil that arise from the rhetoric of Christianity and savagery. The "innate cleverness," the literal meaning of "contrivance" ("Mutterwitz"), is what truly sets apart the two characters, for to an eighteenth-century mind, innate cleverness appeared to be an intrinsic part of blackness, a phantom of the belief that the black mother's body left an imprint on the child (Schiebinger, 396).[14] Since Fiesco perceives Hassan's physical nature as a threat, he struggles to restore some verbal stability through an apt word that can identify the meaning of Hassan's threatening body and calls him "scoundrel," "blockhead," "villain," and "fool" (188). This search for identity proves difficult if not impossible, because the act of naming fails as much as the attempts to see properly. Moreover, Hassan continues to act and, more importantly, to speak, and his dramatic speech disrupts the unity of meaning first by refusing any alliance with evil and then, after Hassan has almost deceived Fiesco, by embracing evilness. Hassan's words ultimately destroy Fiesco's efforts to achieve a unity of perception and signification.

Neil Saccamano describes this narrative strategy as "the willful transgression of a kind of organic unity [in which] words function as both spatially deployable marks and signifying marks" (53). Words can not only arrest meaning but can also undermine its construction, carrying meaning away or altering it when used by other speakers or in other contexts. Words can bring closure and, at the same time, can postpone it forever. Therefore, as Schiller depicted Hassan by assigning meaning to him while simultaneously distancing him from this meaning (evilness), he achieved an aesthetic complexity, the result of a confusion of figural speech with literal sense, or metaphor with body. This strategy affects Fiesco, the outcome of the scene, and the perception of Hassan throughout the play. Hassan's words continually transgress the pattern of identification articulated verbally ("Mulai Hassan, a Moor"), perceived visually, and imagined through the persistence of conflicting notions of the human body. When Hassan's speech relates to Fiesco's visible actions, the dramatic constellation reflects the nonunity between expressible intent and visible action.[15] Only at the end of act 1, scene 9, can the identity of speech and body be restored, constructed as a bond between the two characters. Fiesco reaches out to Hassan and says: "Give me thy hand—thou shalt serve me" (190). Here, Hassan's dark body, a penetrating marker of difference, expresses Fiesco's intention. Hassan's body signifies Fiesco's darkness of mind, which is diametrically opposed to a part Fiesco is expected to enact—the enlightened hero of bourgeois drama with his clear sense of historical purpose and progress. The thus dramatized interior struggle augments Fiesco's aesthetic effectiveness: "[The] conscious distance from his role, the awareness of the role character, increases his scope of action and makes him superior to the other characters" (von Mücke, "Play," 8). Yet the struggle marks also a crisis of perception. Fiesco's thoughts will disturb the republican idea—just like the materiality of permeable bodies affected, according to eighteenth-century popular belief, the unity of an individual organism.

SUSPENDING COLOR: MONEY AND EXCHANGE

The drama shatters the evolving constellation of color by introducing money. In act 2, scene 4, Hassan comes back from Genoa, where he has spied for Fiesco, and reports on an imminent revolt against the government. Despite their deep hatred of Doria, they have little hope of replacing him since his only suitable successor, Fiesco, has behaved like a fool. But dramatically, both Genoa's impending rebellion and Fiesco's ensuing anger yield to Hassan's observations about the effects of money. Still impressed by the reception he received in Genoa, Hassan realizes that money has the symbolic power to transcend skin color: "What a scene it was! Zounds! I almost acquired a relish for benevolence. They caught me round the neck like madmen. The very girls seemed in love with my black visage, that's as ill-omened as the moon in an eclipse. Gold, thought I, is omnipotent: it even makes the Moor look fair" (2.4; 207).

Meant to buy information and access, money transcends its own material exchange value. Money even suppresses the fear of blackness; the inhabitants simply let go of their negative attitude toward Hassan, the "Moor." They used to describe him by interpreting the color of his skin and the effects of his body, but now that he has money, they compare him to themselves and to the economic community they have created, to a a social rather than a sensual, physiological, or environmental constellation. No longer indicating the actual value of an object for which a monetary equivalent is paid, money signifies a social status. It guarantees a discourse in which everyone—because of money's symbolic power—can partake. By entering this system Hassan frees himself from the burdensome materiality of his body. By making him an equal of the people of Genoa, money whitens Hassan's face, albeit not literally. As a symbol, money designates the bourgeois individual as a member of an economic community, while its circulation helps to exclude nonmembers such as villains and thieves. The symbolism links personhood—the figure of Man—and value. Simultaneously, this symbolism allows "man" to detach himself from other systems of signification, such as the language of body perception. Accordingly, money reasserts the aesthetics of distinction by suspending the forces associated with physicality and immanence. The dual function of money reflects the epistemological transformation that characterized late eighteenth-century culture: though still aspiring to the accurate and distinct representation of "Classical language," monetary signs became increasingly self-referential and thus share important features of "Modern languages" (Gray, "Buying into Signs," 1, 12). They regulate and represent relationships among people; they regulate the bourgeois public sphere, while affirming sovereign individuality.

Against Totalitarian Aesthetics

A thus-constructed sovereign individual defines the remainder of the second act; scenes 7–9 condense aspects of the entire drama. Beginning with Fiesco's declaration that the conspiracy must be his own, the scenes highlight his greed for power, his vision, and his hatred. A fable narrates Fiesco's vision of himself as the future ruler of Genoa:

> The business of the state was all arranged in separate departments. Wolves were the financiers, foxes their secretaries, doves presided in the criminal courts, and tigers in the courts of equity. The laws of chastity were regulated by goats; hares were the soldiers; lions and elephants

had charge of the baggage. The ass was the ambassador of the empire, and the mole was appointed inspector-general of the whole administration. [. . .] The tiger murdered innocents while robbers and assassins were pardoned by the doves. And at the last, when each had laid down his office, the mole declared that all were well discharged. The animals rebelled. "Let us," they cried unanimously, "choose a monarch endowed with strength and skill, and who has only one stomach to appease." And to one chief they all did homage. Genoese—to one—but (*rising and advancing majestically*) that one was—the lion! (2.8; 214)

The fable mirrors the political conflicts in which Fiesco finds himself. Here one of the play's central aesthetic representations, the image of Genoa's political reality and its republican aspiration, intersects and overlaps with an aesthetic image within the play, a tableau of an animal republic turned animal kingdom. Unfit for democracy, the animals have chosen monarchy under a dignified lion, incidentally from Genoa; similarly, Fiesco intends to seize the republican idea and install himself as the sole ruler. In a most transparent way, the soliloquy expresses Fiesco's intention of becoming Genoa's elected dictator. By living up to the ideal of Enlightenment clarity, this representation allows spectators to recognize the fable's political dimension and to translate its message into the reality of both on-stage and off-stage communities. However, in order to imagine and adequately represent his position as Genoa's future ruler, Fiesco likens Genoa to an individual human body, comparing society to an organism that functions because of the supplementary nature of its individual parts but that is controlled by the head, or intellect. Thus, the soliloquy renders the aesthetics of individuality, making its material basis, the organic body, and ideal equivalent, man, the foundation of Fiesco's image of himself in relation to the community.

In the third act that follows, several scenes metaphorically reflect Fiesco's fantasy of becoming part of the imaginary body of Genoa's community, revolving as they do around discussions of the nature of political power. Especially act 3, scene 2, echoes the images of body in Fiesco's earlier soliloquy, when he contrasted himself to the common people whose weak bodies and small souls must be subjugated to the sublime mind. Here again Fiesco ascertains his own superiority, although he concedes that he and the people share the "anatomical structure" of human existence, namely, head and body, mind and soul. Recalling a nightmare, he describes the commoners as a mob and, using graphic, bodily images of unrestrained passions, wounds, and animalistic destruction, he proposes plans for quelling these rebellions and reining in the people. His words nevertheless convey a sensible uneasiness about the impending totalitarian power in that he assures the audience that he is speaking of imagination, not reality. Eventually though, he works toward the scene's culmination when his personal ideals of leadership fuse with the essence of life: "What thoughts are these which transport the astounded mind beyond its boundaries! Prince! To be for one moment Prince has absorbed the marrow, the essence of existence. 'Tis not the mere spectacle of life, but the content that defines life's worth!" (235).[16]

Fiesco's rhetoric draws on images of the human body as the speech relates a metonym of the body, "the marrow of existence," and refers to what personal existence "contains." This individuality constitutes the "substance of life"; it opposes life's form, its unfolding through interaction with other people on the stage of human existence. Ultimately, the self-contained organic body forms the foundation of Fiesco's self-assured, sovereign role as future ruler of Genoa; but he achieves this identity of speech and action only after he has safely restrained the unruly body of the people, their wild passions and the material threats that emanate from the rebellious crowd. Very much as Hegel's abstract, philosophical subject of history will face the meandering, engulfing materialities of the African jungle roughly fifty years later, unable to ban their penetrating view from the philosophical text, Fiesco faces a manifestation of color's materiality: the anonymous, undisciplined people, preserved in and through the still-present fear of permeable, osmotic bodies. Appropriately then, Fiesco's last words in this scene are "I am resolved," indicating that he is determined to seek political power (235). Set on unity of action for himself, Fiesco insists on an identity that evolves from the structural sameness between himself (the "substance") and the state (the "form"). Such an identity correlates with a totalitarian image of power. A product of signification whose mode coincides, aesthetically, with the symbol, this imagery absorbs the totalitarian potential from its material ground, the self-contained ("organic") body of the individual. In this respect, the imagery shares the "unmediated theatricality" of Schiller's "The Stage as Moral Institution," a principle that consists in "confounding aesthetic and moral concepts" (von Mücke, "Play," 15).

Although the fantasy of dictatorship constitutes the ideal to which Fiesco aspires, his insistence on playing a role undermines the totalitarian impulse of this aesthetic construct. The role-play produces an aesthetic effect that "question[s] the immediate identification of the audience with the events on stage." This effect emanates as much from Hassan's dubious implication in the plot as it results from Fiesco's and Verrina's clashing characters and "styles," which von Mücke has identified as the locale of *Fiesco*'s aesthetic complexity and transitional role in Schiller's overall dramatic production (17). Throughout the play, Hassan's entering the stage repeatedly challenges the wholeness and organic unity of Fiesco's vision of future political power. Therefore, in order to realize his ideal, Fiesco must solidify his own dramatic position. So depicting Hassan's role in a well-defined image that can be kept at a safe distance seems paramount, given what we know about the narrative strategies used by traveler-authors and philosophers. As chapters 3 and 4 have shown, they tamed the immediacies produced through sensual perception—the deceptive impressions, the bodies—in the texts they wrote.

Consequently, immediately after narrating the fable, Fiesco sets out to tame Hassan's body and thus "the Moor's" influence. Up to this point Hassan's character has carried an enormous semiotic complexity, but now the iridescent "Moor" fades away as Fiesco dissolves the bodily fears that were associated with blackness. As he exclaims "Haß-an!," he eradicates the character's threatening corporeality and replaces corporeality with the linguistic expression for "Let hatred begin!" (202).[17] Simultaneously, since the exclamation momentarily holds the spectator's primary visual engagement in the action on stage, the exclamation shifts the primary perceptual register from seeing to hearing. As hearing excels and surpasses vision, Hassan's dramatic function changes as well, first coming to the fore in act 3, scene 9. Before that, by partaking in the exchange of money, Hassan has detached himself from the symptoms that betrayed the perceptual, sexual, and communal fear of the permeable body. Now, by naming him, Fiesco cuts off the material origin of the linguistically expressed hatred: the superstition and popular knowledge associated with blackness. He separates word and thing, which in turn allows Hassan to deliver alternative dramatic scenarios.

Paradoxically, as Fiesco's exclamation makes Hassan the individualized target of hatred, a character who opposes everyone else as their Other, it also liberates Hassan from being Fiesco's helper. The fact that he is no longer locked in the semiotic and structural function of signifying Fiesco's dark mind is perhaps best expressed by Fiesco's remark, "The Moor has done his deed, the Moor may go" (3.4; 241). Detached from Fiesco and emancipated from his own materiality— the dangerous black body—Hassan is now able to interfere with the other characters' actions and become the protagonist of his own drama. Alternatively, the still-present associations derived from Hassan's body continue to produce opposite effects, pervading the play with chaos. Gianettino Doria suddenly perceives Hassan as a dangerous agent who freely travels without order and direction and asks, "Are all the devils of hell let loose at once?" (2.14; 220). Evidently the material threats associated with blackness persist in the imagination, even if their origin has been thoroughly obstructed. The dramatic action remains chaotic beyond Doria's exclamatory question until it finally settles in the constellation of Fiesco and Gianettino Doria as protagonist and antagonist, respectively. Though unarticulated, Hassan's chaotic effect on the drama also points to the ultimate conclusion: once the chaos is finally contained, the threatening materiality of his body ("the Moor") vanishes.

In the end, Hassan unveils Fiesco's conspiracy. Kalkagno, who has observed Hassan's visit at Doria's house, warns Fiesco (4.8). Though Fiesco refuses to believe Kalkagno, he eventually must realize that his confidant spoke the truth when Hassan is brought before him, carrying a note from Doria acknowledging having known about Fiesco's plans (4.9). Appearing shocked, Fiesco speaks of wanting to strengthen the monarchy—against the wishes of Genoa's republican citizenry and much to Verrina's dismay. Ultimately, Verrina states what he wants the spectators to recognize that Fiesco will let down the republic. Nevertheless, Fiesco continues his dubious play and sets Hassan free.

Verbal exchange and stage appearances produce a significant aesthetic effect at this juncture in the drama. In accordance with his aesthetic role, Hassan distances the spectators from the idea of the republic since both republican representatives, Verrina and Fiesco, inadvertently reveal their ambition under Hassan's gaze; they betray their intention to become totalitarian rulers. By Hassan's disrupting identification either with Verrina's or Fiesco's plans for Genoa, his role emphasizes not only the difference between art and life, but by claiming responsibility for the chaos in Genoa's streets, his role also underscores his aesthetic importance within the drama, simultaneously forsaking any political agency in Genoa and beyond (5.7). For Hassan likewise symbolizes a meandering, undefined threat affecting communities and an aesthetic instrument: the character embodies and reproduces alterity. Rejected by the major political agents, Hassan retreats to his aesthetic role, remaining a dubious force at the drama's core though his dramatic agency is smashed. In the world of drama, in order for the action to come to a close, the other characters must curtail Hassan's actions rather than allowing the play to dissolve into complete chaos, so in act 5, scene 10, Fiesco's friends hang him.

Several scholars have described the beginning of Hassan's dramatic agency—the moment when he is finally cut off from Fiesco and, by extension, from materiality—as an instance of "sovereign subjectivity" (Kluger; Sadji; Stern). While this position emanates from a conception of the individualized body, its aesthetic potential lies in contrasting individuality with a notion of blackness that condenses the dangerous traces of permeability. Schiller effectively used this epistemological ambiguity, setting up a dynamic that pits Hassan's dramatic agency against his aesthetic role. As a result, the immediacy of identification is often forestalled and the aestheticization of politics prevented. In moments when the play foregrounds the idea of identifying with the tableau presented—that is, when it suggests perceiving the dramatic action as an anticipation of politics—Hassan undermines this idea. The character distances the community of spectators from the community on stage by weighting different dramatic options (betraying Doria [4.8] or betraying Fiesco [4.9]) and by musing about belonging, exclusion, and identification with communities through religion (3.7). Though these moments create suspense through reflection, the character continues to connote potential chaos, suggesting that he must and will be confined.

To read Hassan, one of *Fiesco*'s most important characters, according to the model I have presented here points to an epistemological situation in which people could relate, perceptually as well as historically, to the notion of an osmotic body. Aesthetically this historical juncture entailed a notion of community that, though drawing on the idea of the individual body, did not imply an exclusively specular relationship between audience and stage, allowing instead for an undivided interchangeability. Therefore, Schiller's play marked indeed a transitional moment in aesthetics (cf. von Mücke, "Play," 11, 17). In moments when the drama emphasized the idea of play and illusion (*Schein*) and thus anticipated the programmatic intent of *Aesthetic Education*, Hassan ensured that the audience does not confuse play and reality. While constantly stating verbally that he played with the other actors on stage, his blackness signified the fundamental difference between the action on stage and the audience's perception. Fiesco and Hassan duplicated *on stage*, via a semiotics of color, that which defined the audience's relationship to the stage: a specular distance determining an ideal without ever extinguishing the difference between fiction and reality.

Ultimately, Schiller's play *enacted race* as an epistemologically complex and contested construct. *Fiesco* thus captures a moment that is rarely accessible in such originality but rather through its effects and permutations in the subsequent classification and use of race in theater. The dramatic production (i.e., conceptualization) of race differed from its instrumentalization in abolitionist plays and in plays where black (female) characters obstructed both genre structure and the aesthetic impact of bourgeois tragedy, such as Ernst Rathlef's *Die Mohrinn zu Hamburg* (The Moorish Woman of Hamburg; 1775), Karl Ziegler's *Die Mohrinn* (The Moorish Woman; 1801) or—in comedic variation—Karl Gotthelf Lessing's *Die Mätresse* (The Mistress; 1780). In contrast, in *Fiesco* blackness evolved as part of aesthetics as knowledge formation, surpassing in its complexity the *deus ex machina*-role of the Moor in Klinger's *Sturm und Drang* (Storm and Stress; 1776–77); here the character dissolves the dramatic conflict while at the same time defining the historical coordinates of the dramatic action.[18]

Ultimately, chronicling the dramatic genealogy of race provides important insight into the transformation of ethnic and national communities into racial communities. Focusing on the nexus of historically changing and confounding notions of the body, sense perception, and the aesthetic formation of communal and individual identities may seem reductive, because it abstracts from social, economic, and geographical conditions that played a part in eighteenth-century constructions of race. But the concept of race could comply with the notion of individual, human integrity and equality only after people learned to cope with color-induced difference through sublime experiences (cf. Sautermeister, 182).

Unsettling effects of perception are converted within community, which itself is defined by the structural sameness of its individual members and which models a different race accordingly. In this respect, the concept of race acquires not only a dissecting, differentiating power, but also entails a compensatory role. Clearly and explosively, the first designations of "race" attempted to make sense of a noncoevalness of perception, material experience, and intellectual sublimation. This birth within aesthetics suggests that the aesthetic realm has truly played a foundational role in the formation of race and the racisms of modernity, and could not be further removed from its postulated apolitical essence.

6

READING HISTORY, SEEING SELVES:
THE TURN TO THE MODERN

The last four chapters leave off where the narration of modern ethnicity begins. They suggest a context for reexamining the heterogeneous, multifaceted ways in which eighteenth-century writers engaged and represented cultural alterity in German-language texts; they offer a glimpse of how these writers began to conceptualize a prenational German identity, even if it manifested itself only locally and in the imaginary realm. In the process, a changing dynamic between reading and seeing the ethnic emerged as the discursive marker of divergent stories, histories, and images. Racial, ethnic, and national communities constituted themselves in what appears to have been an intrinsically aesthetic act. Yet is there a precise moment when the visual superseded the textual, when color suppressed texture in representing cultural difference? When was alterity banned to the realm of poetic abstraction? When did distant locales become the national subject's Other?

Though readers will immediately recognize their rhetorical nature, these questions warrant pondering. Ultimately, they will take us back to the beginning of this book, to Hegel's *Philosophy of History*. Hegel's narration constructs patterns—of identity and difference, of progress and *telos*, of ethnicity and history—that have become a foil against which discussions of modern (and postmodern) alterity have evolved while simultaneously submerging alternate modes and forms of perception. In this sense *The Philosophy of History* marked a point of inception. Accordingly, the rhetoric of identity and difference offers one angle from which to undertake a concluding discussion of reading and seeing—or texture and color—in the representation of ethnic alterity, a point of departure for mapping the ongoing task of a cultural analysis of modernity's past. In pursuing this angle, I will first turn to two other eighteenth-century philosophers whose work has

sparked discussion of ethnicity, race, and cultural alterity: Immanuel
Kant (1724–1804) and Johann Gottfried Herder (1744–1803).

*   *   *

Nowhere in this book have I attempted to argue for a neat progression toward the visually constructed narrative of Self and Other; however, I have begun to lay bare a discursive shift that ultimately resulted
in epistemological transformations—and the dominance of Self-Other
in modern formulations of ethnic alterity. This shift manifests itself
also in Kant's and Herder's anthropological writings. A separate book
could be devoted to their texts, analyzing in detail the authors' use of
visuality and textuality in writing about cultural alterity and going
beyond David Bindman's consideration of Kant's and Herder's writings on race in relation to iconographic manifestations of beauty and
ugliness, "unity of mankind" and "fragmentation" (esp. 163–73).
Here, a more cursory look at a few pertinent texts must suffice. I will
briefly discuss the rhetorical patterns in Kant's pre-*Critique* writings
on aesthetics and ethnicity, *Beobachtungen über das Gefühl des Schönen
und Erhabenen* (Observations Regarding the Feeling of the Beautiful
and the Sublime; 1764); on race, *Von den verschiedenen Racen der
Menschen* (On the Different Races of Humans; 1775); and in his
Anthropology from a Pragmatic Point of View (1798) and his account
of Africa from *Physische Geographie* (Physical Geography; 1802).[1]
These essays reflect a fluid epistemological situation, especially a
changing intersection with Kant's *Critiques*, as well as the ever-evolving
teaching situation at Königsberg University that influenced Kant's
emphases and interests (see Larrimore, "Race," 102–03). Whereas in
chapter 5, I sought to substantiate an aesthetic notion of race on the
basis of Kant's discussion of the sublime and the beautiful in his
Critique of Judgment, here I will focus on the distinction between
anthropological and aesthetic concepts. After all, though Kant's
Critique resonated with aesthetic constructions of race in the late
eighteenth-century "staging" of bodies, Kant himself "banned"
descriptions of race, nation, and ethnos (*Volk*) from his *Critiques*
(Meg Armstrong, 213, 223).

　　Similarly, excerpts from Herder's *Reflections on the Philosophy of
History of Mankind* (1784–85) and *Briefe zur Beförderung der
Humanität* (Letters on the Advancement of Humanity; 1796) help
illustrate the shift from text to color, from reading to seeing the ethnic.
This shift positions Kant's writings as the beginnings of a modern
philosophical discourse on race and racism (e.g., Eigen/Larrimore,

3–4, 35–120; Hentges) and inflicts rhetorical breaks on Herder's text. By emphasizing this rhetorical aspect, I propose to advance existing scholarship that has focused on the Eurocentrism implied in both Kant's classification of races and Herder's famous description of China as a mummy. As such criticism presupposes conceptual clarity and existing categories for describing culture that are intrinsically modern—that is, concepts that evolved later and sometimes perhaps even in conflict with the narrative dispositions of the texts by Herder and Kant that they seek to explain—I hope to clarify the discursive beginning of this Eurocentric perspective. I intend, therefore, to delineate aspects of what Russell Berman calls "a distinction between Kantian and Herderian descriptions of culture" and which he equates roughly "with an elaboration of a universal space of a physical cosmos in which cultural material plays at best a peripheral role," and the "universality of human capacity for culture" (65).[2]

Finally, my argument brings to the fore the distinct patterns of reading and seeing alterity in late eighteenth-century culture, suppressing some perceptual instances and textualizing others. In order to render the materialities of culture peripheral, all immediacy, sensual effects, and random impressions have had to be ignored. Conversely, the proclamation of cultural diversity within a paradigm of universalism has required, at the very least, acknowledgment of a variety of perceptions and representations. The results are representations of ethnic alterity that only retroactively have been organized according to modern concepts of understanding—race, difference, and identity; superiority and inferiority; history and progress—and often in conjunction with establishing the canon of (German) national literature and philosophy. In other words, Kant's and Herder's position vis-à-vis Eurocentrism (and each other) is complex. For example, Herder never quite abandoned the universal texture in which everything referred—in the form of commentary or translation—to a divine entity, as John Zammito insinuates when retrieving the theological underpinnings of Herder's anthropology. Zammito likewise asserts that Kant had devised a pre-*Critique*, empirical philosophy that may very well have led him to a thoroughly anthropological path à la Herder (*Birth*, 6, 11). I will take this dual observation as a point of departure in examining rhetorical and narrative patterns in the construction of "races" and "mummies."

Kant's various categorizations of race and his thoughts on culture and nations evolved over time. His racial thinking shows nuance and conceptual differentiation, no matter how labored and loathsome its expression is (Hentges, 48–53; Zantop, 70; Zammito, *Birth*, 344–45).

In fact, Kant's classifications display remarkable similarities to Blumenbach's system of racial categories. In 1775, when Kant wrote his treatise on race, Blumenbach rejected a classification "by skin color, observed temperament, or supposed hairlessness," making him appear to represent the "antithesis to Kant's racial theories" (Zantop, 70; Bindman, 162–63, 178; see Zammito, "Policing," 41). However, like travelers circumnavigating the globe, he began to use aesthetic language when reading the different skin colors as expressions of beauty and ugliness (Hentges, 49–50). By 1803 he clearly defined race and racial variations as deviations from an original prototype; as such, they were inherited, perpetuated through procreation, and preserved in the organism of a body perceived as whole and impenetrable. Within this classification, which bears all the epistemological traces of the modern age of history, there was no room for osmotic explanations except as a climate-induced modification of the racial type. As Blumenbach identified five races, he positioned the "Caucasian" or white "race [as] the original or middle race," and located the "Mongolian and Ethiopian race" on opposite ends, defining them as "extreme deviations" of whiteness. The "American race" and the "Malayan race of the South Sea," he claimed, occurred between the middle race and the respective extremes. Blumenbach assumed neither an outright superiority of whiteness (like Meiner), nor an oppositional dichotomy of whiteness and blackness (like Kant; *Handbuch*, 70; see Zantop, 71–72; Bindman). But he shared with Kant not only a particular local (i.e., German) epistemological situation and a common set of influences, but also the rhetorical invocation of the body as organism (see Shell, 58–59) and of climatic influence. Unlike Kant, he actually performed anatomical research that led to an emphasis on the skull as a criterion for racial distinction (Zammito, "Policing," 43–49).

We call upon the dichotomy of black and white, developed in *On the Various Races of Humans,* when we think of Kant as the precursor of modern racism. This dichotomy intersects with other characteristics of Kantian thought about ethnic alterity—with cognitive maps, imitation, and aesthetic productions of race—and at times threatens to undermine them. And yet since Kant developed racial ideas in anthropological texts, usually in conjunction with geography and climate, it is useful to distinguish these ideas from the "veiled" or suppressed discussions of cultural alterity in his later aesthetic writings. By examining this difference, I suggest distinctions similar to those made with respect to politics, history, and community in Kant's pre-*Critique* philosophy as well as in his *Critiques* (Hess, 195–207).

Even the Kant of the pre-*Critique* phase differs from the other authors I have discussed in this book in one main respect: unlike in Schiller's and Camper's writings or in the travelogues, we never witness *the process* of visual perception in Kant's writings on race, anthropology, and geography. To be sure, as Meg Armstrong has argued, the precritical beautiful and sublime materialize as "a product of an aesthetic disposition inherent in sexual, national, and historical characteristics" (213). But we never see the reverse in Kant's texts: an individual, a subject, or, for that matter, a racial body in the making, produced as an effect of beauty or sublimity (213). Rather, Kant outlined beautiful and sublime qualities, personality, and ethnic dispositions for certain aesthetic experiences in his early essay *On the Beautiful and the Sublime*. He supplemented these dispositions with a catalogue of expressions, images, and characteristics possessing the basic qualities he defines as degrees of the beautiful or the sublime. These facets can be observed in ethnic or national characteristics (*Nationalcharaktere*); however, the interrelations between the aesthetic experiences of one individual, people, or nation and the expression of beautiful or sublime traits in another are not immediate or affective. For example, as Kant likened "brown color and black eyes" to the sublime and "blue eyes and blond" to the beautiful, he did not predict respective experiences in the perceiving subject (213) as Burke, Mendelssohn, and several scientists perpetuating their theories did.

Despite his discounting of visual processes, Kant recognized the importance of graphic images, insisting that he had to substitute with description what he was unable to draw or depict in etchings or other visual media: "[H]e who is lacking Hogarth's tools must replace through description what the picture lacks in expression" (*Werke* 2:214).[3] He listed examples of noble and foolish, adventurous and grimacing actions and images, all of which represent modifications of the beautiful and the sublime. In one section, "On National Characters," he assigned these characteristics to peoples and nations, beginning with Europe. Praising the Germans for their inclination toward both the beautiful and the sublime, Kant mocked their tendency to imitate the French, their fashion-obsessed contemporaries who were incapable of exuding essence. Notably, he used rhetorical strategies that remind us of the discourse surrounding travel. Like travelogue authors, who depicted European societies and colonial powers in meticulous detail while categorizing native cultures very broadly, Kant differentiated among the traits of European nations. He observed that despite a common texture—religion—national dispositions prevailed in Europe and differentiated over time (243–52). His picture of the rest of the world is less distinct in that he conflated attributes—national, anthropological, and those resulting from imaginary geographies—in his discussion of non-Europeans (352–56; see Shell, 63).

Kant accounted for alterity but strove for systematic categories based on a fixed process of perception (which is not traceable). The resulting images portray emotions but do not evoke them—they are carefully demarcated, engendering framed and lifeless representations detached from their material origins. They await the philosopher's interpretation. This focus on the aesthetic quality of beautiful and sublime objects is particularly evident in his descriptions of China and Africa. Kant claimed that all portraits of the Chinese contained distortions, "foolish grimaces," representing the "unusual and unnatural that cannot be found anywhere else" (252).[4] He invoked the metaphor of a static painting whose grotesque and grimacing nature projects a "failed sublime" (214). Similarly, as he attributed childishness and foolishness (a pitiful form of beauty) to "the Negroes of Africa," he began to sketch an insurmountable difference between whites and blacks that would henceforth define his racial thought (252, 214). However, in *On the Beautiful and the Sublime*, Kant did not derive these distinctions from the effects of skin color on the human eye, but from supposedly innate, pathological differences that he retroactively applied to temperament and signified through color (see Zammito, "Policing," 39).

Already in this early essay, Kant's descriptions hinted at the emerging paradigm of historical progress since he singled out China's unique position—which contemporaries began to qualify as historical stagnation—and proclaimed Africa's eternal seclusion from history, education, and advancement, anticipating Hegel's imagery of the "children's land." China warranted territorial boundaries and a discreet identity; its representation was unique in the world and extraordinary for their age (252), while Africa appeared as a primitive, sensual mass, worthy of ridicule, emotionally stagnant (253). But we also notice more subtle distinctions: whereas the image of China draws on connotations of distortion, Africa's image is defined by a deceiving yet engulfing color. Kant awarded nation-status to China, while considering the African continent one homogeneous ethnic entity. Overall, while he certainly sought to provoke an intellectual reaction to the images he used in his writing, the reader cannot construct or deduce the image in either case. The image is given to us—a priori, so to speak.

As if to underscore this point in *On the Various Races of Man*, Kant stated bluntly: "I believe it is only necessary to *presume* four races in order to explain all the perpetual differences that present themselves at first glance" (*Werke* 2:432; my emphasis).[5] A systematic delineation of classifying language precedes this statement, culminating in the oppositional rhetoric that juxtaposes whites and blacks. Throughout his argument, as he further distinguished the races, Kant never questioned the essential quality of the "white race" and "the Negro race," claiming instead that "considering them as the basic races is obvious" (433). He was more elaborate in his definition of a "Hunnish or Mongolian race" and a Hindi race, struggling perhaps to justify his rationale for the division (skin color, facial features). He immediately delineated several variations. Rhetorically, I suggest, this hasty amplification served to suspend the unreliable impression of a fleeting moment, the fundamental instability that the awareness of bodies incited.

In a way, the rhetoric here erases the remnants of older body perceptions, for even the bodies' response to their environment and climate, central to Kant's delineation of races in the subsequent portion of his essay, is mediated. He introduces an element that underscores the integrity and isolation of the modern body, the preexistence rather than the formation of individuality as concept: the amount of phlogiston in the body—not an actual interaction of the body with its environs—determines skin color, race, and racial temperament (Hentges, 54–56). Though Kant read oily skin, hair, facial features, and scent as physical, mutually influential responses to climate, he considered the "excess of phlogiston" the cause of the blacks' racial characteristics (438; Hentges, 56). He thought that the other races possessed smaller amounts of phlogiston, while the lack of phlogiston determined whiteness and its inherent qualities: "[T]he complete dissolution of iron in bodily fluids proves the strengths of this particular branch of humanity, above all else" (440). This logic has, of course, striking implications. First, Kant implemented a cognitive figure juxtaposing the white race and *all other races*. Second, he nevertheless constructed blackness as the ultimate opposite. It evolved into the signifier for "non-white" through the context: mythologically and metaphysically, white and black represented oppositional colors. In Kant's argument, blacks possessed the highest amount of phlogiston. Furthermore, in "explaining" blacks' restricted location in Africa, he isolated blackness geographically.

When commenting on the alleged superiority of whites, Kant conceded a lack of expertise, admitting that he was venturing into unfamiliar epistemological territory and merely speculating (440). It is obvious, however, that for him the concept of race depended on the concept of individual identity, on an image of a human being in possession of his body, although he never stated this epistemological and conceptual context explicitly. Kant's attempts to demarcate categories and, ultimately, the "truth" were always a quest for this body and its "possession." Allowing for "representation," the modern body conjures up the metaphors that express the act of representing, which for Kant meant "to exteriorize or to posit outside oneself, to visualize and to define" (Weissberg, 50–51).[6] The sharp delineation of the modern body fueled Kant's certainty about the individual subject's integrity and its representation (cf. Shell, 58).

The ensuing rhetoric, oscillating between innate preformation (*vorgebildet*) and development (*Auswicklung*) not only underscores this claim, but also places Kant firmly within the larger context of eighteenth-century philosophical and aesthetic thought that progressed from "the body to the mind's imagination."[7] In transcending the physical foundations of human existence, it culminated in the lasting idea of the Enlightenment: development according to a preconceived image (*Bildung*) and projected as the imagination (*Vorstellung*) of historical progress. In this respect, Kant's text on race simultaneously initiated and concealed a break between anthropological writings and the aesthetic discourse of the *Critique of Judgment*. Once the aesthetic feeling of the beautiful and the sublime was reconfigured as an act of the perceiving subject, race—especially blackness—disappeared as a "named or articulated term" from Kant's cultural practice. Only then, paradoxically, did race-based individual and communal identities persist. It is at this juncture—in the space where racial, ethnic, and cultural dispositions disappeared, race being produced *ex negativo*—that we witness an intrinsically modern moment: classifying categories are transformed in an aesthetic act. Or, as Meg Armstrong puts it: "[Kant's] erasure of the nationalistic or cultural bases of aesthetic judgment in his later work, and the effort to distinguish pure and impure judgments, prefigure[d] the hiddenness of aesthetic and metaphorical ['non-scientific'] constructions of difference in dominant discourses of race and gender in the nineteenth century" (223).

Accordingly, Kant's writings fall into two groups, even if they evade the distinction into a precritical and critical period (cf. Weissberg, 93). In his *Anthropology*, which appeared later than the *Critiques*, Kant abstracted from the category of race and turned to differentiations among people and nations in order to develop a historically inflected narrative of cultural hierarchies. "Race," according to Zammito, "belonged to [physiological anthropology (i.e., the study of temperament)] which would make it epistemologically problematic for him [Kant] to infer at all from physiology to culture in this domain [of pragmatic anthropology]" ("Policing," 39). In his *Physical Geography*, Kant projected an image of Africa that reminds us of a compilation of characteristics transmitted by eighteenth-century travelers, while anticipating the self-contained and isolated, impenetrable landmass, which would define Hegel's view in his *Philosophy of History*.

Unlike his contemporaries, who dealt with the immediacy of visual effects, Kant was content with the contained image, the representation that lent itself to interpretation. Yet if we attempt to transpose his philosophical language into that of popular science, anatomy, and literature, Kant's thinking mirrored that of his contemporaries in many ways. Like them, he appears to have been torn between accepting anatomical sameness and dealing with perceptual differences, even if his formulations of this problem were different in that he tried to reconcile the rationalist (and aesthetic) text of a priori categories with what he saw. As vision constituted a direct reflex of the sensuality of his own body, Kant's solution consisted in a categorical subjection or "taming" of the latter (e.g., Böhme/Böhme). This gesture influenced, of course, the idea of community. The "bodily" sensation of individuals had to give way to the aesthetic common sense; only then could they be part of the community. Only in the aesthetic sphere were individuals free "from the subjection of its individual body to its senses" (Hess, 230), from the perception of disruptive alterity. If we follow this logic, the visual signatures of race can be transcended, though they can never quite disappear. As Kant's texts perpetuated the simultaneous rejection of sensual immediacy and recourse to the wholeness and integrity of the modern body, they delineated identity and difference categorically. Caught between these dichotomies, Kant could not completely shed the colors of black and white so characteristic of his pre-*Critique* phase.

Herder's writings, especially the *Reflections* and the *Letters*, represent a slightly different, more complex scenario. Peter Hallberg sees Herder's texts as speaking of the irreducible diversity within an overall culture of marginalizing difference (293), and I suggest that diversity applies to Herder's treatment of perceptual modes as well. In the *Reflections*, hailed as "one of the great monuments of eighteenth-century ethnography and ethnology" (Zammito, *Birth*, 345), Herder developed a powerful rhetoric based on images of the body. His writing drew on the modern concept of the body as organism fully engaging the new epistemology to delineate the uniqueness of human beings while rejecting anatomical features, skin color, or genetic origins—in short, scientific data—as criteria for separating humans from one another:[8]

> Lastly, I could wish the distinctions between the human species, that have been made out of a laudable zeal for discriminating science, not carried beyond due bounds. For instance, some have thought fit to employ the term "races" for four or five divisions originally made because of country or complexion, but I see no reason for this appellation. Race refers to a difference of origin, which in this case either does not exist, or, in each of these countries and under each of these complexions, comprises very different races. For every people is one people, having its own national form as well as its own language: the climate, it is true, marks each, or spreads over it a slight veil, but not sufficiently to destroy the original national character. (7)

Herder emphatically rejected the classifying impulse and the racial varieties that natural scientists had produced, calling them "overeager," "arbitrary," and wrong. A firm believer in Creationism, Herder envisioned the unity of the human organism as an idea that could help conceptualize a people's history and development, culture and procreation, in perfect agreement and symmetry with the land they inhabited (Mielke, 212). He believed humanity and nature to be one and race to be a superfluous category because it would only supplant a far superior one, namely the ethnic or national community or *Volk* (*Werke*, 13:257). He believed that the latter persists and regenerates itself throughout history, engaged in self-discovery and embracing inner diversity, and that national communities in turn become open to "an exchange of ideas between different communities" (Spencer, 255), a proposition that could indeed offer a new perspective on rejuvenating the imperative of enlightened universality, were it not for the neglect of the complex power configurations that emerge in the course of a people's history.

Elsewhere—in the "Negeridyllen" (Negro Idylls)—Herder engaged race in ways that tied him to the late eighteenth-century discourse on abolitionism and noble savagery, with its underlying racial dichotomy and historically envisioned progress of civilization and cultures (*Werke*, 18:224–34). By that time race had become a divisive category as much as slavery was a historical fact. Part of the 114th letter on the *Advancement of Humanity*, the idylls—a grouping of five didactic poems—reflect Herder's keen awareness of historical circumstance, especially his knowledge of slavery in the United States and the Caribbean slave revolts (Buck-Morss).[9] The poems refer to his ethical indictment of (religious) colonialism, xenophobia, and slavery, specifically his claim that the injustice of slavery would lead to a violent revenge driven by stereotypes and hatred. They are prefaced by an introduction that ends with an anecdote: " 'Why do you pour water over my head?' said the dying slave to the missionary—'So you'll be saved'—'I don't want to be in a heaven full of whites!' responded the slave, and he turned away and died. Dark history of humanity!" (224). Here, strictly defined, sociologically shored-up boundaries between white and black bodies generate conflict and a clash of identities. But their superficial resolution, paired with actions of resistance, will not alter the hierarchies and differentials of power. As the poems pick up on the rhetorical structure of the anecdote, they produce what critics have called Herder's "ambivalent humanitarianism" (Musgrave, "Herder"). Just as he posited racial difference and dependencies, however regrettable, as laws of history, the poems' fictional slaves internalize the position of inferiority and Otherness that Herder assigned to them. The poems suggest, in the end, that the slaves will obey the power inflicted upon them, remaining voluntarily "locked" in their historical place (e.g., "The Right Hand," "The Brothers," 226–28).

The "Negro Idylls" blur the boundaries among blackness, Africa, and slavery—all concepts that had been conflated in German literature and philosophy by 1796. Though showing Herder's advocacy of abolition, they also expose the problematic underpinnings of the Idealist narrative of history when confronting "the deeds and events of history" (Bernasconi, 177): the slave revolt of the 1790s in Haiti, as well as the situation in German lands. Relying on his experiences in the Baltic (Arens, 26), Herder identified historical instances, mainly in Eastern Europe, where Germans became colonizers, while portraying them also as a colonized people. In fact, Herder construed the historical belatedness of the German nation as "the Germans' association not with the colonizers but with other colonized and oppressed people" (Zantop, 95). In this respect, the "Negro Idylls" are even more telling. They shed light on Herder's thought in relation to Hegel's *Philosophy of History*. On one hand, Herder clearly differed from Hegel: eighteenth-century slavery, based on a historically contrived racial dichotomy of white and black, Europe/America and Africa, could not be sublated after all, but would erupt in violence. On the other hand though, Herder seemingly accepted the logic of the Hegelian narrative of history; when telling the story of black misrecognition and misidentification, he adopted Hegel's position on blacks as inferior beings who could not—but were nevertheless expected to—relate to the *telos* of history. Picking up on his account of Africa in the *Reflections*, where he concluded that Africa was the natural place for black people, Herder ultimately concurred with the many statements made about Africans and their nonperfectibility by his contemporaries (see also Zantop, 75); like Hegel, he thought Africa to be a "children's land." Thus, Herder's text links narratologically the plea for abolition to the historization of blackness and Africa. He feels obliged to insert his voice because inferior intellects could not recognize the logic of history and thus prevent the violent disruption of progress (see Buck-Morss). What distinguishes Herder's overall narrative from Hegel's is the insistence on cultural diversity and the autonomy of individual cultures, which would be severely diminished, even eradicated through interfering narratives of Self and race.

Another passage of the *Reflections* forms a critical link among the sources of my argument in this study, namely, the eleventh book, devoted to the East and South East Asian continent and containing Herder's reading of China. Rolf Goebel has described this passage as a self-conscious reflection on the act of writing and representation, where Herder encountered the central paradox of writing about a people's history on the basis of texts, that is, mediated access—rather than a people's stories, conversations, daily life, that is, ethnographic fieldwork (18). But Herder's text also chronicles the rupture between a textual and visual organization of knowledge and its effects on conceptualizing ethnic difference. The detailing of demographic facts, the admiration for both infrastructure and the balance of society, and a commentary on Chinese wealth accumulation dominate the first portion of Herder's piece. Conveying a fascination with sophisticated manners, the account leads to an assessment of laws, claiming that the Chinese legal system was founded upon natural ethics, which, in turn, drew on the sacred books of tradition. But suddenly Herder's text cuts off description. Switching abruptly into the grammatical subjunctive to imply doubt, the author wonders whether there could be a more perfect civilization than the Chinese: "The entire empire would be (like) a house, full of virtuous, well-raised, diligent, moral, and happy children and brothers." Eventually he answers his own rhetorical question by calling this perfect impression a "painting" (*Werke* 14:6).

Far from carrying the negative connotation of Kant's "grimace," Herder's choice of words nevertheless signals distortion. The text not only alludes to deception and illusion, but also amplifies a moment in Herder's writing where the depiction of *visuality* and the reference to traditional *texts* intersect; it is a moment full of conflicting discursive powers. By conjuring up older accounts, commenting on the impact these texts should have had, and denouncing them through an implication of falsity, Herder's text engenders a concept of history and marks a caesura, suggesting that knowledge about China must be—or already has been—reorganized. The resulting image resurrects a textual archive, the early eighteenth-century missionary reports; in allowing for Herder's critique of a pervasive "disbelief," it simultaneously establishes the alternative basis for constructing China. Identifying a people's ethnic origins and characteristics, their habitat and their history formed impulses for a revision; however, rather than advocating a Chinese point of view in writing Chinese history (Goebel, 18), these impulses pointed to an altered way of perceiving China. Not incidentally, the text presents another graphic metaphor connoting the perceptual complexity of Herder's writing: all the characteristics of the Chinese, "stand clearly before our eyes" (*Werke*, 14:7). From now on, the seeing European could verify the ethnographic turn. Visuality was not at all suspect; on the contrary, visually perceivable evidence became the signature of authenticity when constructing ethnicity. Meanwhile Herder the philosopher clung to textual authorities when recommending that both idealized and overtly critical accounts of Chinese civilization be compared to authoritative Chinese and European sources. The result would be a textual mediation, comprising the ultimate truth (7).

Herder's text captures this epistemological threshold by presenting its argument as part of the emerging texture of historical thinking, no matter how entrenched its author was in theological hermeneutics (Goebel, 16). His ultimate goal was to explain what he considered historical stagnation. In the course of the argument, however, anthropocentric, instinct-driven underpinnings of Herder's thought surfaced. Invoking the concept of race, Herder began by describing the Chinese through racial classifications that, though common at the time, were in flux with respect to their application to China's inhabitants. Like Kant before him, Herder considered the Chinese people to be a hybrid race. But unlike Kant, he interpreted the people's customs, politics, and public ethics as a direct reflex of their biological origins, which brought him closer to a common *public presentation* of Blumenbach's system of racial classification: though Blumenbach did not overtly emphasize this kind of biological anthropology in the text of *Beyträge zur Naturgeschichte* (Contributions on National History; 1806), the popular editions were frequently illustrated with images depicting the Chinese as peasants and craftsmen surrounded by architecture and, not surprisingly, a wall.

Herder's *Reflections* introduced the name "Mongolian" in reference to the inhabitants of China and commented on the "half-Tatarian despotism and Tatarian servitude" allegedly present among the people, considering each of these characteristics evidence of the manners and genetic disposition of the Chinese (*Werke*, 14:8). The thus-conceived nature expressed itself not only in the organism of the nation but also in its discreet parts, in individual persons, and, even more so, in the exterior, ornamental markers of their way of life (i.e., dress and food, arts, the organization of domestic life, etc.). Simultaneously, in naturalizing these social, cultural, and behavioral patterns, the text invoked visible characteristics in the description of humans. It resurrected the biology-infused narrative impulse behind the *Reflections*: the human drive to distinguish oneself, to set oneself apart and surpass, in terms of historical progress, other people, without ever negating their own distinct individuality and ethnicity.

In Herder's text there is no sublation of alterity, only difference in the identity of historical progress. Once anchored in the process of history, the name "Chinese" returns as well. Taken together, the various narrative patterns racialize Herder's ultimate depiction of the Chinese in *Reflections*. He concocted an image that he essentialized at the same time: "They were and remained Chinese, a people with small eyes, a flat nose, and a broad forehead, endowed by nature with little facial hair, big ears, and a big gut; what this ethnic organism could produce it did, and nothing else can be expected of it" (8). A far cry from Herder's denouncing of race as a productive way to describe cultural alterity, this depiction signals his succumbing to images. He stated that the painted characters reproduced in beautiful books "unnerved their users [and] turned thoughts into images" (14). Henceforth, these images would become indicators of Herder's conflicted position vis-à-vis cultural diversity: they were intrinsic to belief in the universal expression of ethnic diversity, a diversity where every people deviated from the idealized Greeks of the past; they implied, or at the very least lent themselves, to hierarchical interpretation of cultures; and finally, these images also reflected Herder's aspirations of an "aesthetic man," the ultimate move toward an epistemology centered on the body (Bindman, 163–69, esp.169).

Simultaneously, another discourse emerged that further defined and complicated the tension between visuality and textuality in the *Reflections*: Herder's thoughts on the Chinese language. On one hand, this focus threatened to undermine the visual signatures of ethnic, racial, and cultural difference; on the other, Herder's reconsideration of language elevated another perceptual dimension to a primary means of locating alterity: the aural sense with aural perceptivity becoming a distinguishing feature of the Chinese (8). In the course of his argument, Herder sharply separated the tonal aspects of the Chinese language from the graphic, even pictorial, nature of the signifying sign, allowing spoken Chinese to become the signifier of insurmountable otherness and keeping the Chinese character as part of the universal texture of a world that could be read eventually. Herder presumed that the tonal system would forever remain inaccessible to Europeans, whereas characters could be deciphered, were it not for their sheer number (8–9).

China was thought to express an inassimilable distance through its language: perceptually and psychologically the association of multiple tones with one character allegedly shut out Germans from ever understanding China, so that cultural alterity manifested itself as difference: insurmountable, nonrepresentable, forever "other." At the same time the stability of the Chinese characters meant stagnation. Like Leibniz and his contemporaries, Herder assumed that a people's social organization and ethical action reflected the principles of language, consequently construing texts as a material basis for any possible history (9–10, 13). Texts composed of pictorial characters could signify only one state of existence, one ethical imperative, in short, one textual truth. In prescribing one way of reading, Herder asserted, Chinese texts precluded historical thinking; neither characters nor texts nor the unfolding stages of society were susceptible to change (15). He also concluded that a profound temporal difference between Europe and China became evident in these texts: with only one discernable meaning, Chinese texts could not harbor the seeds of renewed self-discovery, linguistic decay, and rebirth as Europe's evolving languages and texts, nations, and powers could.

Ultimately, though these statements arose in conjunction with a reorganization of vision and text, they contain a not-so-subtle antivisual argument. In critiquing Chinese characters for their pictorial qualities, said to capture deteriorated and dead ideas, Herder presumed that linguistic stagnation means cultural and ethnic difference—which led him to his infamous description of China as a mummy. In turn, he thought of historical progress as a narrative of overcoming visual stages, of transcending images of stability, believing that the distinction between the tonal and pictorial qualities of the Chinese language hid an epistemological threshold, concealing not only an understanding of inassimilable linguistic and historical, in short, cultural, alterity, but also the epistemological prerequisite for conceptualizing alterity in such a way: visuality as a dominant paradigm. Furthermore, compared with other eighteenth-century texts, Herder's transformed the relationship of aurality, visuality, and the symbolic access to history. Unlike Leibniz and his contemporaries, who appreciated Chinese characters for their intercultural communicability and considered them the ultimate expression of a perfect natural order and stability, Herder read them as an expression of an ethnic obsession with perceptual detail and radical otherness (13).

By highlighting a representational gap within the Chinese language itself, Herder went beyond those of his contemporaries who depicted China mainly as a state of historical stagnation and provided the linguistic or theoretical parallel to poetic sketches of fleeting sounds. His reading "explained" the idealization of the Chinese language—and by extension the Chinese territory—as a space that escaped the torment of temporality and representation. Thus Herder's text resembles a transitory moment in "The Wheel of Fate" in which torturous sounds represent the subject's discomfiture in the world; yet unlike in the treatise—where this moment ceases—Herder sought to arrest it. Whereas "The Wheel of Fate" proposed a unity of life and death and, by locating the recognition of death in a Chinese realm, demonstrated another mode of restoring the coherence between the Eastern and Western hemispheres, Herder's text produces no Romantic image. But it evinces true Romantic potential in its ability to envision alterity as promise. Such an ideal, existing beyond any universal coherence of world and not depending on any inscription of ethnic identity, made difference permanent. In this sense, Herder's alterity of fleeting sounds signaled Romantic chaos and infinite signification, rather than the ideal space of Romanticism's textual Orient.

The tentative elevation of hearing over seeing finds its correlation in Herder's *Letters on Humanity*, in which he denigrated the cold brutality of a classifying eye ("the coldest, most exteriorizing, most superficial sense") while celebrating the poetic dimension of the ear ("a deeper, more powerful [. . .] sense"; 18:27).[10] He posited that both senses differentiate and classify, and it is in and through the senses that a people's character, its ethnicity, expresses itself. Going back to the physiological theories first presented by Albrecht von Haller, Herder's valuation of all senses, especially their comprehensive interplay or mutual vibrations (18:27), sheds new light on the role of archived knowledge about osmosis, the environs, and climate in the discursive constructions of racial thought, steering us away from the visually defined signatures of race and the biological narrative that presumably endowed these signatures with historical truth. In Herder's narrative, hearing—in its transcendence of corporal boundaries and the confinement of visuality—became the prerequisite for an adequate representation of ethnic and cultural difference, without prejudice. And yet, Herder, perhaps more than any other of his contemporaries, relied on a historicity that developed naturally and doubtlessly depended on images of corporal unity and limitations. To him, a nation was clearly defined against a state and government administered by humans, against political contracts between individuals and community, and against human-centered rationality; for him, a nation always evolved over time, like an organism. And yet "listening" to each other makes an "exchange of ideas" between nations possible; "listening" turns cultural alterity into a productive experience, restoring the idea that perceived difference is a positive force in the universe.

*   *   *

Kant, Herder, Hegel—all three philosophers influenced present day study of cultural alterity and ethnic, racial, and national identity. Hegel's formulation of Self-Other has, for better or worse, defined postcolonial scholarship to date; he, however, was only a symptom of his time, evoking numerous, equally expressive counterparts in philosophy, scientific and literary prose, and poetry. At the same time, alternative models for constructing alterity did exist. As I have attempted to show in this book, they were contested (and eventually eclipsed) in the eighteenth century, but not without leaving traces in texts written around 1800. In this concluding section I will therefore turn to a small corpus of texts that help us map the treatment of China and Africa in fiction of that time. Some revel in the visual constitution of Self and Other, simultaneously preserving and rejecting eighteenth-century encounters with Africa; some revolve around China as text, a figure that underwent a process of partial deterritorialization: metaphorically, by engaging death and overcoming personhood, and literally, by extending the reach of the mythical text to other Asian cultures. Whereas the latter group addresses the metaphysical or philosophical problem of temporality, the former projects physical difference, usually through a black body in opposition to a white body. By teasing out points of conflict, intersection, and mutual transcendence between these two narrative approaches, we can enhance our understanding of identity and difference as dominant cognitive figures of modernity. We will recognize, in the end, a philosophical web, or texture that ties in not only Hegel, but also Kant and Herder.

In one group of texts, visuality underlined the centrality of Self. Stories and images related Selves aesthetically, either through the abject condition of the black body, which manifested itself in such metaphors as material danger, ugliness, and dramatic death or through the erection of a new aesthetic ideal, white Greek sculpture (Purdy, "Whiteness," 86–87). Often prose fiction and drama responded to extratextual elements, realizing—like Herder in "Negro Idylls"—that racial conflict presented itself colored in black and white; among the antislavery texts, the following stand out: August von Kotzebue's *The Negro Slaves* (1796), Heinrich von Kleists's *Die Verlobung in St. Domingo* (The Betrothal in Santo Domingo; 1811), and Caroline Auguste Fischer's *William the Negro* (1817). Fischer's story expresses very lucidly the processes through which racial identities were thought to be produced and culturally codified, differing sharply from Kleist's *Betrothal*, which constantly obscures racial attributions and visual signatures in the narrative up to the point where racial Selves—the white stranger, Gustav, and the black "mulatto," Toni—are literally destroyed and the narration falls apart. In Kleist's novella, narrative closure is possible through the act of memorializing a love that could not survive the identification imposed by skin color and race, and through the novella's participation in the discourse on miscegenation, by thwarting the danger by means of the deaths of the protagonists (Gilman, *On Blackness*, 47; Zantop, 155–58). In contrast, Fischer's text created rigid divisions and "truisms" to preempt any possibility of lasting contact and intimacies. Like its European counterparts, *William the Negro* reflects on the complicated relations between races by narrating romance—involving the love triangle of William, a black noble savage, his teacher/master, Sir Robert, and Molly, a beautiful white girl—through the lens of Caribbean revolutions and slave revolts (Nussbaum, *Limits*, 240). What intrigues me about the story is the elevated, defining role of *visuality* in the narrative construction of race, geographical space, and gender, presenting us in turn with an amplification of the nexus of public sphere and domesticity.

The tale creates a tableau-like image of Molly, who seems mute yet of robust health, rare beauty, and in perfect tune with nature. Making wonderful music, Molly attracts spectators, among them William, who, infatuated with her singing, remains hidden, an "invisible listener." But this initial equilibrium between image, voice, and listener breaks down when William is introduced to the readers as "the young Moor from the neighborhood," who perceives the racial difference between himself and Molly as insurmountable: "How often, how gladly he would have fallen at her feet, had he not seen his own black face every time in the brook that meandered through the meadow behind the garden" (355). William contrasts his self-recognition with

Molly's ideal whiteness, while the narrator leaves whiteness unnamed, merely paraphrasing it as the blush of Molly's cheeks, the heavenly blue of her eyes, and the blond shine of her hair (355). The narrator provides us with a character tableau of William, detailing his personal history from captured slave to educated "noble savage," before sealing in the visual dichotomy through William's words, "Alas, why am I black. Molly, you divine white girl!" (356). Like numerous other fictional characters, William finds himself at the juncture where racial difference and the postulate of universal equality intersect, where the nexus of aesthetics and history is formed. Expected to aid the Caribbean revolution after finishing his education, William exposes the century's contradictions: embodying at once the symbolic invisibility of blackness (and Africa) in Europe's ideal domesticity and Enlightenment and the actual visibility of black skin, William's position carries the signature of race (Bhabha).

In the course of the story, the visual economy of racial difference is rearranged, spatially as well as historically. William and Molly confess their affection for each other, but when William finally introduces his bride to Sir Robert, his teacher and fatherly friend, the young girl and the older man are "struck as if by lightening" when their eyes meet (360). What Molly and Sir Robert only intuit at first, William instantaneously recognizes, concluding that Molly and Robert belong together. Perceiving the white man and the white woman as a beautiful ideal, he sees himself as inferior, "animal-like," and "ugly." Through a pronounced act of viewing, the literary character internalizes a societal and historical position that Herder had ascribed to the slaves in his "Negro Idylls" and that Homi Bhabha would identify 150 years later as the postcolonial predicament of misrecognition: William puts himself into a position of private inferiority while rededicating himself to the public task of the Caribbean revolution ("Remembering," 115). Similarly, by representing the symbolic superiority of the white foster father, the visual construction of European paternity becomes the narrative's *telos*. This aesthetic ideal is symbolized in Sir Robert and Molly's marriage and their two children, and in William's decision to entrust Sir Robert with the upbringing of his black son, born in St. Domingo to a black woman. Ensuring the paternal dimension of both the bourgeois subject and society's future, this ideal extends Sir Robert's role as the father of the revolution and of Enlightened paternalism, which began with William's education decades earlier. And it extends to William, as he succumbs to the late eighteenth-century ideal of race separation in becoming a black surrogate who fulfills the white postulate of public political activity.

Like Kotzebue's drama and Kleist's novella, Fischer's story suggests that racial identities supplant ethnic or national origin by pointing, on one hand, to the situation of the slave revolts, which contemporaries, including Herder, saw as an expression of racial anger. On the other hand, the fact that such fictional characters often pose as European underscores the fragility and illusionary quality of German ethnic and national identity in eighteenth-century fiction (Zantop, 95). But Fischer's story reminds us also of the other contexts for constructing Germanness—vis-à-vis China and Africa—which I have examined in this book. No matter whether Germanness appeared as an expression of Enlightenment universalism, as an experiment in enlightened erudition and the public sphere, or in relation to gender, reading, and travel, it manifested itself as an "absent" reality. Germanness longed for the fantasy of fiction, the thought experiment, and the idea, before constituting itself as community. (This displacement is perhaps most pronounced in my reading of "bodies on stage," where community inadvertently comes into existence, albeit not as nation but as race.) By veiling themselves, "German" subjectivities stood in contrast to Hegel's Self of history, which found its *telos* in the "Germanic World," and Kant's discussion of race and nation which, at the very least, anticipated the prominence of Germanness in racist thought (Shell, 56; Zammito, *Birth*, 345).

A small but significant number of texts evaded the visual signatures of race and "corporeality," taking us back to the second locale of this book, Asia. Originating among the early German Romantics (1794–1805), these texts turned to India to resolve—poetically as well as philosophically—the unsettling experience of modernity. They either allude to India when constructing an archival but otherwise abstract "Orient" to constitute the mythical point of reference in Romantic historiography and theory of representation, or they depict what they regard as the core of India—Brahmanism—and revolve around motifs connoting religious and philosophical practice. In Heinrich Wackenroder's *Wunderbares morgenländisches Mährchen von einem nackten Heiligen* (Wondrous Oriental Tale of a Naked Saint, 1799), the sage, preoccupied with and tortured by time, eventually escapes temporality by literally dissolving in the air. Under the influence of music, he lets go of his body; in the very moment that his physical gestalt ceases to exist, he dispels the adverse effects of differentiation and modernity. Expressing the infinite potential of signification, sound enables—very much like Herder's rendering of the aural side of Chinese—the transcendence of limits, while isolating and mystifying the result. Similarly, the bourgeois traveler in Karoline von Günderrode's *Geschichte eines Braminen* (Tale of a Brahmin, 1805) achieves a blissful state of existence by surrendering to the introspective and contemplative stage of Brahmanism, enhanced by literally moving through geographical space toward India. As the traveler gradually sheds the traces of utilitarian business, political, and communal engagement on his journey, he erases any discord between himself and the world. Whereas this discord manifests itself in the traveler's body—as well as through his alienation from his surroundings, which has both individualizing and isolating effects—contemplation tames the distracting effects of life, culminating in the transcendence of body.

Though staging the body as a metaphor of human existence and pain, both stories dissolve physical suffering by rendering the body invisible, either literally or figuratively. By dispelling visuality, they restore the textual foundation of the relation to Asia that had characterized Leibniz's and Wolff's writing. These new texts abandoned reading as the primary mode of constituting subjectivity, transforming instead all senses into a poetic texture. Responding to the fracturing results of late eighteenth-century political, historical, and epistemological developments, Romantic subjects aspired to "heal"— however phantasmagorically—the rift between humans and nature, individual and society. As poetic renderings of "temporality," "bourgeois existence," and "representation" became evidence of the perceived fragmentation of modern life, textual Asia emerged as the substrate for the metaphor of "the Orient," a space where differences could be reconciled. (Of course, in its emphasis on the Western world's geographical counterpart, Romanticism's oriental tale demarcated difference *per se*.) However, in Romanticism both the textual tradition and the geographical origin of Hinduism directed the formation of the narratives' reservoir of images. Around 1800, the "absent text" of Hinduism gained a prominent role in establishing a decipherable relation between Europe and Asia, creating a bond that could sustain a narrative of universalism and prepare the new myth of the nineteenth century: Indo-Europeanism as a philological foundation for Aryanism (see Figueira 8–88; Murti 2–9). Therefore, by engaging another textual tradition of Asia, early Romantic texts continued to weave the imaginary texture of Enlightenment universalism, although it had lost its rationalist, asensual impetus.[11] By countering the teleological narrative of German Idealism, early Romanticism recalled the perceptual-representational archive suppressed in Hegel's *Philosophy*. Romantic texts also evoked Herder: his distinction between listening to a language and reading its characters, his use of concepts and metaphors ("mummy") that inscribe a stable image and, finally, his recognition of the infinite potential that comes with an "escape" from identification. Herder's *Reflections* can thus form another backdrop—and an alternative to Hegel—against which to examine the traces of multifaceted expressions of eighteenth-century alterity.

That these traces persist in modernity—and indeed in today's culture—has been the implied premise of scholarship on "exoticism" and "primitivism," even if their eighteenth-century roots have been eclipsed. Carefully delineating the patterns of seeing and spatial recognition at the epistemological center of Carl Einstein's work on "primitive art" (e.g., *Negerplastik* [1915]), Andreas Michel observes patterns of producing the African that are incongruent with other, contemporary models of defining black ethnicities (e.g., colonialism, exhibition culture, or sexuality) which point, of course, to the symptoms of modernity—and their manifestations in political history, consumer culture, and the medical field—that arose in the aftermath of Kant and Hegel and resemble what David Pan calls "progressivist vision" (4). Pan, too, invokes the counterpoint of such vision when proposing that "the primitive does not designate something foreign but familiar, though perhaps repressed" (4). Therefore, I believe that since the eighteenth century constitutes a decisive epistemological foundation for the thinking of progress, it must also become a crucial element in ascertaining the epistemological status of primitivism as a critique of modernity (cf. Pan, 4).

Perhaps we need to go even further and consider our reliance on visually inflected languages as a reflection of textual prohibition. Eckard Nordhofen defines "exotic" in a way that supports the persistence of a perceptual tension between vision and textuality. Claiming that the exotic is sensual in nature, made up of vivid images, colors, and smells, and marked by an almost animalistic state of human existence, he contrasts this idol-like construct of the exotic with philosophy. It is the philosophical impulse, the aspiration to achieve pure recognition that sustains the (originally biblical) prohibition of worshipping false idols. This conclusion leads Nordhofen to interpret exoticism as a psychological and cultural response to a prohibition that was forced upon people by a text whose roots go back to the "original text" of Western culture, the Bible, whose hermeneutics became a model for philosophy; like the original text, philosophy suppresses images by taming them through language.

This argument touches on several issues that I have addressed and refined in *Reading and Seeing Ethnic Differences*. On one hand,

Nordhofen adopts a long-standing assumption that the ethnic must be understood as a homogeneous figuration, a unitary Other of a Self, while suggesting that constructions of ethnic difference reflect the relationship between perception and representation on the other. By projecting an essential incommensurability of imagery and philosophy, of vision and text, Nordhofen aligns the exotic realm with imagery and vision while associating the European home with philosophy and text. As sensuality *per se* turns into Otherness within this logic, rationality constitutes Selfhood, and Nordhofen restores, at last, the homogenous configuration Other-Self à la Hegel. But implied in his argument is also a compressed history of visuality in Western thought: its rise as the new guarantor of knowledge in the last quarter of the eighteenth century, followed by visuality's simultaneous magnification and dispersal at the beginning of the twentieth century. (That the exotic might constitute a conceptual parallel to the dominance of new visual media—which arose in compensation for and opposition to vision's overall decline vis-à-vis epistemological certainty—must remain a mere suggestion at this point.[12]) However, Nordhofen does not consider that in the last quarter of the eighteenth century a new narrative of identity and difference engulfed philosophy and was founded on neither the rudimentary texture of Scripture nor the cognitive assertion of the Cartesian ego. Rather, it was defined by vision and humans' imaginary perception of Selfhood. As vision embraced the symbolic power of a textual tradition while suppressing its material foundation, the text itself created the new, modern texture of History and Man (see Stafford).

But where does that leave us here and today? How can we go about utilizing the genealogical foundations, which eighteenth-century cultures provided in the narrative of modernity, rather than perpetuating their eclipse? Is there any potential advantage to detouring to the oppositional narratives of primitivism and exoticism, to cultural periods and movements that at once defy and intensify the logic of Self-Other? Such questions about the historiography of literature and culture bring into focus again the purpose of this book, namely to work toward a historically more refined understanding of a series of conceptual pairs—cultural alterity and ethnicity, identity and difference, individual and community—rethinking their relationship through modes of perception and representation.

I hope that this book will be seen as an attempt to take the relationship between texts and visuality seriously, to recognize how this relationship shapes our extratextual world and the language we impose on it. It is an attempt to unearth and highlight alternative stories, an effort to counter the dominance of Self-Other and expose its historicity. It is also a call for alternative ways of perceiving alterity and (re)constructing it. This book bears, therefore, the seeds of other studies, exposing the fissures of a monolithic text, the fragility of Self, and, last but not least, the limitations of our own historical moment. It hopes to turn to a new page in reading and seeing the fictions and realities of life.

NOTES

INTRODUCTION

1. See Said's own reflections in "*Orientalism*, An Afterword"; Arif Dirlik's exemplary essay on Asians' participation in the Orientalist project, "Chinese History and the Question of Orientalism"; and Timothy Brennan's piece "The Illusion of a Future" that appeared in *Critical Inquiry*, Spring 2000 issue. Brennan argues convincingly that neither *Orientalism* nor its fruitful reception would have been possible without the particular historical constellations in U.S. academia and politics in the late 1970s and early 1980s. In contrast to these studies, all of which are firmly grounded in the traditions of U.S. academia, Jürgen Osterhammel presents a distinctively German perspective. Recently, Katherine Arens has demanded a thorough reexamination of Said's account vis-à-vis the German situation and eighteenth-century studies. Her article resonates with my present, independently conceived project.
2. The formulations are borrowed from von Mücke, *Virtue*, 7 (all additions mine).
3. In developing this argument, I have relied on the wealth of research on German and European (pre) colonialism, nationalism, and/or racism, as well as theories of visuality and textuality. While I weave my critical reading of these studies into my model analyses, I believe my study to be different with respect to the period it covers and/or with respect to its conceptual and methodological focus. For example, Figueira addresses aspects of China as a culture of textuality with respect to the nineteenth-century concept of Aryanism (and latent anti-Semitism), whereas Zantop focuses on colonial fantasies as an important instrument in imagining German communities. I follow perhaps most closely Berman's argument as he disputes the assumption that eighteenth-century culture is either one of Empire or one of Enlightenment. Instead, he shows how both are inevitably linked. However, none of the existing studies pursues a contrastive reading of different perceptual modes.

1   HEGEL AT THE LIMITS OF DISCOURSE

1. Aspects of the editorial history influenced my choice of *Vorlesungen* in volume 12 of the *Theorie-Werkausgabe*. I decided that this edition reflects perhaps most accurately the actual lectures as far as they can be reconstructed

from Hegel's notes and notes taken by his students. This text does not account sufficiently, however, for evolving elements in Hegel's thought.

2. The edition of *The Philosophy of History* used here misleadingly translates the section title as "The German world" (341).

3. I differ from Spivak, who is interested in questions of rhetoric and the rhetorical instantiation and elimination of the native informant, that is, a voice that escapes the colonial (and, by the same token, the postcolonial) gesture.

4. This is very much in line with the turn to modernity as described by Foucault, especially in *The Order of Things* and *The Archaeology of Knowledge*. Accordingly, the concept of functionality is closely linked to wholeness; it is dependent on the possibility of perceiving an object as an organism and interpreting it as such.

2   THREADS OF A TEXTURE: LEIBNIZ'S TRANSLATION OF CHINA

1. Only one of Leibniz's treatises, *Essays in Theodicee*, was published during his lifetime. Cook and Rosemont do not include "Mystery" among the Chinese writings, which I consider an omission.

2. Cf. Foucault, The *Order of Things*, on the enactment and effects of rhetorical paraphrase, especially: "This primacy of the written word explains the twin presence of two forms which, despite their apparent antagonism, [were] indissociable in sixteenth-century knowledge. The first of these [was] a non-distinction between what [was] seen and what [was] read, between observation and relation, which result[ed] in the constitution of a single, unbroken surface in which observation and language intersect[ed] to infinity. And the second, the inverse of the first, [was] an immediate dissociation of all language, duplicated, without any assignable term, by the constant reiteration of commentary" (39).

3. I am aware of the broad and homogenizing designation "Chinese philosophies." Leibniz himself was vague apart from the explicit references to Confucianism in his writings on rites (Cook/Rosemont, 67–74) and in his *Discourse*. This reception is in line with the missionaries' privileging of Confucianism over Taoism and Buddhism (see Glasenapp, 117–77; Ching/Oxtoby, 175).

4. Since my interest in Leibniz is confined to his textual constructions of China, I do not enter this debate between philosophers and Sinologists on Leibniz's philosophical innovations.

5. Deleuze has developed a notion of reading with respect to Leibniz's monadology; however, my present use of "reading" is not related or otherwise indebted to Deleuze's argument, because Deleuze is interested in the singularities of the Baroque and its influential mathematical and architectural space, not in the intercultural space Leibniz created (cf. Deleuze, 3–13, 55).

6. Cf. Fenves, who attributes to Leibniz's worldview the conviction that "the peoples of Europe and those of China [had] a distinct advantage over all other nations" ("What 'Progresses,' " 15).

7. Leibniz proceeded to evaluate Longobardi's readings, trusting that his translations were more accurate because he intended to refute the Chinese sources (79).

8. See my chapters 6 and 1, respectively.

9. See also p. 39 here.

10. To quote Ames more fully: "First, tradition has it that the Sage-rulers of antiquity observed regularity and order implicit in the natural process and sought to devise formal rules of conduct, or li, that would enable human beings to make the same cosmological patterns explicit in their own lives. These formal behaviors, serving to structure human life within and integrate it without, are a microcosm of the liax (veins, fibres) of the macrocosm" (50).

11. Leibniz's recourse to Chinese philosophies can consequently be understood as a search for a system that perfectly represented the idea of prestablished harmony. Although in Leibniz's view, ancient Chinese scholars did not define the preestablished harmony by naming it or by developing conceptual frameworks to explain it, the postulate of harmonious existence was implied in the structure of Chinese philosophical concepts and the polar ideas of macro- and microcosm (see Ames, 41). Polarity structures Chinese thought and is reflected, for example, in the complex meanings of different characters for "body" in the Chinese language. The various characters resemble each other as they signify the relationships between part and whole, physical and spiritual, but it is their polar nature that is relevant to Leibniz's account of the *Li* (cf. Ames, also regarding the philosophical invention of the *Li*).

12. At one point Leibniz discusses the example of two clocks in perfect agreement and likens them to the correspondence between the soul and the body, suggesting that the clocks—just like the body and the soul—are "constructed with so much skill and accuracy that one can be certain of their subsequent agreement" despite their essential differences. He proceeds to define preestablished harmony: "Thus there remains only my hypothesis, that is, the way of pre-established harmony, through a prior divine artifice, which has formed each of these substances from the beginning in such a way that by following only its own laws, laws which it received with its being, it nevertheless agrees with the other, as if there were a mutual influence" ("Postscript," 148).

13. Cook and Rosemont proceed rather cautiously in their reading of the binary arithmetic. They consider it, on one hand, the strongest evidence of Leibniz's ecumenical intentions; on the other, they emphasize the scientific importance of being able to represent the creation of something out of nothing (see 17). David Porter asserts that Leibniz gave up on his project of discovering or creating a universal language (50), and Eco emphasizes the coincidental discovery of calculus in the course of a project intended to produce a universal language (68–75).

14. Leibniz dealt extensively with decimal progression; after all, he is considered the inventor of infinitesimal as well as differential calculus.

3   READING SOVEREIGN SUBJECTIVITY
VIA CHINA

1. In keeping with Wolff's efforts to democratize scholarship, the German version was included, complete with a new preface, and I base my argument on it and cite it as the *Lecture on Chinese Ethics*, using the rough, incomplete English translation in Ching/Oxtoby when it is reliable (145–86). When it is not, I cite the German text (*Rede*). For comparative purposes, see also Hsia, 42–72.

2. See, among others, Immanuel Kant, "Beantwortung der Frage: Was ist Aufklärung?"; Matthias Metternich, "Etwas über Aufklärung." Cf. also twentieth-century critical analyses of Enlightenment reflexivity in relation to temporality, awareness of presence, and projection of future. A case in point is the infamous exchange between Foucault and Habermas, documented in Michael Kelly, 17–156.

3. See Ching/Oxtoby for a historical placement of these concepts (xii–xiii, 1–60). Wolff had access to and referred to Noel's translations of Confucius's writings, and following Noel's classification, Wolff included the two books among the classics (Ching/Oxtoby, 175.) Approximate life dates for Confucius are 552–479 BCE and for Chu Hsi 1130–1200, the latter during the climax of Neo-Confucianism during the Sung Dynasty (960–1279) in later Imperial China.

4. Weber's understanding of filial piety seems not much different from *piousness*, often an overly demonstrative exhibition of religious affiliation and loyalty to religious teachings.

5. Eventually these fictions were played out in the retroactive installment of the legendary bourgeois King—the *Bürgerkönig*—who not only embodied the father of the house, but who was the father of the house "Germany."

6. This is a revised—and I believe more nuanced—conclusion, compared to older scholarship that simply assumes an unbroken tradition from Wolff to Tiefurt (cf. Ursula Aurich; Berger).

7. A late eighteenth-century review in the *Allgemeine Deutsche Biographie* states that the second volume was promised but never completed, suggesting that this was due to Seckendorff's premature death in Prussian service in 1785 (33:519). Nevertheless, bibliographic records list the novel consistently as "in two volumes." The text itself provides no indication that the novel actually comprised two volumes; rather, the preface hints at one volume (whose unsatisfactory end, however, makes the text appear to be a fragment).

8. At this point I will not address questions of gender, although Kittler suggests gendered versions of these oppositions. Nor will I discuss the links between origin, visuality, and the maternal voice (cf. von Mücke, "Introduction," *Virtue*).

9. The story ends with an encounter with another stranger, whose right of passage has been violated by Tschaong-tse. They fight, and Tschoang-tse, who is injured, is brought to the stranger's house. Though the story ends with "to be continued," another part was never published in the journal.

4 DETAILED ETHNICITY: PERCEPTION AND GENDER IN TRAVEL ACCOUNTS

1. The representation of China as text facilitated the representation of India's Hinduism, the textual origin of which would become a fantasy and reference point for German Romanticism.

2. *Der Teutsche Merkur* was edited by Christoph Martin Wieland and modeled on its French namesake, the *Mercure de France*, and because of its enormous success, was published monthly. It became one of the first venues of literary criticism that featured translations, a phenomenon that is particularly relevant in the present context.

3. An actual source text has never been located. I consider the reference to a "French authority" an attempt to legitimate the writing process rather than an indication of an actually existing source. Since Germany was far from being a colonial power in the eighteenth century, the authenticity of travel reports was often assured through the reference to French or British "sources" (cf. Sadji; Eigler/Kord, 6–7).

4. See Peter Kolb's preface to his account of the natives of the Cape of Good Hope: "He was sent to the Cape because of his erudition [. . .] somebody to travel there who was indeed capable of scientific observations" (b1). He was a German trained in basic sciences. The first German-language edition of his work was published in 1719 and was followed by a Dutch edition a year or two later, which has sometimes led to confusion regarding his linguistic and national origin. Even contemporaries considered him a "Dutch author" (Cf. Cossigny, 19).

5. This depiction may even mark the origin of a stereotype that since has pre-occupied Western thought: the nexus of blackness, seduction, and sexuality, later also associated with primitivism and the female prostitute. According to Martin, black prostitutes had been in Germany since the eighteenth century (173). The formation of the cultural imagery revolved onaround the South African Saartje Baartman (the "Hottentotvenus"), who was publicly exhibited as "a heavy-arsed heathen" between 1800 and 1815 (see Gilman, "Black Bodies, White Bodies," 206; also Martin, 467; Sharpley-Whiting, 16–31).

6. Hull uses this term in chronicling the public debates on sexual excess and transgression and the transposition of fears onto the anti-masturbation campaign (258–66).

7. Referring to their physical nature, the author associates Creoles with blacks. Creole women appear intrusive and sexually transgressive toward white men, thus resembling the black woman on the ship. To express innate hybridity, the text regresses from discursive regulation to unmediated perception. Unlike the depiction of the Negro woman, which symbolized the social transgression from private into public space, the Creoles' image included sensations and the material, pre-semantic essence ascribed to color. Their sexual practices are modeled on a material exchange between their bodies and their environs which fuels the sexual economy of supply and demand allegedly ruling on the island (77). See also chapter 5 here.

8. See Martin for a summary of the names used for black people since the Middle Ages, especially 81–89.

9. Cf. also Foucault's discussion of the opposition between "disciplined" and "marked" (198).

10. See also Pratt, who clearly distinguishes between superiority and subjugation. In my opinion the present account marks the threshold of subjugation, which signifies a textual dynamic and is different from superiority, an indication of socio-economic power.

11. These travelogues contain implicit reflections on a competing literary discourse, fashionable literature (*Modeliteratur*), which was interested neither in supporting traditional ideals of knowledge formation nor in offering models of identification. Instead, fashionable literature reflected the fleeting interests and preferences of the reading public. (It is here that the details' discursive circulation comes full circle, taking on the connotation of femininity.) Judging by the numbers, travel literature contributed aggressively to the fashionable portion of literature. Nevertheless, these travel accounts betray a subtle uneasiness with fashion, stemming perhaps from the awareness that obsession with exteriorities and dress leads to stylistic ornaments that inhibit the narrative flow.

12. The conclusion that travelers attempted to find commonalities in order to construct a homogenizing image for maximized narrative efficiency contradicts Agnew's thesis on island ethnology, geographical separation, and defiance of racial taxonomies (89–91).

13. Figuratively speaking, it is this cognitive map that distinguishes Forster's position and intention as author of the *Voyage around the World* from his position as translator-author of *Cook's Third Voyage*, where his insistence on authorial reputation and success competes with the ironclad principle of cognition "without fiction" (cf. Berman, 21–64).

5   Bodies on Stage: Late Eighteenth-Century Aesthetics of Blackness

1. To a certain degree, Paul Gilroy's argument against "visual signatures" of race implies an aesthetic foundation of race, though he pays little attention to the historical and genealogical development of the concept.

2. This dual notion of aesthetics continues to influence David Bindman's *Ape to Apollo*. Although he accounts for the "aesthetics of the perceiver" (51–58), Bindman's study of aesthetics and race in eighteenth-century Germany focuses largely on iconography and thus privileges the aesthetic qualities of the perceived object.

3. Many studies of race and dichotomies of skin color in the late eighteenth century presupposed an absolute concept of "man" based on the biologically defined unity of personhood and its correlative philosophical Self.

Often these studies implied that the formation of this concept preceded the modern notion of race but would eventually transcend it. Yet the idea of man's universally human emancipation arises, as I have begun to argue in this book, only as an effect of eighteenth-century cultural transformations, compensating for a crisis in perceiving alterity (see Honegger; Gilman, *On Blackness without Blacks*, 19–35; Schiebinger; Zantop, especially 121–61; to a lesser degree also Mielke; Sadji, *Negermythos*).

4. H.-J. Schings focuses on melancholy and boredom as adversarial influences on the formation of bourgeois group identities. Though eighteenth-century theories of melancholy influenced connotations of black skin, they are not the primary explanation of the century's aversion to blackness.

5. The premise of coevalness, that is, structural and institutional parallels in the delineation of modern categorizations of gender and race, dominated the history of science, sometimes leading to conflation and the interchangeable use of these categories in cultural analysis (e.g., "woman" is to "man" what "blackness" is to "whiteness"); more importantly, these equations were treated as a cultural "given," that is, their epistemological genealogies were ignored. However, we may infer important insights into eighteenth-century shifts in body perception and their influence on theories of race from this tendency to assume a parallelism between race and gender. For example, in discussing the beginnings of modern anthropology, Claudia Honegger claims that the sciences were late in establishing a woman's anthropology, basing this on the fact that eighteenth-century anthropologists dealt for about twenty years with classifying race but not with gender. In other words, she implies that these classifications would have occurred simultaneously had they been based on analysis of a body's inside, the anatomical structure of the skin and so on. The suggestion is perhaps, then, that the body's interaction with the environment—its osmotic nature—remained a dominant paradigm in theories of race. Thomas Laqueur's study seems to support this conclusion as well: he maintains in his theory of sex that the "economy of fungible fluids (in an osmotic body) transcends sex and species boundaries" (36).

6. Personal religious beliefs and justified concerns about being banned from public lecturing because of blasphemy may well explain his use of archaic rhetorical structures.

7. In German literally: "Durch die Zergliederungskunst dem Auge darstellet" ("Rede," 25).

8. This observation adds further depth to the "figuration of the individual," the historical dimension of which I began to characterize in my reading of Hegel and contrasted with a reading of its cognitive identification in Wolff and in Weimar court society. While I have so far used the construction to discuss the self-stylization of the philosopher as a sovereign subject, Foucault has long since outlined the "ethical potential," meaning that individuality requires a new distribution of power, which allows for discussions

of equality and hierarchy, in a concealed as well as in an open manner (Foucault, *Discipline*, 91).

9. Their interrelations furthermore offer a glimpse into the emergence of both racial and national iconography through physiognomy and suggest that the subject gained prominence not just because of influential proponents such as Lavater, but also because of wide popular acceptance and invocation in theater (Bindman).

10. Cf. also Theweleit, who discusses seventeenth- and eighteenth-century efforts to mediate through pictures the effects of "real women" (332–46).

11. Schiller was well aware of the aesthetic potential of physiognomic thought and, by suggesting an intrinsic relation between moral character and physical appearance, incorporated physiognomic knowledge in the description of several stage characters. He depicts morally despicable characters as ugly while emphasizing the immediate, positive influence of noble intention on the outer beauty of humans (see *Werke und Briefe*, 2:1016).

12. See also chapter 4 of this book and Sutherland for the most recent accounts of German collaboration with slavery, and, especially, of Baron Schimmelmann as a slave trader ("Staging Blackness," 101–11).

13. German original: "Teufel—bitt' um Vergebung" (*Werke und Briefe*, 2:336).

14. In the late eighteenth century, physical contact with and closeness to the mother's body were considered a defining element in the child's development, influencing the build, posture, and emotional constitution of the human being. According to Schiebinger, blacks were considered to be more heavily influenced by their mothers simply because black women carried their children on their back or hip, often for several years, even at a historical juncture when an unrestricted exchange between environment and body was no longer intelligible.

15. Or, as Saccamano writes: "What this [simile] lets us read is that the recognizable body guaranteeing the truth of the figure can be yet another figurative disguise" (51).

16. "Ha! welche Vorstellung, die den staunenden Geist über seine Linien wirbelt!—Ein Augenblick: Fürst: hat das Mark des ganzen Daseins verschlungen. Nicht der Tummelplatz des Lebens—sein Gehalt bestimmt seinen Wert" (*Fiesko* 382).

17. The English translation cannot convey the connotations expressed through the alternate spelling in the German original. However, the translation emphasizes that Fiesco counts on the masses, hoping that they will augment his hatred (*Fiesco*, 202; *Werke und Briefe*, 2:362).

18. In Emmanuel Schikaneder and Wolfgang Amadeus Mozart's opera *Die Zauberflöte* (*The Magic Flute*; 1791), Monastatos—"a Moor"—fulfills, at least in part, a similar aesthetic function. He personifies irrationality, a dubious yet physical presence of Nemesis (Schiller, *Werke*, 2:991); he perpetuates fears of dangerous sexuality associated with the black,

osmotic body when he attempts to rape Pamina; he inflicts terror on Papageno because of the view (blackness) he presents; he in turn is terrified by Papageno, thus linking blackness to the unnatural disguise of the birdman. He does not, as Nicholas Till claims, embody Pamina's "pre-social sexual desires" (285). However, as the opera brings out a multitude of epistemological issues, it is much too complex for adequate consideration here, let alone by a nonmusicologist (see Till, 270–319).

6   READING HISTORY, SEEING SELVES: THE TURN TO THE MODERN

1. I use the German originals of Kant's texts with the exception of his *Anthropology*, which is readily available in several reliable translations, and *Critique of Judgment*. Quotations from Herder's *Reflections* are modified and expanded upon whenever the edition omits passages from the original. All other translations are my own.
2. See Eigen and Larrimore for a welcome addition on the topic of race in Kant. Their edition contributes a refined understanding of the complex epistemological situation that fueled Kant's thinking and pinpoints threshold moments and parameters in the conceptual emergence of "race."
3. A recent essay by Eigen has opened up a new subset of research devoted to the eighteenth-century challenge of representing race visually through the mimetic representation of an individual. Since the image was judged by its quality of resemblance, it was left to the beholder to decipher "race."
4. I interpret the German original as referring to depictions of Chinese people and artwork by Chinese people, the latter including self-portraits and paintings in general.
5. Whereas Zammito uses the rhetoric of presumption to emphasize the differences in the revised version of the essay (1777), I am more interested in the implication that one should assume the racial matrix in order to classify what one sees.
6. See also Weissberg, 34–55, on the genealogy of the text (-body) as a result of Kant's attempt to "possess" the human body.
7. See chapter 5; *The German Invention of Race* reiterates this oscillation, especially in reference to Haller's theory of preformation (74); however, in my opinion, no one has pointed out the link to aesthetics.
8. See especially the rhetoric in books 3 through 5 of *Reflections*.
9. The 114th letter contains detailed notes on Herder's historical sources and references to geography (e.g., Delaware) and politics (the slave revolt in Haiti).
10. Herder conceded that the ear also gave rise to superstition (27).

11. I cannot fully explore the fact that Romanticism, including its notion of the Orient, also underwent an at least partial re-Christianization. Katherine Arens has discussed this phenomenon, especially "the Europe of Romantic Christianity" that became a driving force in Edward Said's (and subsequent) formulations of "Orientalist attitudes" (21–22).

12. See Martin Jay; Assenka Oksiloff's *Picturing the Primitive* suggests that the exotic has compensatory qualities.

BIBLIOGRAPHY

Abbeele, George van den. *Travel as Metaphor*. Minneapolis: University of Minnesota Press, 1992.

Agnew, Vanessa. "Pacific Island Encounters and the German Invention of Race." In *Islands in History and Representation*. Ed. Rod Edmond and Vanessa Smith. London: Routledge, 2003. 81–94.

Allen, Amy. "Foucault's Debt to Hegel." *Philosophy Today* 42.1 (1998): 71–80.

Allgemeine Deutsche Biographie. 56 vols. Leipzig: Duncker und Humblot, 1875–1912.

Ames, R.S. "The Meaning of Body in Classical Chinese Thought." *International Philosophical Quarterly* 24.1 (1984): 39–53.

Arens, Katherine. "Said's Colonial Fantasies. How Orientalism Marginalizes Eighteenth–Century Germans." *Herder Yearbook: Publications of the International Herder Society* 7 (2004): 11–29.

Armstrong, Meg. " 'The Effects of Blackness': Gender, Race, and the Sublime in Aesthetic Theories of Burke and Kant." *The Journal of Aesthetics and Art Criticism* 54.3 (1996): 213–36.

Armstrong, Nancy. *Desire and Domestic Fiction*. New York: Oxford University Press, 1987.

Ashcroft, Bill, and Garet Griffiths. *Post–Colonial Studies: The Key Concepts*. London: Routledge, 2000.

Aurich, Ursula. *China im Spiegel der deutschen Literatur des 18. Jahrhunderts*. Berlin: Ebering, 1935.

Bal, Mieke. "Reading the Gaze: The Construction of Gender in Rembrandt." In *Vision and Textuality*. Ed. Stephen Melville and Bill Readings. Durham, NC: Duke University Press, 1995. 147–76.

Barck, Karlheinz. "Amerika in Hegels Geschichtsphilosophie." *Weimarer Beiträge* 38.2 (1992): 274–78.

Barnouw, Dagmar. "Eräugnis: Georg Forster on the Difficulties of Diversity." *Impure Reason: Dialectic of Enlightenment in Germany*. Ed. W. Daniel Wilson and Robert Holub. Detroit: Wayne State University Press, 1993. 322–43.

Bartkowski, Frances. *Travelers, Immigrants, Inmates: Essays in Estrangement*. Minneapolis: University of Minnesota Press, 1995.

Baston, Thomas. *Thoughts on Trade and a Publick Spirit*. London, 1716.

[Beniowski, Graf Moritz August]. *Des Grafen Moritz August von Beniowski Reisen durch Sibirien und Kamschatka über Japan und China nach Europa. Nebst einem Auszuge seiner übrigen Lebensgeschichte*. Aus dem

Englischen übersetzt und mit Anmerkungen von J. Reinhold Forster. *Magazin von merkwürdigen neuen Reisebschreibungen* 3 (1790).

Berger, Willy Richard. *China-Bild und China-Mode im Europa der Aufklärung*. Cologne: Böhlau, 1990.

Berman, Russell. *Enlightenment or Empire: Colonial Discourse in German Culture*. Lincoln: University of Nebraska Press, 1998.

Bernasconi, Robert. "With What Must the Philosophy of World History Begin? On the Racial Basis of Hegel's Eurocentrism." *Nineteenth-Century Contexts* 22.2 (2000): 171–202.

Bersier, Gabriele. "The Education of a Prince: Wieland and German Enlightenment at School with Fénelon and Rousseau." *Eighteenth-Century Life* 10.1 (1986): 1–13.

Bhabha, Homi. "Interrogating Identity: The Postcolonial Prerogative." *Anatomy of Racism*. Ed. David Theo Goldberg. Minneapolis: University of Minnesota Press, 1991. 183–209.

———. "Remembering Fanon: Self, Psyche, and the Colonial Condition." *Colonial Discourse and Postcolonial Theory: A Reader*. Ed. Patrick Williams and Laura Chrisman. New York: Columbia University Press, 1994. 112–24.

Bindman, David. *Ape to Apollo: Aesthetics and the Idea of Race in the 18th Century*. Ithaca: Cornell University Press, 2002.

Blumenbach, Johann Friedrich. *De Generis Humanis Varietate Nativa*. Goettingae: Typis Frid. Andr. Rosenbuschii, 1775.

———. *Handbuch der Naturgeschichte*. 10th ed. Göttingen: Diederichsche Buchhandlung, 1821.

———. *Über die natürlichen Verschiedenheiten im Menschengeschlecht*. Leipzig: Breitkopf und Härtel, 1798.

Bode, Wilhelm. *Der weimarische Musenhof 1756–1781*. Berlin: Mittler & Sohn, 1920.

Bohm, Arnd. "Goethe and the Romantics." *The Literature of German Romanticism*. Ed. Dennis Mahoney. Rochester, NY: Camden House, 2004. 35–60.

Böhme, Hartmut, and Gernot Böhme. *Das Andere der Vernunft*. Frankfurt a. M.: Suhrkamp, 1983.

Borchert, Angela. "Gelegenheitsdichtung und Geselligkeitsdichtung an Herzogin Anna Amalias Hof in Weimar und in Tiefurt (1754–1807)." PhD diss., Princeton University, 2002.

Brennan, Timothy. "The Illusion of a Future: Orientalism as a Traveling Theory." *Critical Inquiry* 26.3 (2000): 558–83.

Brentjes, Burckard. *Anton Wilhelm Amo: Der schwarze Philosoph in Halle*. Leipzig: Koehler & Amelang, 1976.

———, ed. *Antonius Guilielmus Amo Afer aus Axim in Ghana: Student, Doktor der Philosophie, Magister Legens an den Universitäten Halle, Wittenberg, Jena 1727–1747*. Halle: Martin-Luther-Universität Halle-Wittenberg, 1978.

Bruford, W.H. *Culture and Society in Classical Weimar*. Cambridge: Cambridge University Press, 1962.

Buck-Morss, Susan. "Hegel and Haiti." *Critical Inquiry* 26.4 (2000): 821–66.

Burke, Edmund. *A Philosophical Enquiry into the Origin of Our Ideas of the Sublime and the Beautiful.* Oxford: Oxford University Press, 1990.

Burney, Ian Adnan. "Viewing Bodies: Medicine, Public Order, and English Inquest Practice." *Configurations* 2.1 (1994): 33–46.

Butler, Judith. *Gender Trouble.* New York: Routledge, 1990.

Camper, Peter. "Lecture on the Origin and Color of Blacks." In Meijer, *Race and Aesthetics.* 183–92.

———. "Rede über den Ursprung und die Farbe der Schwarzen gehalten in Groeningen auf der anatomischen Schaubühne den 14. November 1764." *Sämtliche kleinere Schriften die Arzneykunst und fürnehmlich die Naturgeschichte betreffend.* Leipzig: Crusius, 1787. 24–49.

Caplan, Jay. *Framed Narratives: Diderot's Genealogy of the Beholder.* Minneapolis: University of Minnesota Press, 1985.

Carretta, Vincent, and Philip Gould, eds. *Genius in Bondage: Literature of the Early Black Atlantic.* Lexington: University Press of Kentucky, 2001.

Ching, Julia, and Willard Oxtoby, eds. *Moral Enlightenment. Leibniz and Wolff on China.* Nettetal: Steyler, 1992.

Chow, Rey. *Women and Chinese Modernity. The Politics of Reading between East and West.* Minneapolis: University of Minnesota Press, 1991.

C.J.W. "Beytrag zur Geschichte des gefleckten Menschen." *Der Naturforscher* 22 (1787): 123–28.

Clifford, James. *The Predicament of Culture: Twentieth-Century Ethnography, Literature, and Art.* Cambridge, MA: Harvard University Press, 1988.

Cook, Daniel J., and Henry Rosemont Jr., eds. *Gottfried Wilhelm Leibniz: Writings on China.* Chicago: Open Court, 1994.

Cossigny, Carpentier de. *Reise nach China und Bengalen.* Mit einer Landkarte. *Magazin der merkwürdigen neuen Reisebeschreibungen* 22 (1801).

Crump, Thomas. *The Anthropology of Numbers.* Cambridge: Cambridge University Press, 1990.

Dawson, Raymond. *The Chinese Chameleon.* London: Oxford University Press, 1967.

Debon, Günther. "Freiherr von Seckendorff als Du Fu." *China zu Gast in Weimar: 18 Studien und Streiflichter.* Heidelberg: Guderjahn, 1994. 51–78.

Deleuze, Gilles. *The Fold: Leibniz and the Baroque.* Minneapolis: University of Minnesota Press, 1993.

"Der Chinesische Sittenlehrer." In *Das Journal von Tiefurt.* 79–81. 112–14.

Dirlik, Arif. "Chinese History and the Question of Orientalism." *History and Theory* 35.4 (1996): 96–118.

Douthwaite, Julia V. *Exotic Women: Literary Heroines and Cultural Strategies in Ancient Regime France.* Philadelphia: University of Pennsylvania Press, 1992.

Duden, Barbara. *The Woman beneath the Skin. A Doctor's Patients in Eighteenth-Century Germany.* Cambridge, MA: Harvard University Press, 1991.

Dyer, Richard. *White.* London: Routledge, 1997.

Eco, Umberto. *Serendipities.* New York: Columbia University Press, 1998.

Eigen, Sara. "Self, Race, and Species: J. F. Blumenbach's Atlas-Experiment." *German Quarterly* 78.3 (2005): 277–98.

Eigen, Sara, and Mark Larrimore, eds. *The German Invention of Race.* Albany: State University of New York Press, 2006.

Eigler, Friederike, and Susanne Kord. *The Feminist Encyclopedia of German Literature.* Westport, CT: Greenwood Press, 1997.

Elias, Norbert. *Die höfische Gesellschaft.* Frankfurt a. M.: Suhrkamp, 1969.

El-Tayeb, Fatima. *Der Diskurs um "Rasse" und nationale Identität.* Frankfurt a. M.: Campus, 2001.

Fenves, Peter. *Arresting Language: From Leibniz to Benjamin.* Stanford: Stanford University Press, 2001.

———. "What 'Progresses' Has Race-Theory Made since the Times of Leibniz and Wolff?" In *The German Invention of Race.* Ed. Eigen and Larrimore. 11–22.

Figlio, Karl M. "The Metaphor of Organization: A Historiographical Perspective on the Bio-Medical Sciences of the Early Nineteenth Century." *History of Sciences* 14.1 (1976): 17–53.

———. "Theories of Perception and the Physiology of Mind in the Late Eighteenth Century." *History of Sciences* 13.3 (1975): 177–212.

Figueira, Dorothy. *Aryans, Jews, Brahmins: Theorizing Authority Through Myths of Identity.* Albany: State University of New York Press, 2002.

Fischer, Caroline Auguste. *Kleine Erzählungen und romantische Skizzen.* Ed. Anita Runge. Hildesheim: Olms, 1988.

———. "William the Negro." *Bitter Healing.* Trans. and ed. Jeannine Blackwell and Susanne Zantop. Lincoln: University of Nebraska Press, 1990. 349–68.

Forster, Georg. *Kleine Schriften zur Völker- und Länderkunde. Georg Forsters Werke. Sämtliche Schriften, Tagebücher, Briefe.* Vol. 5. Ed. Gerhard Steiner. Berlin: Akademie-Verlag, 1985.

———. *Reise um die Welt. Georg Forsters Werke. Sämtliche Schriften, Tagebücher, Briefe.* Ed. Gerhard Steiner. Vols. 2 and 3. Berlin: Akademie-Verlag, 1965.

———. *Voyage around the World. Georg Forsters Werke. Sämtliche Schriften, Tagebücher, Briefe.* Vol. 1. Ed. Gerhard Steiner. Berlin: Akademie-Verlag, 1968.

Foucault, Michel. *The Archeology of Knowledge.* New York: Pantheon, 1972.

———. *Discipline and Punish: The Birth of the Prison.* New York: Vintage, 1979.

———. *The History of Sexuality.* New York: Vintage, 1990.

———. "Of Other Spaces." *Diacritics* 16.1 (1986): 22–27.

———. *The Order of Things: An Archeology of Human Sciences.* New York: Vintage Books, 1973.

Friedrichsmeyer, Sarah, Sara Lennox, and Susanne Zantop, eds. *The Imperialist Imagination: German Colonialism and Its Legacy.* Ann Arbor: University of Michigan Press, 1998.

Gilman, Sander. "Black Bodies, White Bodies: Towards an Iconography of Female Sexuality in Late Nineteenth-Century Medicine and Literature." *Critical Inquiry* 12.1 (1985): 204–42.

———. "The Hottentot and the Prostitute: Toward an Iconography of Female Sexuality." *Difference and Pathology. Stereotypes of Sexuality, Race, and Madness.* Ithaca, NY: Cornell University Press, 1985. 76–108.

———. *On Blackness without Blacks: Essays on the Image of the Black in Germany.* Boston: G. K. Hall, 1982.

Gilroy, Paul. *Against Race: Imagining Political Culture Beyond the Color Line.* Cambridge, MA: Harvard University Press, 2000.

Glasenapp, Gerhard von. *Die fünf Weltreligionen.* Munich: Diederichs, 1964.

Goebel, Rolf F. *Constructing China: Kafka's Orientalist Discourse.* Columbia, SC: Camden House, 1997.

Goethe, Johann Wolfgang. *Goethes Werke.* Hamburg: Christian Wegner Verlag, 1966–1972.

Goetschel, Willi, "Epilogue: 'Land of Truth—Enchanting Name!' Kant's Journey at Home" In *The Imperialist Imagination: German Colonialism and Its Legacy.* Ed. Friedrichsmeyer, Lennox and Zantop. Ann Arbor: University of Michigan Press, 1998. 321–36.

Goldberg, David Theo, ed. *Multiculturalism: A Critical Reader.* Oxford: Oxford University Press, 1994.

Gray, Marion. *Productive Men, Reproductive Women: The Agrarian Household and the Emergence of Separate Spheres during the Enlightenment.* New York: Berghahn Books, 2000.

Gray, Richard. *About Face: German Physiognomic Thought from Lavater to Auschwitz.* Detroit: Wayne State University Press, 2004.

———. "Buying into Signs: Money and Semiosis in Eighteenth-Century German Language Theory." *German Quarterly* 69.1 (1996): 1–14.

Green, Malcolm, and Hedwig Schmidt-Glintzer. *A Treasure House of Books: The Library of Duke August of Brunswick-Wolfenbüttel.* Wolfenbüttel: Herzog August Bibliothek, 1998.

Griep, Wolfgang, and Hans-Wolf Jäger, eds. *Reise und soziale Realität am Ende des achtzehnten Jahrhunderts.* Heidelberg: Carl Winter Universitätsverlag, 1983.

Grimm, Jacob, and Wilhelm Grimm. *Deutsches Wörterbuch.* 1893. Munich: dtv, 1984.

Grimminger, Rolf, ed. *Deutsche Aufklärung bis zur Französischen Revolution 1680–1789.* Munich: dtv, 1980.

Günderrode, Karoline von. *Der Schatten eines Traumes.* Neuwied: Luchterhand, 1981.

Gwilliam, Tassie. "Cosmetic Poetics: Coloring Faces in the Eighteenth Century." In *Body and Text in the Eighteenth Century.* Ed. Kelly and von Mücke. Stanford: Stanford University Press, 1994. 144–59.

Haas, Norbert. "Sehen und Beschreiben." In *Reise und soziale Realität am Ende des achtzehnten Jahrhunderts.* Ed. Wolfgang Griep and Hans-Wolf Jäger. Heidelberg: Carl Winter Universitätsverlag, 1983. 1–13.

Habermas, Jürgen. *Strukturwandel der Öffentlichkeit.* Neuwied: Luchterhand, 1965.

Hähnel, Birgit. " 'Skin/Deep': Unterschiedliche Perspektiven in der Repräsentation schwarzer und weißer Frauenbilder in der zeitgenössischen Kunst." In *Beschreiben und Erfinden.* Ed. Hölz and Schmidt-Linsenhoff. 173–95.

Hallberg, Peter. "The Nature of Collective Individuals: J. G. Herder's Concept of Community." *History of European Ideas* 25 (1999): 291–304.

Harris-Schenz, Beverly. *Black Images in Eighteenth-Century German Literature.* Stuttgart: Heinz, 1981.

Härtel, Helmar. "Duke August and His Book Agents." In *A Treasure House of Books,* Ed. Green and Schmidt-Glintzer, 105–18.

Hartsock, Nancy. "Rethinking Modernism." *The Nature and Context of Minority Discourse.* Ed. Abdul JanMohamed and David Lloyd. Oxford: Oxford University Press, 1990. 17–36.

Heckendorn Cook, Elizabeth. *Epistolary Bodies: Gender and Genre in the Eighteenth-Century Republic of Letters.* Stanford: Stanford University Press, 1995.

———. "The Limping Woman and the Public Sphere." In *Body and Text.* Kelly and von Mücke. 23–44.

Hegel, Georg Wilhelm Friedrich. *The Philosophy of History.* Trans. J. Sibree and intro. C.J. Friedrich. New York: Dover, 1956.

———. *Vorlesungen über die Philosophie der Geschichte. Werke.* Vol. 12. Frankfurt a. M.: Suhrkamp, 1986.

Heimendahl, Echkard. *Licht und Farbe.* Berlin: de Gruyter, 1961.

Helfer, Martha B., ed. *Re-Reading Romanticism.* Amsterdam: Rodopi, 1999.

———. *The Retreat of Representation: The Concept of Darstellung in German Critical Discourse.* Albany: State University of New York Press, 1996.

Henke, Burkhard, Susanne Kord, and Simon Richter, eds. *Unwrapping Goethe's Weimar.* Rochester, NY: Camden House, 2000.

Hentges, Gudrun. "Die Erfindung der 'Rasse' um 1800—Klima, Säfte und Phlogiston in der Rassentheorie Immanuel Kants." In *Colors.* Ed. Tautz, 47–66.

Hentschel, Uwe. "Die Reiseliteratur am Ausgang des 18. Jahrhunderts: Vom gelehrten Bericht zur literarischen Beschreibung." *Internationales Archiv für Sozialgeschichte der deutschen Literatur* 16.2 (1991): 51–83.

Herder, Johann Gottfried. *Reflections on the Philosophy of History of Mankind.* Trans. and ed. Frank Manuel. Chicago: University of Chicago Press, 1968.

———. *Sämmtliche Werke.* Ed. Bernhard Suphan. Berlin: Weidmannsche Buchhandlung, 1887.

Hess, Jonathan. *Reconstituting the Body Politic: Enlightenment, Public Culture, and the Invention of Aesthetic Autonomy.* Detroit: Wayne State University Press, 1999.

Hilbert, David. *Color and Color Perception: A Study on Anthropocentric Realism.* Stanford: Center for the Study of Language and Information, 1987.

Hinderer, Walter, ed. *Goethe und das Zeitalter der Romantik*. Würzburg: Königshausen & Neumann, 2002.

Hölz, Karl, and Victoria Schmidt-Linsenhoff, eds. *Beschreiben und Erfinden: Figuren des Fremden vom 18. bis zum 20. Jahrhundert*. Frankfurt a. M.: Peter Lang, 2000.

Honegger, Claudia. *Die Ordnung der Geschlechter: Die Wissenschaften vom Menschen und das Weib 1750–1850*. New York: Campe, 1991.

Honold, Alexander, and Klaus R. Scherpe, eds. *Das Fremde: Schreiberfahrungen, Schreibformen und kulturelles Wissen*. Berlin: Peter Lang, 1999.

Hsia, Adrian, ed. *Deutsche Denker über China*. Frankfurt a. M.: Insel, 1985.

Hull, Isabel. *Sexuality, State, and Civil Society in Germany 1700–1815*. Ithaca, NY: Cornell University Press, 1996.

Ivanhoe, Philip J. "Filial Piety as a Virtue." *Filial Piety in Chinese Thought and History*. Ed. Alan Chan and Sor-hoon Tan. London: Routledge Curzon, 2004. 353–77.

Jay, Martin. *Downcast Eyes: The Denigration of Vision in Twentieth-Century French Thought*. Berkeley: University of California Press, 1993.

Das Journal von Tiefurt, 1781–1784. Ed. Eduard von der Hellen. Weimar: Verlag der Goethe–Gesellschaft, 1892.

Kant, Immanuel. *Anthropology from a Pragmatic Point of View*. Trans. and intro. Mary Gregor. The Hague: Martinus Nijoff, 1974.

———. *Critique of Judgment*. Trans. Werner Pluhar. Indianapolis: Hackett, 1987.

———. *Werke*. Ed. Akademie der Wissenschaften Berlin: Carl Reimer /de Gruyter, 1905.

Kelly, Michael, ed. *Critique and Power*. Cambridge: MIT Press, 1994.

Kelly, Veronica, and Dorothea von Mücke. *Body and Text in the Eighteenth Century*. Stanford: Stanford University Press, 1994.

Ketelsen, Uwe-K. "Die Anonymisierung des Buchmarktes und die Inszenierung der 'Speaking Voice' in der erotischen Lyrik um 1700." *Literary Culture in the Holy Roman Empire, 1555–1720*. Ed. James Parente, Erich E. Schade, and Georg C. Schoolfield Chapel Hill: University of North Carolina Press, 1991. 259–76.

Kittler, Friedrich. *Aufschreibesysteme 1800/1900*. Munich: Fink, 1987.

Kleist, Heinrich von. *Die Verlobung in St. Domingo. Kleists Werke*. Berlin: Aufbau 1961. 188–227.

Klinger, Friedrich Maximilian. *Sturm und Drang. Werke in zwei Bänden*. Vol 1. Ed. H.-J. Geerdts. Berlin: Aufbau, 1970.

Klüger, Ruth. "Fremdheit, die ich meine: Fremdherrschaft in Kleists 'Hermannsschlacht' und 'Verlobung in St. Domingo.' " *Katastrophen*. Göttingen: Wallstein, 1994. 133–62.

Kluge, Gerhard, ed. *Friedrich Schiller: Werke und Briefe*. Vol 2. Frankfurt a. M.: Deutsche Klassiker Verlag, 1989.

Kolb, Peter. *Beschreibung des Vorgebürges der guten Hoffnung und der darauf wohnenden Hottentotten*. Frankfurt a. M.: n. p., 1745.

Kord, Susanne. "From Werther Cult to Goethe Cult." Unpublished conference talk, ASECS March 31, 2006.

———. "The Hunchback of Weimar: Louise von Göchhausen and the Weimar Grotesque." In *Unwrapping Goethes Weimar*. Ed. Henke, Kord und Richter. 233–72.

Koschorke, Albrecht. *Körperströme und Schriftverkehr. Mediologie des 18. Jahrhunderts.* Munich: Fink, 1999.

Kotzebue, August von. *Die Negersklaven.* Leipzig: Kummer, 1796.

Krell, David Farrell. "The Bodies of Black Folk: From Kant and Hegel to Du Bois and Baldwin." *boundary 2* 27.3 (2000): 103–34.

Krimmer, Elisabeth. *In the Company of Men: Cross-Dressed Women around 1800.* Detroit: Wayne State University Press, 2004.

Kukendall, Ronald. "Hegel and Africa: An Evaluation of the Treatment of African the Philosophy of History." *Journal of Black Studies* 23.4 (1993): 571–81.

Kutter, Uli. *Reisen—Reisehandbücher—Wissenschaft: Materialien zur Reisekultur im 18. Jahrhundert.* Neuwied: Ars Una, 1996.

Kuzniar, Alice. "Hearing Women's Voices in Heinrich von Ofterdingen." *PMLA* 107.4 (1992): 1196–207.

Lacoue-Labarthe, Philippe. *Heidegger, Art, and Politics: The Fiction of the Political.* Oxford: Blackwell, 1990.

Laqueur, Thomas. *Making Sex: Body and Gender from the Greeks to Freud.* Cambridge, MA: Harvard University Press, 1992.

Larrimore, Mark. "Orientalism and Antivoluntarism in the History of Ethics: On Christian Wolff's *Oratio De Sinarum Philosophia Practica*." *Journal of Religious Ethics* 28.2 (2000): 189–219.

———. "Race, Freedom and the Fall in Steffens and Kant." In *The German Invention of Race*. Ed. Eigen and Larrimore. 91–120.

Laugero, Greg. "Infrastructure of Enlightenment: Road-Making, the Public Sphere, and the Emergence of Literature." *Eighteenth-Century Studies* 29.1 (1995): 45–67.

Lavater, Johann Caspar. *Physiognomische Fragmente zur Beförderung der Menschenkenntnis und Menschenliebe.* Leipzig: Edition Leipzig, 1968.

Leibniz, Gottfried Wilhelm. *Discourse on the Natural Theology of the Chinese.* In *Leibniz: Writings on China*. Ed. Cook and Rosemount, 75–138. Chicago: Open Court, 1994.

———."Das Geheimnis der Schöpfung." *Zwei Briefe über das Zahlensystem und die chinesische Philosophie.* Stuttgart: Chr. Belser Verlag, 1968. 19–23.

———. *Lettre sur la philosophie chinoise à Nicolas de Remond. Zwei Briefe,* 34–134.

———. *New Essays on Human Understanding.* New York: Macmillan, 1896.

———. "On the Ultimate Origination of the Universe." *Monadology and Other Philosophical Essays.* Ed. Anne Marie Schrecker. New York: Macmillan, 1965. 84–94.

————. "Postscript to a Letter to Banage De Beauvai." *Philosophical Essays.* Ed. Roger Ariew and Daniel Garber. Indianapolis: Hackett, 1989. 147–49.

————. "Vorrede: Novissima Sinica." In *Deutsche Denker über China.* Ed. Hsia. 9–27.

Leidner, Alan, and Karin Wurst. *Unpopular Virtues: The Critical Reception of J. M. R. Lenz.* Columbia, SC: Camden House, 1999.

Lenz, Jakob Michael Reinhold. *Der Hofmeister oder die Vortheile der Privaterziehung.* Basel: Stroemfeld, 1986.

————. *Der Neue Menoza.* Berlin: de Gruyter, 1965.

Lessing, Karl Gotthelf. *Die Mätresse.* Heilbronn: Henninger, 1887.

Le Vaillant, François. *Le Vaillants Reisen in das Innere von Afrika.* Mit Anmerkungen von Johann Reinhold Forster. *Magazin von merkwürdigen neuen Reisebeschreibungen* 2 (1790).

Lichtenberg, Georg Christoph. "Von den Kriegs- und Fast-Schulen der Schinesen." In *Deutsche Denker über China.* Ed. Hsia. 103–16.

Liu, Yu. "The Jesuits and Anti-Jesuits: The Two Different Connections of Leibniz with China." *The Eighteenth Century* 43.2 (2002): 161–74.

Lode, Imke. "The Body in the Discourses of Colonial Savage and European Woman during the Enlightenment." *Women in German Yearbook* 11 (1995): 205–22.

Loschge. "Beytrag zur Geschichte der ungewöhnlichen Farben des Menschen." *Der Naturforscher* 23 (1788): 213–22.

Lowe, Lisa. *Critical Terrains: French and British Orientalism.* Ithaca, NY: Cornell University Press, 1992.

Luhmann, Niklas. *The Differentiation of Society.* New York: Columbia University Press, 1982.

————. "Das Problem der Epochenbildung in der Evolutionstheorie." In *Epochenschwellen und Epochenstrukturen im Diskurs der Literatur- und Sprachtheorie.* Ed. Hans-Ulrich Gumbrecht and Ursula Link-Heer. Frankfurt a. M.: Suhrkamp, 1985. 11–33.

Lyotard, Francois. "Sensus Communis: The Subject in Status Nascendi." *Paragraph* 11.1 (1988): 1–23.

Martin, Peter. *Schwarze Teufel, edle Mohren. Afrikaner in Bewußtsein und Geschichte der Deutschen.* Hamburg: Junius Verlag, 1993.

Marx, Werner. *Hegel's Phenomenology of Spirit.* Trans. Peter Heath. Chicago: University of Chicago Press, 1988.

Mattenklott, Gert. *Der übersinnliche Leib: Beiträge zur Metaphysik des Leibes.* Reinbek bei Hamburg: Rowohlt, 1982.

Matuschek, Stefan. *Literarische Spieltheorie.* Heidelberg: Carl Winter Universitätsverlag, 1998.

Maupertius. *Venus Physique.* Paris: n.p., 1751.

Mauser, Wolfram. "Freundschaft und Verführung." In *Frauenfreundschaft— Männerfreundschaft: Literarische Diskurse im 18. Jahrhundert.* Ed. Wolfram Mauser and Barbara Becker-Cantarino. Tübingen: Max Niemeyer Verlag, 1991. 213–35.

McCarthy, John. "The Gallant Novel and the German Enlightenment, 1670–1750." In *Anticipation of the Enlightenment in England, France, and Germany*. Ed. A.C. Kors and P.J. Korshin. Philadelphia: University of Philadelphia Press, 1987. 185–217.

Meijer, Miriam Claude. *Race and Aesthetics in the Anthropology of Petrus Camper (1722–1789)*. Amsterdam: Rodopi, 1999.

Mendelssohn, Moses. "Anmerkungen über das englische Buch: On the Sublime and the Beautiful." *Gesammelte Schriften* III.1. Stuttgart-Bad Cannstatt: F. Frommann, 1971. 237–53.

Metternich, Matthias. "Etwas über Aufklärung." *Der Patriot* 1791/92: n.p.

Michel, Andreas. " 'Our European Arrogance': Wilhelm Worringer and Carl Einstein on Non-European Art." In *Colors*. Ed. Tautz. Amsterdam: Rodopi, 2004. 143–62.

Mielke, Andreas. *Laokoon und die Hottentotten*. Baden-Baden: Koerner, 1993.

Montesquieu, Charles de Secondat. *Persian Letters*. Baltimore: Penguin, 1973.

Müller, G.H. "Beschreibung der Haare und Haut des Menschen von Martin Frobenius Ledermüller (1719–1769)." *Hautarzt* 28.1 (1977): 28–31.

Müller, Thomas. *Rhetorik und bürgerliche Identität. Studie zur Rolle der Psychologie in der Frühaufklärung*. Tübingen: Max Niemeyer Verlag, 1990.

Murti, Kamakshi P. *India: The Seductive and Seduced "Other" of German Orientalism*. Westport, CT: Greenwood Press, 2001.

Musgrave, Marion. "Herder, Blacks, and the 'Negeridyllen': A Study in Ambivalent Humanitarianism." *Studia Africana* 1 (1977): 89–99.

———. "Literary Justification of Slavery." In *Blacks in German Culture*. Ed. Reinhold Grimm and Jost Hermand. Madison: University of Wisconsin Press, 1990. 3–21.

Needham, Joseph. *Science and Civilization in China*. Vol. 2. Cambridge: Cambridge University Press, 1956.

Nordhofen, Eckard. "Der greinende Moloch: Philosophische Motive des Exotismus." *Exotische Welten—Europäische Phantasien*. Ed. Institut für Auslandsbeziehungen. Stuttgart: Edition Cantz, 1987. 34–39.

Noyes, John. *Colonial Space: Spatiality in the Discourse of German South West Africa 1884–1914*. Chur: Harwood, 1992.

———. *Hegel and the Fate of Negativity after Empire*. http://www.semioticon.com/virtuals/postcolonialism_2/Noyes%20Hegel.htm (accessed date, October 20, 2006).

Nussbaum, Felicity, ed. *The Global Eighteenth Century*. Baltimore: Johns Hopkins University Press, 2003.

———. *The Limits of the Human: Fictions of Anomaly, Race, and Gender in the Long Eighteenth Century*. Cambridge: Cambridge University Press, 2003.

Observationes. Afst/H A 164. Halle: Franckesche Stiftungen, n. d.

Oksiloff, Assenka. *Picturing the Primitive: Visual Culture, Ethnography, and Early German Cinema.* New York: Palgrave, 2001.

Ong, Walter J. *Orality and Literacy: The Technologizing of the World.* London: Routledge, 1982.

Osterhammel, Jürgen. "Edward Said und die Orientalismus-Debatte: Ein Rückblick." *Asien, Afrika, Lateinamerika* 25.6 (1997): 597–607.

Palumbo-Liu, David. "Schrift und kulturelles Potential in China." In *Materialität der Zeichen.* Ed. Hans-Ulrich Gumbrecht and K. Ludwig Pfeiffer. Munich: Fink, 1993.

Pan, David. *Primitive Renaissance: Rethinking German Expressionism.* Lincoln: University of Nebraska Press, 2001.

Paulinus. *Des Fra Paolino da San Bartolomeo Reise nach Ostindien.* Aus dem Französischen. Mit Anmerkungen von Johann Reinhold Forster. *Magazin von merkwürdigen neuen Reisebeschreibungen* 15 (1798).

Pelz, Annegret. *Reisen durch die eigene Fremde.* Cologne: Böhlau, 1993.

Plotnitsky, Arkady. "Closing the Eye: Hegel, Derrida, and the Closure of Philosophy." In *Agonistics: Areas of Creative Contest.* Ed. Janet Lungstrum and Elizabeth Sauer. Albany: State University of New York Press, 1997. 70–91.

Porter, David. *Ideographia: The Chinese Cipher in Early Modern Europe.* Stanford: Stanford University Press, 2001.

Porter, Dennis. *Haunted Journeys: Desire and Transgression in European Travel Writing.* Princeton: Princeton University Press, 1991.

Pratt, Mary Louise. *Imperial Eyes: Travel Writing and Transculturation.* London: Routledge, 1992.

Purdy, Daniel. "The Discipline of Elegance." Unpublished manuscript. 1997.

———. *The Tyranny of Elegance: Consumer Cosmopolitanism in the Era of Goethe.* Baltimore: Johns Hopkins University Press, 1998.

———. "The Whiteness of Beauty: Weimar Neo-Classicism and the Sculptural Transcendence of Color." In *Colors.* Tautz. 83–100.

"Das Rad des Schicksals." In *Das Journal von Tiefurt,* 83–85, 94–97, 141–43.

Radhakrishnan, R. "Ethnic Identity and Post-Structuralist Difference." *The Nature and Context of Minority Discourse.* Ed. Abdul JanMohamed and David Lloyd. Oxford: Oxford University Press, 1990. 50–71.

Rajan, Gita. "Labyrinths of the Colonial Archive: Unpacking German Missionary Narratives from Tranquebar Southeast India (1706–1720)." PhD diss., University of Michigan, 2001.

Rathlef, Ernst Lorenz Michael. *Die Mohrinn zu Hamburg.* n.p., 1775.

Redfield, Marc. "The Dissection of the State: Wilhelm Meisters Wanderjahre and the Politics of Aesthetics." *German Quarterly* 69.1 (1996): 15–31.

"Reise des Herrn Von M** nach China in den Jahren 1773 und 74." *Der Teutsche Merkur* (1775): 66–83; 132–48; 244–69.

Renouard, Felix de Sainte-Croix. *Reise nach Ostindien, den Philippinischen Inseln und China.* Aus dem Französischen übersetzt von Ph. Chr. Weyland. *Magazin von merkwürdigen neuen Reisebeschreibungen* 32 (1811).

Rivlin, Robert, and Karen Gravelle. *Deciphering the Senses: The Expanding World of Human Perception.* New York: Simon and Schuster, 1984.

[Rochon, Alexis?]. *Des Abbe Rochons Reise nach Madagaskar und Ostindien. Magazin der merkwürdigen neuen Reisebeschreibungen.* Aus fremden Sprachen übersetzt und mit erläuternden Anmerkungen begleitet. Berlin: Voss, 1792.

Rotman, Brian. *Signifying Nothing: The Semiotics of Zero.* Stanford: Stanford University Press, 1987.

Russon, John. "Reading and the Body in Hegel." *Clio* 22.4 (1993): 321–36.

Saccamano, Neil. "Wit Breaks." In *Body and Text.* Ed. Kelly and von Mücke. 45–67.

Sadji, Uta. *Der Moor auf der deutschen Bühne des 18. Jahrhunderts.* Salzburg: Ursula Müller-Speiser, 1992.

———. *Der Negermythos am Ende des 18. Jahrhunderts: Analyse der Rezeption der Reiseliteratur über Schwarzafrika.* New York: Peter Lang, 1979.

Said, Edward. *Orientalism.* New York: Pantheon, 1978.

———. "Orientalism, an Afterword." *Raritan* 14.3 (1995): 32–60.

Sautermeister, Gert. *Idyllik und Dramatik im Werk Friedrich Schillers: Zum geschichtlichen Ort seiner klassischen Dramen.* Stuttgart: Kohlhammer, 1971.

Schaub, Uta. "Foucault's Oriental Subtext." *PMLA* 104.3 (1989): 306–16.

Schiebinger, Londa. "The Anatomy of Difference: Race and Sex in Eighteenth-Century Science." *Eighteenth-Century Studies* 23.4 (1990): 387–405.

Schiller, Friedrich. *Fiesco. Works.* Trans. and ed. Nathan Haskell Dole. Vol. 12. Boston: Francis Niccolls & Company, 1902.

———. *Schiller's Works.* No named translator. Chicago: Belford, n. d.

———. "Was kann eine gute Schaubühne wirken?" *Schillers Werke.* Vol. 20. Weimar: Hermann Böhlaus Nachfolger, 1962. 87–100.

———. *Werke und Briefe.* Ed. Gerhard Kluge. Vol. 2. Frankfurt a. M.: Deutsche Klassiker Verlag, 1989.

Schings, H.-J. *Melancholie und Aufklärung: Melancholiker und ihre Kritiker in Erfahrungsseelenkunde und Literatur des 18. Jahrhunderts.* Stuttgart: Metzler, 1977.

Schlözer, August Ludwig. *Vorlesungen über Land- und Seereisen 1795–96.* Göttingen: Musterschmid, 1962.

Schmidt, Gunnar. "Von Tropfen und Spiegeln: Medienlogik und Wissen im 17. Jahrhundert." *KulturPoetik* 2.1 (2002): 1–23.

Schmidt-Biggemann, Wilhelm. "Aufklärung durch Metaphysik: Zur Rolle der Theodizee in der Aufklärung." *Herder-Jahrbuch/Herder Yearbook 1994.* Ed. Wilfried Malch. Stuttgart: Metzler, 1994. 104–14.

Schor, Naomi. *Reading in Detail: Aesthetics and the Feminine.* New York: Methuen, 1987.

Schrecker, John. *Filial Piety as Basis for Human Rights.* Honolulu: East-West Center, 1995.

Schrecker, Paul, and Anne Marie Schrecker. *Monadology and Other Philosophical Essays.* New York: Macmillan, 1965.

Schubert, Mary Hurst, ed. *Wilhelm Heinrich Wackenroder's Confessions and Fantasies*. University Park: Pennsylvania State University Press, 1971.

Schulte-Sasse, Jochen. "From the Body's to the Mind's Imagination." Unpublished essay. University of Minnesota, 1995.

———, ed. *Gotthold Ephraim Lessing: Briefwechsel über das Trauerspiel*. Munich: Winkler, 1972.

———. "High/Low and Other Dichotomies." *High and Low Cultures: German Attempts at Mediation*. Ed. Reinhold Grimm and Jost Hermand. Madison: University of Wisconsin Press, 1994. 3–18.

Schuster, Ingrid. *Vorbilder und Zerrbilder: China und Japan im Spiegel der deutschen Literatur 1773–1890*. Frankfurt a. M.: Peter Lang, 1988.

Schroer, Karl Julius. "Minervas Geburt. Schattenspiel zu Ehren Goethes in der Schilderung des Herzogs Karl August." *Westermanns illustrierte deutsche Monatshefte* 29 (1885) 57: 754–64.

Seckendorff, Karl Siegmund von. *Das Rad des Schiksals oder die Geschichte Tschon-gsees*. Dessau: Buchhandlung der Gelehrten, 1783.

———. "Über Minervens Geburth, Leben und Thaten." *Goethe Jahrbuch*. Vol. 7. Frankfurt a. M.: Rütten und Lönig, 1886.

———. *Weimarsche Briefe*. Leipzig: Polz, 1865.

Seyhan, Azade. *Representation and Its Discontents: The Critical Legacy of German Romanticism*. Berkeley: University of California Press, 1992.

Sharpley-Whiting, T. Denean. *Sexualized Savages, Primal Fears, and Primitive Narratives in French*. Durham, NC: Duke University Press, 1999.

Shell, Susan M. "Kant's Concept of a Human Race." In *The German Invention of Race*, Ed. Eigen and Larrimore, 55–72.

Smith, Samuel Stanhope. *An Essay on the Causes of the Variety of Complexion and Figure in the Human Species*. Philadelphia: n.p., 1788.

Sömmerring, Samuel Thomas von. *Über die körperliche Verschiedenheit des Negers vom Europäer*. Frankfurt a. M.: Varrentrapp Sohn und Wenner, 1785.

[Sonnerat, Pierre]. *Des Herrn Sonnerats Reise nach Ostindien, und China, in den Jahren 1774 bis 1781 nebst dessen Beobachtungen über Pegu, Madagascar, das Cap, die Inseln France und Bourbon, die Maldiven, Ceylon, Malacca, die Philippinen und Molucken, aus dem Französischen*. Leipzig: W. G. Sommers, 1783.

Sorkin, David. "Reclaiming Theology for the Enlightenment: The Case of Siegmund Jacob Baumgarten (1706–1757)." *Central European History* 36.4 (2003): 503–30.

Spacks, Patricia Meyer. *Boredom: The Literary History of a State of Mind*. Chicago: University of Chicago Press, 1995.

Spencer, Vicki. "Towards an Ontology of Holistic Individualism: Herder's Theory of Identity, Culture, and Community." *History of European Ideas* 22.3 (1996): 245–60.

Spivak, Gayatri Chakravorty. *Critique of Postcolonial Reason: Toward a History of the Vanishing Present*. Cambridge, MA: Harvard University Press, 1999.

Stafford, Barbara Maria. *Artful Science: Enlightenment, Entertainment, and the Eclipse of Visual Education*. Cambridge, MA: MIT Press, 1994.

———. *Body Criticism: Imagining the Unseen in Enlightenment Art and Medicine*. Cambridge, MA: MIT Press, 1991.

———. *Good Looking: Essays on the Virtue of Images*. Cambridge, MA: MIT Press, 1996.

———. "Voyeur or Observer? Enlightenment Thoughts on the Dilemmas of Display." *Configurations* 1.1 (1992): 95–128.

Stern, Dagmar E. "Schiller's 'Die Verschwörung des Fiesco zu Genua': A Blueprint of Democratic Evolution." *Michigan German Studies* 17.2 (1991): 89–98.

Stoler, Ann Laura. *Race and the Education of Desire: Foucault's History of Sexuality and the Colonial Order of Things*. Durham, NC: Duke University Press, 1995.

Sun, Ying. *Wandlungen des europäischen Chinabildes in illustrierten Reiseberichten des 17. und 18. Jahrhunderts*. Frankfurt a. M.: Peter Lang, 1996.

Suphan, Bernhard. "Einleitung." In *Das Journal*, vii–xxxvi. Ed. Hellen.

Sutherland, Wendy. "Black Skin, White Skin, and the Aesthetics of the Female Body in Ziegler's 'Die Mohrinn.' " In *Colors*. Ed. Tautz. 67–82.

———. "Staging Blackness: Race, Aesthetics, and the Black Female in Two Eighteenth-Century German Dramas: Ernst Lorenz Rathlef's 'Die Mohrinn Zu Hamburg' (1775) and Karl Friedrich Wilhelm Ziegler's 'Die Mohrinn' (1801)." PhD diss., University of Pennsylvania, 2002.

Tautz, Birgit. "Autopoeisis of World, Rhetoric of the Orient." *Monatshefte* 95.1 (2003): 59–75.

———, ed. *Colors 1800/1900/2000: Signs of Ethnic Difference*. Amsterdam: Rodopi, 2004.

———. "Cutting, Pasting, Fabricating: Late Eighteenth-Century Travelogues and Their German Translators between Legitimacy, Community, and Imaginary Nations." *German Quarterly* 79.2 (2006): 155–72.

Taylor, Charles. "The Politics of Recognition." In *Multiculturalism*. Ed. Goldberg. 75–106.

Theweleit, Klaus. *Male Fantasies*. Vol. 1. Minneapolis: University of Minnesota Press, 1987.

Thunberg, Karl Peter. *Karl Peter Thunbergs, Ritters des Was-Ordens und Professors der Botanik in Upsala, Reisen in Afrika und Asien, vorzüglich in Japan, während der Jahre 1772 bis 1779*. Auszugsweise übersetzt von Kurt Sprengel. Mit Anmerkungen von Johann Reinhold Forster. *Magazin von merkwürdigen neuen Reisebeschreibungen* 7 (1792): 1–293.

Till, Nicholas. *Mozart and the Enlightenment: Truth, Virtue and Beauty in Mozart's Operas*. New York: Norton, 1993.

Torgovnick, Marianna. *Gone Primitive: Savage Intellects, Modern Lives*. Chicago: University of Chicago Press, 1988.

Tsu, Lao. *Tao Te Ching*. New York: Vintage, 1972.

Utz, Peter. *Das Auge und das Ohr im Text: Literarische Sinneswahrnehmung in der Goethezeit.* Munich: Fink, 1990.

———. "Auge, Ohr und Herz: Schillers Dramaturgie der Sinne." *Jahrbuch der deutschen Schillergesellschaft* 29 (1985): 62–97.

Verstreute Nachrichten von einer Reise in die Südsee—Unternehmungen der Gesellschaft zur Beförderung der Entdeckungen im Inneren Afrikas. Magazin von merkwürdigen neuen Reisebeschreibungen 5 (1791).

von Mücke, Dorothea. "Play, Power, and Politics in Schiller's 'Die Verschwörung des Fiesko zu Genua.' " *Michigan Germanic Studies* 13.1 (1987): 1–18.

———. *Virtue and the Veil of Illusion.* Stanford: Stanford University Press, 1991.

Wackenroder, Wilhelm Heinrich. *Sämtliche Werke und Briefe.* Ed. Silvio Vietta and Richard Littlejohns. Heidelberg: Carl Winter Universitätsverlag, 1991.

Wassermann, H.P. *Ethnic Pigmentation: Historical, Clinical, and Medical Aspects.* Amsterdam: Excerpta medica, 1974.

Weber, Max. *The Sociology of Religion.* Boston: Beacon Press, 1964.

Weigel, Sigrid. "Zum Verhältnis von 'Wilden' und 'Frauen' in der Aufklärung." *Topographien der Geschlechter.* Reinbek bei Hamburg: Rowohlt, 1987. 118–48.

Weissberg, Liliane. *Geistersprache: Philosophischer und literarischer Diskurs im späten achtzehnten Jahrhundert.* Würzburg: Königshausen & Neumann, 1990.

Wellbery, David. *Lessing's Laokoon: Semiotics and Aesthetics in the Age of Reason.* Cambridge: Cambridge University Press, 1984.

———. *The Specular Moment: Goethe's Early Lyric and the Beginnings of Romanticism.* Stanford: Stanford University Press, 1996.

Wertheim, Ursula. *Schillers "Fiesko" und "Don Karlos."* Weimar: Arion 1958.

Wheeler, Roxann. "Betrayed by Some and My Own Complexion: Cugoano, Abolition, and the Contemporary Language of Racialism." In *Genius in Bondage.* Ed. Carretta and Gould. 17–38.

———. *The Complexion of Race. Categories of Difference in Eighteenth-Century British Culture.* Philadelphia: University of Pennsylvania Press, 2000.

Whitlock, Greg. "Concealing the Misconduct of One's Own Father: Confucius and Plato on the Question of Filial Piety." *Journal of Chinese Philosophy* 21.2 (1994): 113–37.

Widmaier, Rita, ed. *Leibniz korrespondiert mit China: Der Briefwechsel mit den Jesuitenmissionaren 1689–1714.* Frankfurt a. M.: Vittorio Klostermann, 1990.

———. *Die Rolle der chinesischen Schrift in Leibniz' Zeichentheorie.* Frankfurt a. M.: Harrasowitz, 1983.

Wieland, Christoph Martin. *Der goldenen Spiegel oder die Könige von Scheschian Sämtliche Werke.* Vols. 7 and 8. Leispzig: Göschen, 1839.

Wilson, W. Daniel. *Das Goethe-Tabu: Protest und Menschenrechte im klassischen Weimar.* Munich: dtv, 1999.

Wilson, W. Daniel. "Intellekt und Herrschaft. Wielands Goldener Spiegel, Joseph II. und das Ideal eines kritischen Mäzenats im aufgeklärten Absolutismus." *MLN* 99.3 (1984): 479–502.

———. "Skeletons in Goethe's Closet: Human Rights, Protest, and the Myth of Political Liberality." *Unwrapping Goethe's Weimar*. Ed. Henke, Kord, and Richter Rochester, NY: Camden House, 2000. 295–309.

Wilsons, James. *Missions-Reise in das südliche stille Meer, unternommen in den Jahren 1796, 1797, 1798 mit dem Schiffe Duff*. Mit zwei Kupfern und einer Landkarte, aus dem Englischen übersetzt/Mit Anmerkungen von Canzler. *Magazin von merkwürdigen neuen Reisebeschreibungen* 21 (1800).

Wolff, Christian. *Gesammelte Werke. I. Abt.: Deutsche Schriften*. Hildesheim: Ohlms Verlag, 1981.

———. "Rede über die Sittenlehre der Sineser." In *Deutsche Denker über China*. Ed. Hsia. 42–72.

———. *Rede über die Sittenlehre der Sineser*. *Gesammelte Werke*, Vol. 21.6.

Woodruff, Charles Edward. *Medical Ethnology*. New York: Rebman Company, 1915.

Zammito, John. *Kant, Herder, and the Birth of Anthropology*. Chicago: University of Chicago Press, 2002.

———. "Policing Poligeneticism in Germany, 1775: (Kames,) Kant, and Blumenbach." In *The German Invention of Race*. Ed. Eigen and Larrimore. 35–54.

Zantop, Susanne. *Colonial Fantasies: Conquest, Family, and Nation in Precolonial Germany, 1770–1870*. Durham, NC: Duke University Press, 1997.

Zedler, Johann Heinrich. *Grosses Vollständiges Universallexikon, 1732–1763*. Graz: Akademische Druck-und Verlagsanstalt, 1961 (online Bayrische Staatsbibliothek).

Ziegler, Karl Friedrich Wilhelm. *Die Mohrinn. Ein Schauspiel in vier Aufzügen. Sämmtliche dramatische Werke*. Vol. 2. Vienna: Hirschfeld, 1802.

Žižek, Slavoj. *For They Know Not What They Do: Enjoyment as a Political Factor*. London: Verso, 2002.

INDEX